CYPRUS

CONSTITUTIONALISM
AND
CRISIS
GOVERNMENT

CYPRUS

CONSTITUTIONALISM AND CRISIS GOVERNMENT

by Stanley Kyriakides

UNIVERSITY OF PENNSYLVANIA PRESS
PHILADELPHIA, 19104

Library of Congress Catalog Number 68-25333

7567
Manufactured in the United States of America

FOREWORD

by

Roy C. Macridis

Myron and Walter Jaffee Professor of Politics

Brandeis University

It takes courage to attempt to unravel the legal, political, and international tangles of the Cyprus situation. Ever since the end of World War II Cyprus has been the most troublesome area in the southeastern Mediterranean—only recently to be overshadowed by the Arab-Israeli dispute; indeed until de Gaulle hoisted his flag of independence, Cyprus was the weakest link in NATO. Pent-up national sentiments that go back to the Byzantine period and the unexpected virulence of nationalism—not peculiar to Cyprus, as events in Canada and in Belgium have indicated—accounted for the armed truce that prevailed in Cyprus for so long.

Underlying the legal arrangements and accommodations in Cyprus is the hard reality of two communities, different in religion, language, and national identity, who simply do not trust each other and find it hard to live together in peace. Their mistrust, often exacerbated by outside interference, may well continue to undermine whatever ad hoc legal and constitutional arrangements are made, unless the Cypriots' two nation-states of origin—Greece and Turkey—can themselves set an example of cooperation. All who are impatient with the conflicts and instabilities in Cyprus must understand that in a world where "big" nationalisms flourish small ones will smoulder, and even dead ones will be kindled to life! Cyprus, in the last analysis, is the sad legacy of a world in which conflict continues in the name of the most tenacious of myths—nationalism.

Professor Kyriakides illuminates for us a major dimension of the Cyprus problem—the political and more particularly the legal one. He traces with remarkable lucidity the political history of the island, including the years before World War II, giving particular attention to postwar developments up to the Zurich agreement. His work is the most accurate and scholarly statement of the Cyprus constitutional question and as such it will remain the best-documented analysis for many years to come.

How enduring the present arrangements are for Cyprus remains to be seen, and the author does not seem to be sanguine: "Any settlement," he writes, "must reflect magnanimity on the part of the Greek Cypriot community and restraint on the part of the Turkish Cypriot community." These are indeed virtues that are hard to come by. But whatever the future may hold for the Cypriots and for all of us who are involved in their problems in one way or another, few will be able to understand the situation without reading this book.

PREFACE

Since December 1963, when intercommunal fighting broke out, Cyprus has been functioning under crisis government. Constitutional government as envisaged in the Constitution, establishing the Republic of Cyprus in August 1960, proved to be unworkable.

The purpose of this study is to examine and analyze the nature and causes of crisis government and the lack of constitutionalism in Cyprus. By lack of constitutionalism, we refer to the absence of a Cypriot political consciousness and the inability of the Greek and Turkish communities to function under constitutional government.

The hypothesis of this study is that crisis government and the lack of constitutionalism in Cyprus is the result of the following major factors: first, the existence of two distinct ethnic communities, Greek and Turkish Cypriot, preserving two distinct ethnic identities; second, the bi-communal mistrust resulting from the persistence of the Cypriot Church-directed *Enosis* movement,[1] which culminated in open bi-communal antagonism before independence; third, the absence of any serious attempts on the part of the British Colonial Administration to promote genuine self-government and bi-communal cooperation; fourth, the unwillingness and inability of the two Cypriot communities to function under the 1960 constitutional framework; fifth, the entrenchment of external interests and the Greco-Turkish involvement in Cyprus.

Culturally, the Cypriot society is polarized into two distinct ethnic Cypriot communities, Greek and Turkish. The Greek Cypriots speak Greek, are Greek Orthodox in religion and identify themselves with the Hellenic tradition; the Turkish Cypriots speak Turkish, are Moslem in religion and identify themselves with Turkey. The two communities have retained and transferred their individual cultural identities into two distinct political cultures. The Greek Cypriots have identified themselves with the Greek tradition and the Turkish Cypriots with the Turkish tradition. The

[1] *Enosis* stands for union with Greece. Throughout this study, *Enosis* is referred to either as *Enosis* movement or "movement."

preservation of two antagonistic ethnic cultures, Greek and Turkish, prevented the development of a distinct Cypriot political consciousness.

The bi-communal structure of the Cypriot society was institutionalized by the 1960 Constitution. However, the Greek and Turkish Cypriots were unable to function under the 1960 constitutional framework. This led to the December 1963 crisis in Cyprus and the severing of Greco-Turkish relations.

There is no serious work dealing with the problem of constitutionalism and crisis government in Cyprus. This study, through a chronological-analytical and case-study method, traces the problem under investigation from its roots to the present. The investigation of this study rests mainly on primary sources; namely, British and Cypriot government documents, United Nations documents, newspapers and interviews of Cypriot government officials. Further, a public opinion survey was conducted and library research as well as secondary sources were consulted. However, secondary sources representing the Greek and Turkish Cypriots, respectively, are highly opinionated and therefore have been carefully scrutinized.

The organization of the divisions in the study is as follows: the Preface sets forth the general purpose, method, and objectives. Chapter 1 provides an historical background to Cyprus and traces the forces which have shaped the character of the Cypriot society. It also analyzes the role of the Greek Orthodox Church of Cyprus in the *Enosis* movement and the resulting Turkish Cypriot objections to *Enosis*. Chapter 2 evaluates the British Colonial Administration's attempts to introduce limited self-government, examines the nature of the British constitutional proposals, their effects on constitutionalism in Cyprus, the involvement of Greece and Turkey, and the resulting Zurich and London agreements. Chapter 3 analyzes the major features of the 1960 Cypriot Constitution, with emphasis on the major provisions leading to bi-communal friction. Chapter 4 examines four major constitutional tension areas through the Parliament, the Executive branch, and the Judiciary, examines the inability of the Constitution to become a common symbol, and the factors leading to the 1963 crisis. Chapter 5 analyzes the nature of constitutional crisis, government in crisis, and bi-communal attitudes toward the crisis. Chapter 6 deals with the Cyprus dilemma as interdependent with external interests, especially those of Greece and Turkey. In the concluding chapter, prospects for constitutional solution in Cyprus are presented. Finally, Appendices A, B and C, the Zurich Agreement, Dr. Fazil Kuchuk's letters to the Secretary-General of the United Nations, and the method of the public opinion survey, respectively, are included.

This work would not have been possible without the help and assistance of many individuals. My family in Cyprus was the guiding inspiration during my research project there, and without their assistance and dedication, it would have been impossible to arrive at a fruitful conclusion.

Cypriot Government officials have been extremely helpful, especially George Kyprianides, Director of the Office of the House of Representatives, who furnished me with the typewritten House debates, as well as with an office to use at my disposal in the House building. My thanks also go to A. Necati Sager, Director of the Turkish Information Center in Nicosia, for the material regarding the Turkish Cypriot point of view; the United Nations officials in Cyprus for facilitating my research; and the officials of the United Nations Mission of Cyprus in New York, especially the Consul General, Dinos Moushoutas, and Demos Hadjimiltis.

The assistance of my colleagues and friends in the improvement of the manuscript has been immeasurable: Professor George Gregory of Seton Hall University read the entire manuscript and made excellent comments and suggestions, which, I am sure, improved its quality; Professor Christopher Kornaros of Briarcliff College helped in the analysis of the Constitution and especially with regard to Chapter 3 of this book; Demetrios Zacharias, my close friend and able statistician, gave me valuable assistance in the preparation and evaluation of the questionnaire. I should also like to extend my appreciation to Professors Gisbert H. Flanz of New York University and Kemal H. Karpat of the University of Wisconsin for all their help and constructive suggestions. Lastly, this book, as it stands, has been made possible by Carol Tunick's enthusiasm and devotion.

New York, N. Y.
February, 1968

S. Kyriakides

CONTENTS

1

CYPRUS IN PERSPECTIVE

Cyprus is a small island in search of an identity. Located in the extreme northeast corner of the Mediterranean, Cyprus covers an area of approximately 3,500 square miles. The population of Cyprus is divided by race, language, and religion. On the island, 78 percent of the people speak Greek and are members of the Greek Orthodox religion. About 18 percent are Turkish-speaking and members of the Moslem religion. The remaining four percent are Armenians, Maronites, and others.[1]

The present difficulties of Cyprus' political life stem, to a large degree, from its diverse historical past. The nature of this historical past has contributed to the development of a bi-communal society and accounts for the lack of a Cypriot national consciousness.

The bi-communal character of the Cypriot society, as it has evolved through the centuries, did not necessarily have to lead to thorny relations among the Cypriots. For example, other societies, such as those in Lebanon and Switzerland, have been able to solve the problem of multi-communalism and have developed a distinct national consciousness. Cyprus, however, has not been able to develop a definite identity of its own.

The purpose of this chapter is first, to examine, in historical perspective, the major forces that have left a lasting impact on the communal character of the Cypriot society; namely, the colonization of Cyprus by the ancient Hellenic world, the Byzantine influence, and the Ottoman rule; second, to examine the nature of the *Enosis* movement under the British rule, which has accentuated bi-communalism and prevented the development of a distinct Cypriot consciousness.

---

[1] According to the 1960 Census, there were 441,000 Greek Orthodox, 104,000 Turkish Moslems, 3,500 Armenians, 7,000 Maronites, and 16,000 others. Cyprus, Statistics and Research Department, *Statistical Abstract* (Nicosia: Printing Office of the Republic of Cyprus, 1963), p. 22.

Cyprus in Historical Perspective

The history of Cyprus can be traced to the neolithic period. For our purposes, we may begin with the ancient Hellenic influence on the character of Cyprus. It is widely accepted by scholars that the first significant influence by the Greeks can be traced to the Mycenaeans during the fourteenth century B.C.[2] This early contact with the Mycenaeans linked Cyprus with a civilization and legends which enabled her to become part of what was later to be known as the Greek world, a characteristic feature that Cyprus was to retain strongly throughout her history.

The connection with the Mycenaeans was strengthened by a great influx of Achaean Greeks to Cyprus in the same century. This influx of Achaeans gave Hellenized Cyprus a new role in the Eastern Mediterranean; with a vitalized economy, she steadily became one of the cultural and commercial centers of the ancient Greek world. Another wave of Greek settlers to Cyprus, which occurred around 1,000 B.C., is often identified with the movements related to the Trojan War. From the legends of this period, historians identify a great number of important settlements by Greek leaders in Cyprus.[3]

Further expansion of the Greek civilization in Cyprus was systematically undertaken by the Cypriot King, Evagoras, in the latter part of the fifth and early part of the fourth century B.C. This continuing expansion of the Greek civilization developed a Greek literary heritage in Cyprus. This was culminated in the foundation of the school of Stoicism in Athens by the Cypriot philosopher Zeno of Kition in the third century B.C.[4]

The above historical phenomena partly explain the recurring Greek Cypriot claim to close affinity with the Greek civilization. Indeed, the Greek Cypriots claim to have retained more ancient

---

[2] Doros Alastos, *Cyprus in History: A Survey of 5,000 Years* (London: Zeno Publishers, 1955), p. 27. For an excellent study of the ancient heritage of Cyprus, see Stanley Casson, *Ancient Cyprus* (London: Methuen, 1937). See also, Louis Palma Di Cesnola, *Cyprus: Its Ancient Cities, Tombs and Temples* (New York: Harper and Brothers, 1878), especially Introduction.

[3] Sir George Hill, *A History of Cyprus* (4 Vols., Cambridge: Cambridge University Press, 1940-1952), II, pp. 82-94.

[4] C. Spyridakis, *A Brief History of Cyprus* (Nicosia: Greek Communal Chamber, 1964), pp. 20-28.

Greek characteristics than the modern Greeks of mainland Greece. The argument goes that in the present Greek Cypriot dialect there are more Homeric words than in the language of modern Greeks in Greece. That Cyprus developed an early Greek heritage, there can be little doubt.[5]

The most important event, however, which molded the feelings of the Cypriots was the introduction of Christianity during the early part of the Roman period. The introduction of Christianity in Cyprus was carried on by Apostles Paul and Barnabas in 45 A.D.[6] By the time the Byzantine Emperor Constantine recognized Christianity in the early part of the fourth century, the great majority of Cypriots had already embraced the Christian religion. This transformation from the Hellenic to the Hellenic Christian tradition brought Cyprus into the Byzantine civilization and marks the beginning of the influence of the Church on the long history of Cyprus. The strong grip of the Church was further advanced when in 488 A.D. Emperor Zeno of Byzantium recognized the Church of Cyprus as autocephalus, (i.e., independent).[7]

The Byzantine pattern of politics was characterized by the closeness of Church-State relations. This pattern of politico-religious alliance, which was also evident in Cyprus, consolidated the Cypriot society under the aegis of the Church.

During the Byzantine period, the pagan towns were turned into cathedral towns. Churches and monasteries were being built throughout the island. By the middle of the sixth century A.D., the Church in Cyprus was in complete command. The pagan past had disappeared; Christianity became the force prescribing the duties of the people.[8]

No other part of the Byzantine world continues to preserve the Byzantine past as strongly as Cyprus. The geographical isolation of the island and the independence of the Cyprus church may be

---

[5] Philip Newman, A Short History of Cyprus (London: Longmans, Green & Co., 1953), pp. 20-30. See also, Gordon C. Home, *Cyprus Then and Now* (London: J. M. Dent, 1960), pp. 225-226. See also, Hill, *op. cit.,* pp. 58-81.

[6] John Hackett, *History of the Orthodox Church in Cyprus,* (in Greek), trans. Ch. I. Papaioannou (3 Vols., Athens: Sakellariou and Eleftheriou, 1923-1932), I, p. 9.

[7] *Ibid.,* pp. 42-44.

[8] Alastos, *op. cit.,* pp. 121-122.

the reasons why this is so. It is in this context that we find the Church-State marriage continuing in the political life of Cyprus. Therefore for over fifteen centuries the Church has remained powerful and influential. Its overwhelming influence over the Greek Cypriot population resulted in the development in Cyprus of a Christian spirit of brotherhood linking her with the rest of the Greco-Byzantine world.

With the end of the Byzantine rule in Cyprus, the dominant position of the Greek Orthodox Church diminished. Under the Lusignan Dynasty, which lasted almost three-hundred years (1192-1489), the Church of Cyprus suffered unprecedented oppression and was in grave danger of elimination.

The Orthodox Church of Cyprus was brought under the direct control and influence of the Church of Rome. The fourteen Dioceses, which formed the basis of the organization of the Church of Cyprus during the Byzantine period, were abolished.[9] The affairs of the Orthodox Church were placed under the new administrative structure of the Latin Church. The Orthodox bishops came under the direct control of the newly established Latin Bishoprics. The election of an Orthodox Archbishop was forbidden, and a Latin Archiepiscopal See became the center of authority.[10] The spiritual subordination of the Orthodox Church of Cyprus was accompanied by financial domination as well.

The humiliation of the Church of Cyprus by the Church of Rome eliminated the grip of the Greek Orthodox clergy over the Greek Cypriot population. When the Ottomans took over the island in 1571, the Cypriot Orthodox Church was in an extremely precarious position.

Under the Ottoman rule, the most important single factor resulting from religious toleration, was the elevation of the Orthodox Church of Cyprus. The Archbishops of Cyprus were employed as instruments of control over all Christian subjects in Cyprus.[11] The Orthodox Church of Cyprus, unlike the Latin Church, which had

[9] Hackett, *op. cit.*, I, p. 141.

[10] Spyridakis, *op. cit.*, p. 47. For a detailed examination of the Church of Cyprus under the Latins, see Hackett, *op. cit.*, I, especially pp. 83-213.

[11] Claude Delaval Cobham, *Excerpta Cypria: Materials for a History of Cyprus* (Cambridge: Cambridge University Press, 1908), pp. 268-269. See also, Newman, *op. cit.*, p. 172.

become powerful under the Venetian rule, was permitted by the Ottomans to reestablish its dominant position in religious, social and economic affairs over the Christian Cypriot population. There are responsible writers who believe that the reestablishment of the Church to its preeminent position saved it from Latinization. Latinization might have occurred if the oppressive measures which were carried out by the Latins were not culminated by the Ottoman rule.[12]

What strengthened the Church's position even more, was the fact that the Ottomans allowed their subjects to set up their own schools. This denominational autonomy, under the Millet system,[13] enabled the Orthodox Church to direct the education of the Cypriot Christian community. Thus by shaping the educational organization and molding the curriculum of the Christian schools, the Church leadership nurtured the Byzantine and Hellenic heritage.

By 1660 the Archbishop and the Bishops of Cyprus were recognized by the Porte[14] as representatives of the Christians in Cyprus.[15] In a sense, they were recognized as unofficial guardians of the Christian community. The reason for the Church's elevation by the Porte was the maladministration by the local Pashas.[16] Taxation was heavy and the depopulation of the taxpaying Greeks was mounting owing to oppressive measures and to famine.[17] This move of the Porte was intended, on the one hand, to satisfy the clamor of the Cypriots, and on the other, to check the excesses of the local Pashas. As a result, the Archbishop could send petitions with his own signature directly to the Sultan without having to consult the local Ottoman governor. This factor greatly enhanced the power of the Church.

In 1754 the Grand Vezir issued a firman [18] by which he appointed the Bishops as Kojabashis, or Official Representatives and Supervisors of the Christians of Cyprus, with direct access to the Porte. At

---

[12] Chrysostomos A. Papadopoulos, *The Church of Cyprus Under the Turks,* (in Greek) (Athens, 1929), p. 4. See also, Hackett, *op. cit.,* I, pp. 224-228.
[13] For a comprehensive study of the Ottoman Empire, see Wayne S. Vucinich, *The Ottoman Empire, Its Record and Legacy* (Princeton: Van Nostrand, 1965), *passim;* Anthony Dolphin Anderson, *The Structure of the Ottoman Dynasty* (Oxford: Clarendon Press, 1956), *passim.*
[14] "Porte" refers to the Government of the Ottoman Empire.
[15] Alastos, *op. cit.,* p. 269; Hackett, *op. cit.,* I, p. 258.
[16] "Pashas" refer to governors of provinces in the Ottoman Empire.
[17] Harry C. Luke, *Cyprus Under the Turks 1571-1878* (London: Oxford University Press, 1921), pp. 31-39.
[18] "Firman" refers to a decree issued by the Ottoman Sultan.

the same time, the Archbishop was recognized as Ethnarch or politico-religious leader of his ethnic community. In this politico-religious capacity, the Archbishop was to play an increasingly important role in the political life of Cyprus.[19]

The ascendancy of the Bishops and the Archbishop continued until the Greek War of Independence in 1821. During this period, the Ottoman authorities took strict measures to suppress any Cypriot participation in the Greek War of Independence. According to Sir George Hill, a former priest from Greece went to Archbishop Kyprianos of Cyprus in 1819. He enrolled the Archbishop in the *Philike Hetaireia*[20] and got from him a promise of moral support.[21] This involvement of the Cypriots in the Greek War of Independence brought reaction from the Ottomans. The governor of Cyprus, Küchük Mehmed, having implicated the Greek Cypriots in the revolution, recommended the execution of all leading Christians. There followed a large-scale massacre on the island on July 9, 1821, in which the Bishops were beheaded, and the Archbishop hanged.[22] This in effect eliminated the powerful position of the Church.

Another important consequence of the Ottoman rule in Cyprus is reflected in the character of the Cypriot society. The origins of the present Cypriot-Turkish community can be traced to the armies of Sultan Selim II. After taking control of the island, some 20,000 of Sultan Selim's soldiers were awarded assistance and permanent residence on Cyprus.[23]

When the Ottoman rule ended in 1878, the Turkish Cypriot Moslems formed approximately one-fourth of the total population of 190,000.[24] When the British took over Cyprus under the Convention of Defensive Alliance with the Ottoman Empire,[25] Cyprus was distinctly bi-communal. The immediate effect of the British

---

[19] Hill, *op. cit.,* IV, p. 316; Hackett, *op. cit.,* I, pp. 292-293.
[20] "Philike Hetaireia" refers to the organization which initiated the Greek Independence movement.
[21] Hill, *op. cit.,* IV, pp. 123-124.
[22] Georgios Kepiades, *Memoirs of the 1821 Tragic Events in Cyprus,* (in Greek) (Alexandria, 1888), pp. 15-30.
[23] Alastos, *op. cit.,* p. 258.
[24] Cyprus, Statistics and Research Department, *Statistical Abstract, op. cit.,* p. 22.
[25] For an excellent analysis of the Cyprus Convention, see Dwight E. Lee, *Great Britain and the Cyprus Convention Policy* (Harvard Historical Studies, Vol. XXXVIII, Cambridge: Harvard University Press, 1934).

presence on the island was the intensification of bi-communalism. This can be seen in the context of the *Enosis* movement.

The British Rule and the Enosis Movement Through World War II

This section examines the nature of the *Enosis* movement in order to show its negative effects on the development of a distinct Cypriot personality. Although the movement was not systematically launched until the British took over Cyprus, the idea of *Enosis* antedated British rule. In fact, *Enosis* has been linked to the idea of Hellenic expansionism, the revitalized spirit of the Byzantine tradition, as exemplified in the modern Greek movement of "Megali Idea."[26]

The actors of the movement were the Greek Cypriots, through the leaders of the Greek Orthodox Church of Cyprus, who conceived the British presence on the island as an opportunity to accomplish their long-desired aspiration to unite with "Mother Greece." The Greek Cypriots' desire to unite with the rest of the Greek world was based on the deep conviction that the Greek Cypriots were part of the Hellenic world, since they spoke the same language, practiced the same religion, and were identified with the same culture and tradition.[27]

Regarding the Greek Cypriot conviction about their Hellenic tradition, Sir George Hill writes:

> Of the three main factors: race, language, and religion, which contribute to Cypriot nationality the first, paradoxical as it may seem, is the least important.[28]

---

[26] "Megali Idea" or Great Idea refers to the nationalistic desire of modern Greece to recreate the Byzantine Empire under Greek hegemony. For a comprehensive study of Modern Greek nationalism, see Adamantia Pollis Koslin, *The Megali Idea: A Study in Greek Nationalism* (Johns Hopkins University, unpublished Ph.D. dissertation, 1958).

[27] For literature expounding the Greek feelings of the Greek Cypriots, see the following: Zenon G. Rossides, *The Island of Cyprus and Union with Greece* (Nicosia: The Ethnarchy Council, 1954), especially pp. 5-20; Savvas Loizides, *Cyprus Demands Self-Determination* (Athens: National Committee For Self-Determination of Cyprus, 1956), pp. 5-7; Achilleus K. Emilianides, *The Greekness of Cyprus,* (in Greek) (Nicosia: Mouson Press, 1944), *passim;* K. Pana, *Cyprus is Greek: 3,000 Years of Greek Life,* (in Greek) (Athens, n.d.), *passim.*

[28] Hill, *op. cit.,* IV, p. 488.

On the other hand, Sir Ronald Storrs, a former Governor of Cyprus, in his *Memoirs* wrote:

> The Greekness of Cypriots is in my opinion indisputable . . . A man is of the race of which he passionately feels himself to be.[29]

This feeling of "Greekness" by the Greek Cypriots can thus be explained in terms of their devotion to the ancient Greek heritage, and to their attachment to Byzantium and Eastern Orthodox Christianity.

The institution personifying this Greco-Byzantine tradition was the Church of Cyprus. During its long history, the Church was successful in combining religion and language and fostering the idea of "Greekness" in the Greek Cypriot community. It must be remembered that during the Ottoman rule the Church was the only dominant force in the socio-political life of the Greek Cypriots.

Through its privileged position as the religious and political spokesman for the Greek Cypriot Christian community, along with its predominant role in the field of education, the Church, on the one hand, implanted and preserved the feelings of Hellenism and on the other hand, fostered the growth of modern Greek nationalism. An article in the *Times of London* places this unique character of the Church in its proper perspective:

> The Church is the organ of his nationality and the . . . Ecumenical Patriarch its embodiment . . . This sentiment has shown a remarkable power of absorbing and making Greek in language and thought stocks that may be really Anatolian, and no more Hellenic in blood than, say, the Great Cappadocian fathers, who are the legitimate glory of the Orthodox Church . . . A Cypriot may be anything by blood, but being Orthodox he thinks of himself as Greek.[30]

Thus, it was natural for the Church to become the spearhead of the *Enosis* movement; it was the only institution able to appeal to the national sentiments of the Greek Cypriot community, which had already been imbued with Greek culture.

---

[29] Sir Ronald Storrs, *The Memoirs of Sir Ronald Storrs* (New York: G. P. Putnam's Sons, 1937), p. 495.

[30] *The Times* (London), May 5, 1928; quoted in Hill, *op. cit.*, IV, p. 489 fn.

Because of the very nature of the *Enosis* movement, its effects on developing a distinct Cypriot personality have been significantly negative: First, by its demands for union with Greece, the Church emphasized and kept alive the distinct differences of the two ethnic communities of Cyprus, namely, Greek and Turkish Cypriots. In turn, the *Enosis* demand invited reaction from the Turkish-Moslem Cypriot community, which opposed the Church's drive; second, the Church's traditional privileged position as a political spokesman for the Greek Cypriot community discouraged the growth of any serious opposition to *Enosis* within the Greek Cypriot community. This factor contributed to the movement's becoming monolithic, thereby discouraging any possibilities for alternatives—namely, the encouragement of Cypriot self-government; third, the unwillingness of the British Colonial Administration to accede to the *Enosis* pressures resulted in bipolarization of the Greek Cypriot community and the Colonial Government. This has led to constant friction, which has defeated any attempts to promote a genuine understanding in self-government. In effect, the Legislative Council, established under the 1882 Constitution for Cyprus[31] failed to become a training ground for self-government. To the contrary, it became a political forum for the *Enosis* agitation.

What emerges out of the presentation of the *Enosis* drive is the powerful and predominant role of the Church. The Church's demand for union with Greece seems to have been a systematic attempt to prevent the development of a distinct Cypriot personality.

From the very beginning of the British rule, the demand for *Enosis* placed the Church in the forefront of the movement. When the first British High Commissioner, Sir Garnet Wolseley, arrived in Cyprus on July 12, 1878, the Church of Cyprus, through its Archbishop, welcomed him as follows:

> We accept the change of government in as much as we trust that Great Britain will help Cyprus as it did the Ionian Islands to be united with Mother Greece, to which it is naturally connected.[32]

Thus, the pattern of the Greek Cypriot demands for *Enosis* has

[31] C. W. J. Orr, *Cyprus Under British Rule* (London: Robert Scott, 1918), pp. 95-113.
[32] *Ibid.*, p. 160.

been set from the start. By and large, although peacefully conducted, the *Enosis* movement can best be described with one word —persistence.

Hardly a year went by without the Greek Cypriots, under the aegis of the Church, finding a way to express their deep desire to unite with Mother Greece.

In 1880, when Greece was mobilizing and preparing for war against Ottoman Turkey, the Greek Cypriots not only expressed their support and enthusiasm, but sent more than 150 volunteers to help the Greek expedition. The Archbishop also sent a letter to the King of Greece, expressing the Cypriot solidarity with Mother Greece. Needless to say, the British Administration issued a Cyprus Neutrality Order in Council on May 18, 1881, to calm the enthusiastic Greeks of Cyprus.[33]

In 1887, the Greeks of Cyprus boycotted the celebration of the Queen's Jubilee. To minimize the English celebration on the island, the Church leadership held meetings in more than six hundred Churches and demanded "Union with Greece." [34]

In 1889 the first *Enosis* delegation was formed. Under the leadership of Archbishop Sofronios, the delegation went to London to present the grievances of the Cypriots to the British government and to reiterate the Cypriot's demands "for their national cause." [35]

In 1895, there was a great deal of agitation for *Enosis*. The Archbishop of Cyprus, on the one hand, protested to the High Commissioner against the heavy taxes; and on the other, he encouraged protest meetings in Cyprus demanding union with Greece.[36] At a significant protest meeting in Limassol, held on April 28, 1895, the meaning and the strength of the *Enosis* movement was revealed in the following resolution, typical of numerous resolutions passed throughout the island:

> The Hellenic people of the district of Limassol, in concord with the rest of the Hellenic people of the island, who form the great majority of the whole population has always de-

[33] Hill, *op. cit.*, IV, p. 411.
[34] *Ibid.*, p. 498.
[35] Nikos Kranidiotis, *Cyprus in the Struggle for Freedom,* (in Greek) (Athens, 1957), p. 27.
[36] Philios Zannetos, *History of the Island of Cyprus,* (in Greek) (3 Vols., Larnaca: Philokalias Press, 1910-1912), II, p. 846.

> sired, desires and will desire one and only one solution and today solemnly demands the union with Hellas to which it belongs by race and blood be effected with the least possible delay.[37]

When Greece again declared war on Ottoman Turkey in 1897, thousands of Greek Cypriots went to Greece to join the Greek forces. It is estimated that a total of 6,318 Greek Cypriots fought along with the Greeks against the Ottoman Turks. Their heroism was widely acclaimed by the press: "with the Cypriot volunteers in the war, Cyprus was a proud participant in the national cause." [38]

In 1899 when Crete was placed under a Greek High Commissioner, *Enosis* agitation erupted in Cyprus. Under the direction of the Church, there were numerous demonstrations throughout the island. The intensity of the emotional ferment is reflected in the report submitted to the Commissioner of Limassol by his Chief of Police:

> Limassol, May 9, 1899
> During the whole week, only Greek flags were seen floating over Limassol. On the grounds of the Stadium there were only Greek flags; the churches . . . displayed only Greek flags . . . On the arrival of the Greek Consul and the Bishop of Kitium at the Stadium, the Greek National Anthem was played and the people stood up . . . Cheers were repeatedly called for—the King of Greece . . . but no cheers were called for the Queen.[39]

That the Greek Cypriot's demands for *Enosis* accentuated bipolarity, can be understood from the protests by the Turkish Cypriot community of Cyprus.[40] In 1895 when Greek Cypriot

---

[37] Quoted in Hill, *op. cit.,* IV, p. 500.
[38] Kranidiotis, *op. cit.,* p. 32; Pana, *op. cit.,* p. 93.
[39] British Public Record Office, C.O. 883/6, quoted in *History Speaks: A Documentary Survey* (Nicosia: Turkish Communal Chamber, 1964), pp. 19-20.
[40] Turkish Cypriot arguments often emphasized that Cyprus never belonged to Greece; and if the island was to be returned to any other power, it should be returned to Turkey, which controlled the island before the British. See Vergi H. Bedevi, *Cyprus Has Never Been A Greek Island* (Nicosia: Cyprus Turkish Historical Association, 1964), pp. 12-14. See also, Cyprus Turkish Information Centre, *Turks Say No To Enosis* (Nicosia, n.d.); also, Turkish Communal Chamber, *A Report on Cyprus* (Nicosia, 1965), pp. 21-27.

agitation was intensified, the Turkish Cypriot community headed by the Mufti[41] of Cyprus, Ali Rifki Eff., submitted the following petition to the Chief Secretary:

> A great number of the Moslems have attended the Mufti's residence and requested us to bring their complaints to the Government, and to ask the adoption of the necessary steps . . . we pray in the name of all the Moslem inhabitants that the Government may take such measures as to prevent the occurrence of things causing the excitement of the Moslems.[42]

The strong disapproval of the Greek Cypriot demands for *Enosis* by the Turkish Cypriot community can be seen in the following two petitions to the Secretary of State for the Colonies:

> The feeling that the Mohammedans will not agree to the Administration of Cyprus leaving the people to Greece is unanimous. If our Island be united to an unjust Administration which is not yet civilized, this Administration will increase the oppressive conduct and manners of our Greek fellow-countrymen, which are well known to Your Excellency . . . If it be absolutely necessary, in the opinion of the Government of England, that the Island should be given up, in order to preserve our lives, property and honour, the favour is humbly asked that it may restore it to the Ottoman Government.[43]

> As regards the cession of the Island to Greece, or the conversion of the present Administration to some other shape, in accordance with the views of our Greek compatriots, it being obvious that the mischievous proclivities and conduct of our Christian fellow-countrymen, that are known to you . . . it is not possible for the Moslem community to share the same views with them in this matter. In case of it being necessary by the illustrious British Government to abandon the Island, we all pray and solicit, in the name of justice that . . . the Island may be restored to our august sovereign, our illustrious Caliph and Monarch the ever-lasting Ottoman Empire . . .[44]

The conflicting positions of the two Cypriot communities resulting from the *Enosis* movement were also reflected in the Legislative

---

[41] "Mufti" refers to a Moslem religious leader.
[42] British Public Record Office, C.O. 67/91, quoted in *History Speaks, op. cit.,* pp. 12-13.
[43] *Ibid.,* C.O. 883/6, quoted in *History Speaks,* p. 38.
[44] Ibid., C.O. 883/6, quoted in *History Speaks,* pp. 39-40.

Council. In a sense, the two communities prevented the Legislative Council from becoming a training ground for self-government and thereby laying the foundations for the development of a Cypriot consciousness.

THE NATURE OF THE BRITISH ADMINISTRATION AND THE ENOSIS MOVEMENT

By an Order in Council on September 14, 1878,[45] the British Administration established a Legislative Council. The Council consisted of the High Commissioner "and not less than four or more than eight other members, one half being officials and the other unofficial." [46] All the members were to be nominated by the High Commissioner. In general, this Constitution was consistent with British colonial policy whereby the Crown had complete control over legislation.

The British Administration, in an attempt to pacify the Greek Cypriots, initiated more "liberal" reforms. The 1882 Constitution, established by an Order in Council in March, 1882,[47] was intended for this purpose. This Constitution established a new Legislative Council, consisting of eighteen members in total, twelve of which were elected and six officially appointed. The presiding officer of the Council was the High Commissioner or the senior official member present with the privilege of one vote. The twelve elected members were allocated proportionally according to the population of the "Christian and Moslem" communities. There were nine Christian and three Moslem members in the Council.[48]

In a great number of matters, the Cypriots could initiate discussion in the Council. The Council's discussions, however, were subject to certain reservations. The salary and the expenses of the High Commissioner and the official members of the Council together with the question of the Tribute[49] could not be discussed in the Council.

---

[45] Zannetos, *op. cit.*, II, pp. 72-76.
[46] Orr, *op. cit.*, p. 95.
[47] *Ibid.*, p. 96.
[48] *Ibid.*
[49] Under the *Cyprus Convention,* Britain undertook to pay to the Porte an annual Tribute. The amount of money to be paid was calculated to represent the excesses of revenue over expenditure in Cyprus, on the average, for the

The two ethnic communities reacted with mixed feelings toward the new Council. Archbishop Sofronios sent a telegram to the Colonial office expressing the delight of the Greek Cypriot population.[50] For the Turkish Cypriots, this Council was interpreted to be the first step toward *Enosis.* In a petition to the Colonial Office, the Cypriot Moslem population opposed the reform and expressed the fear that the Greeks would not respect the Turkish rights:

> Our forefathers occupied this island more than three hundred years ago . . . Ever since that time we have been the ruling element . . . The Legislative Council which is hereafter the basis of the Administration will ultimately become a prelude to the independence which is the motto constantly repeated by our Christian compatriots . . . We know perfectly well that her Britannic Majesty's Government make laws according to the capacity and requirements of every place, and we once more desire to repeat that the project of proportional representation in the Legislative Council is in every respect detrimental to our rights and destructive to the safety we now enjoy. We consequently take the liberty to solicit your Lordship to be pleased to amend according to the principle respected *ab antiquo* the franchise in question, which is incompatible with local requirements and which if enforced will absolutely compel us all to leave the Island for some other place.[51]

When the Constitution was put into practice, however, the attitudes of the two ethnic communities toward the Legislative Council were soon to be reversed. The Greek Cypriots began to object to the Council's character, and the Turks to support it. Evidently this change of attitudes resulted from the inherent character of the Legislative Council. That is, the six official members together with the three elected Turkish members could offset the nine Greek members. The High Commissioner's casting vote tilted the balance in favor of the Government.

---

five years preceding the 1878 *Cyprus Convention.* The Tribute money, which was extracted from the Cypriots, was 92,799 sterling pounds per year. From the very beginning, this added tax was a source of friction between ruler and ruled. There were constant complaints against this "unfair taxation" because the Cypriots felt they were forced to pay a Tribute for a transaction of "change of administration" without their consent. For an extensive analysis of the Tribute, see Orr, *op. cit.,* pp. 46-64.

[50] Storrs, *op. cit.,* p. 497.

[51] Orr, *op. cit.,* pp. 97-99.

The Greek Cypriots looked upon this new political arrangement as nothing more than a "Toy Parliament." For some political analysts, this Constitution was looked upon as a "sham gift" [52] through which the British could facilitate their domination.

This pattern of colonial government in Cyprus represented a substantial departure from normal constitutions of Crown colonies. These colonial constitutions always provided for an absolute official majority. In the case of Cyprus, the British Administration depended on the three votes of the Turkish ethnic minority to offset the nine elected votes of the Greeks. It seems that the new Council of the 1882 Constitution not only did not provide a base for bi-communal cooperation but promoted animosity between the two ethnic communities.[53] The structure of the Council was such that the government depended on the Turkish minority for the Legislative Council to function. This practice fostered divisiveness between Greeks and Turks. From the very beginning, the Greek members became the permanent opposition to the British-Turkish alliance.

The Council increasingly acquired a new feature. It tended to become a forum for the Greek Cypriots to demand reforms and majority rule and to agitate for *Enosis*.[54] The Greek elected members took every opportunity to promote the cause of *Enosis* through resolutions in the Legislative Council. What facilitated the occasional passing of the *Enosis* resolutions, was the irregular attendance of the Turkish Cypriot Representatives.[55] Thus, on May 7, 1903, the Greek Cypriots passed a resolution stating that the "Cypriot people and the Council hoped to be guided by the noble English nation, which it hopes will grant justice through Union with Mother Greece." [56] This resolution was strongly opposed by the two

---

[52] This idea is expressed in the *Edinburgh Review,* Vol. CLXXII (1891), p. 453: "The Cyprus Constitution was a sham gift. The giver gave nothing. The recipient received that which he did not want, and was unable to put to any good use, and the gift has had the fate of all shams. It has made the giver contemptible and the receiver ungrateful." Quoted in Hill, *op. cit.,* p. 419.

[53] This is indicated in Newman, *op. cit.,* p. 207: "This situation was not satisfactory since it tended to foster instead of to allay the racial animosity between the two sections of the population."

[54] Alastos, *op. cit.,* pp. 323-324.

[55] Hill, *op. cit.,* pp. 511-513.

[56] Kranidiotis, *op. cit.,* p. 35.

Turkish Representatives of the Council. The absent Turkish Cypriot member returned on June 18, 1903, and moved that the High Commissioner should take note that the Turks of Cyprus were opposed to the Greek resolution and that if Cyprus was to be abandoned, it should be ceded to the Ottoman Empire, its lawful owner. The Greek members protested these proposals, but the motion was carried anyway on July 6, 1903 aided by the casting vote of the High Commissioner.[57]

The existing rift in the Legislative Council between the government and the governed often necessitated legislation by order in council. To offset the British Turkish alliance in the Council, the Greek Cypriot members often resorted to tactics of their own. Most common were their attempts to reduce budget estimates; to call for majority rule in the Council and to crown their tactics with demands for "Union with Greece." The British Administration, however, was unwilling to meet these demands and the Council's basic character remained unchanged.

The *Enosis* movement took a new form after 1914, when Ottoman Turkey entered World War I on the side of the Central Powers. By an order in council on November 5, 1914, the British annexed Cyprus and declared the 1878 Cyprus Convention invalid.[58]

In 1915 the British government made an offer to cede Cyprus to Greece, provided that the latter enter the war on the side of Serbia against Bulgaria. This cession never materialized, but it had significant effects on the *Enosis* movement. It invited increased agitation from the Greek Cypriots within and outside the Legislative Council. The Greek Cypriots pointed to the offer as proof of recognition of their *Enosis* demands.

Under the Treaty of Lausanne on July 24, 1923, Turkey officially recognized the 1914 British annexation of Cyprus. When Cyprus became a Crown colony, on March 10, 1925,[59] the agitation by the Greek Cypriots persisted.

---

[57] Hill, *op. cit.,* pp. 512-513.

[58] Royal Institute of International Affairs, *Cyprus, Background to Enosis* (London: Chatham House, 1958), p. 2.

[59] Newman, *op. cit.,* p. 209. Until 1925, Britain was directing the governmental affairs on Cyprus through a High Commissioner. When Cyprus officially became a Crown Colony, Britain's highest official became the Governor.

The British Colonial Administration's opposition to the Greek Cypriot demands was based on a number of tactical arguments: that the Cypriots were not Greek; that the Turkish minority would have to be considered in any change of political status; and that England had no intention of changing the status of Cyprus.[60]

At the same time, the British government instituted certain changes in the Legislative Council. By an order in council on February 6, 1925, the Legislative Council was increased from eighteen to twenty-four members. The new distribution increased the Greek Cypriot elected members to twelve. The Turkish Cypriot elected members remained the same.[61] This redistribution was understood to reflect more accurately the population proportion. But in spite of the changes, the balance in the Council remained the same as before. The official members were increased to nine and together with the three Turkish Cypriot elected members could again offset the Greek Cypriot majority.

The new British arrangement in the Legislative Council did not satisfy the Greek Cypriots, for it failed to provide for majority rule. Furthermore, the British unwillingness to consider the *Enosis* demands, led to a more systematic and organized drive by the Church leadership.

THE ORGANIZATIONAL ACTIVITIES OF THE CHURCH LEADERSHIP IN THE ENOSIS MOVEMENT

In December 1921, a political organization known as the National Assembly was established to unite all Greek Cypriots under the Archbishop and to promote "Union with Greece." The executive arm of the National Assembly was the National Council. It consisted of forty-six members. The Archbishop, three Bishops, and the Abbot of Kykko were ex-officio members of the Council. The other forty-one members were elected by the various organizations in Cyprus.[62] In addition, all the Greek members of the Legislative Council participated in the affairs of the National Council. This was a complete consolidation of the Greek Cypriot

---

[60] Kranidiotis, *op. cit.,* pp. 42-44; Alastos, *op. cit.,* p. 344.
[61] *Royal Institute of International Affairs, op. cit.,* pp. 3-4.
[62] Stanley Mayes, *Cyprus and Makarios* (London: Putnam Press, 1960), p. 169.

community under the aegis of the Church. In a sense, the National Council began to function as the Greek counterpart to the Government's Legislative Council.

Under the auspices of the National Assembly and its executive organ, memorials, deputations and delegations were initiated to promote the cause of *Enosis*. In addition, the organization's foremost policy was directed toward non-cooperation with the British Colonial Administration. This can be seen in the position of the National Assembly toward Britain's educational policy in Cyprus.

When Britain assumed control of Cyprus, it did not set up a central system of education. Reflecting the British philosophy at the time, the British administration's educational policy in Cyprus was characterized by decentralization.

Two separate Boards of Education were established in Cyprus, one for the "Christian community" and another for the "Moslem community." [63] The two communal Boards of Education controlled the general direction of the schools in their respective communities; the setting up of their curriculum; the appointment and payment of their teachers, and the selection of text books.

Both communal Boards of Education were strongly influenced by their respective religious leadership. On the one hand, the Orthodox Archbishop headed the Greek Board of Education, and on the other, the Mufti had an influential voice on the Turkish Board of Education. The effect of such a system was that Education in Cyprus was essentially a bi-communal tool.[64]

In the context of the *Enosis* movement, Education for the Greek Cypriot community represented the means of "Keeping alive the national (Greek) feeling." By controlling education, the Orthodox Church, on the one hand, was able to nurture the Greek

---

[63] W. W. Weir, *Education in Cyprus* (Nicosia: Cosmos Press, 1952), p. 26.

[64] In the Turkish Cypriot schools, for example, religious instruction took up a large proportion of the school hours. After the 1922 Kemalist revolution in Turkey, the curriculum in the Turkish Cypriot schools was directed toward nurturing the new Turkish nationalism. See Weir, *op. cit.,* pp. 35, 78-79. In the Greek Cypriot schools, great emphasis was placed in teaching classical language and history. The average Greek Cypriot teacher felt a great obligation to introduce the student to the Greek cultural heritage and the glory that was Greece. See Weir, *op. cit.,* pp. 113-127; Penelope Tremayne, *Below the Tide* (Boston: Houghton Mifflin, 1959), pp. 106-107.

Cypriot youth with the Greco-Byzantine heritage;[65] and on the other, it strengthened its grip on the Greek Cypriot community.

The *1923 Education Law* gave authority to the Government over teaching appointments and salaries.[66] This law was intended to give the Government more active participation in administering elementary education. No attempt was made, at this time, to change the curriculum. The Archbishop continued to head the Greek Board of Education.

However, the *Education Law of 1923* invited strong reaction on the part of the National Assembly and the Church leadership, accusing the British of attempting to "de-Hellenize" the Greeks.[67] The protests by the National Assembly were further intensified as a result of the *1929 Education Law*. Under this Law, elementary school teachers were made civil servants. Their appointments, promotions, discipline and payments were brought under the control of the Government.[68]

Again these new educational changes were strongly criticized by the National Assembly and the church leadership as detrimental to the continuity of the Hellenic culture:

---

[65] Dr. Costas Spyridakis, a leading Greek Cypriot intellectual and presently the Minister of Education, wrote "The Greek schools of Cyprus are the cultural and national nurseries of the Greek population of the island . . . Their national consciousness is also stimulated so that they may become heralds of the national ideals and aims of the Greek people of the island." Costas Spyridakis, *The Greek Secondary Education of Cyprus* (Nicosia: The Cyprus Ethnarchy Office, 1959), p. 20.

[66] Weir, *op. cit.*, pp. 28, 94.

[67] The Greek Board of Education protested: ". . . [this law is] opposed to the real and expressed will of the Church of Cyprus and the Greek Cypriots; [it abolishes] the rights of the people to elect the educational committees and to administer the schools and . . . [it] also endanger(s) the national education of the Greek Cypriots. Cleovoulos I. Myrianthopoulos, *Education in Cyprus From The British Occupation 1878-1946* (Limassol: Papatsiakou Press, n.d.), p. 100; quoted in Weir, *op. cit.*, p. 94.

[68] Sir Ronald Storrs, the then Governor of Cyprus, explains the reasons why he felt the *1929 Education Law* was necessary: ". . . the method of appointing, transferring and dismissing teachers, male and female, by the Greek members of the Council was open to grave objections. The politicians too often exercised their power for political or petty personal aims. The teacher was usually the only educated man in the village; as a political agent he was, therefore, almost indispensable to the politicians, who were exclusively town-dwellers. Being dependent upon the politicians for advancement in his profession he had to serve the political purposes of his masters. The system was bad, but had been tolerated partly because the Government had lacked the financial means to pay the teachers itself." See Storrs, *op. cit.*, p. 530.

> The new Law [1929] regarding education interferes with our education . . .
> (1) the Greek people protest against this law by which their national education is enslaved.
> (2) they declare that they have the same feeling [towards education as they do towards] their religion; that they consider their children educated only when education is free from government interference.[69]

It is evident that the Church used the National Assembly to serve a dual role for the Greek Cypriots. On the one side, it became the focal point of opposition to the British Administration as in the case of the Educational Laws. On the other, it became the source of demands for sweeping reforms. These demands resulted from Greek Cypriot frustrations in the Legislative Council.

Consequently, the Church leadership sought reforms in the Legislative Council in order to relieve the Greek Cypriot frustrations. In 1929 a Greek Cypriot deputation under the leadership of the Bishop of Kition went to London and demanded the following reforms:

> (a) The representatives of the people in the Council should have unlimited legislative power regarding all local matters except such as affected the general interests of the Empire. The Council to consist only of elected members the two elements of the population being represented in proportion to their number.
> (b) In the Executive Council . . . the majority should be persons elected by the Legislative Council from its own members or outside persons; only three British born officials should participate in the executive; (the chief secretary, the attorney general and the treasurer).
> (c) The governor to have only the right to disallowance in the ratification of laws.
> (d) The decision of the Executive should bind the governor.
> (e) The King in Council should not legislate for the Island, save in extraordinary cases provided for in the Constitution.[70]

These demands, however, were rejected by the British Government.

The rejection of the Greek Cypriot demands for legislative re-

[69] *Eleftheria* (Nicosia), December 18, 1929; quoted in Weir, *op. cit.*, p. 98.
[70] Hill, *op. cit.*, pp. 430-431.

forms further alienated the Church leadership from the British Colonial Administration. This alienation increased the importance of the National Assembly to the Greek Cypriots. Thus, in January 1930, the National Assembly voted to form The National Organization. Ex-officio members of The National Organization were the Archbishop, the Bishops and the Greek Cypriot members of the Legislative Council. There was created a three-member Executive Committee, headed by the Archbishop.[71]

By 1931, when the uprising took place, The National Organization was regarded by the Greek Cypriots as their legitimate constitutional organ.

THE NATURE OF THE 1931 UPRISING AND THE ENOSIS MOVEMENT

The general causes which led to the 1931 uprising were the economic problems, the rift over taxation in the Legislative Council, and the Tribute.[72]

The economic crisis was in fact part of the depression which dominated all Europe in the 1920's. The unrest was intensified by extensive unemployment. Thousands of workers lost their jobs in the asbestos and copper mines; debts were mounting and the value of agricultural products, the main lifeline of the Cypriot economy, dropped to a low ebb. To meet extremely increasing deficits, the government found it necessary to increase taxation. Unable to do this in the Council, the government reverted to executive orders. The whole Cypriot population suffered under these economic conditions and the atmosphere became increasingly tense.[73]

The economic tensions resulted in a falling-out within the Legislative Council. On April 28, 1931, a Turkish Cypriot member of the Council voted with the Greek Cypriots to defeat a proposed increase in taxation of 20,000 pounds sterling.[74] It was evident

---

[71] Zannetos, *op. cit.*, II, p. 125. See also, Kranidiotis, *op. cit.*, p. 44. Kranidiotis quotes the objectives of The National Organization as "consolidating the efforts of the Greek Cypriot people towards their national objective the union of Cyprus with Mother Greece."

[72] See *supra*, fn. 49, p. 13.

[73] Alastos, *op. cit.*, pp. 349-350.

[74] Regarding the Turkish Cypriot member of the Council voting along with the Greek Cypriots, Sir Ronald Storrs, the then Governor of Cyprus, gave the following account: "Unfortunately, the Turkish Consul, Assaf Bey, a

that the reliance of the British authorities on the Turkish Cypriot members in the Legislative Council collapsed. The tax increase had to be imposed by an Executive Order.

The imposed tax increase, coupled with the ill-timed announcement in the British Parliament in July 1931 that the Tribute collected from the Cypriots went into a sinking fund for the Ottoman loan of 1855,[75] led to the "Manifesto" and the October 1931 uprising. The Manifesto was issued by the Bishop of Kition. It was a direct result of the rift within the Legislative Council and the imposition of the tax increase.

Frustrated in the Legislative Council, the Greek Cypriot members met secretly in the village of Saitta, in mid-September 1931 to discuss a common course of action. They proposed civil disobedience and refusal to pay taxes.

The decisions of the Greek members of the Legislative Council were taken up by The National Organization.[76] In a series of meetings, the Organization was unable to reach a decision. In its last meeting, the Bishop of Kition presented his Manifesto. The Manifesto was accepted, and it was agreed that all Greek Cypriot members of the Legislative Council would meet in a week's time to arrange a date for their resignation and the Manifesto's proclamation. In spite of this agreement, the Bishop published his Manifesto the following day (October 17, 1931) and simultaneously submitted his resignation.[77]

---

strong Nationalist and Kemalist, had succeeded in creating a small but active element of opposition to the loyal Turkish majority. I discovered his intrigues and reported them to the Government, who procured his recall, but not before he had so influenced the Turkish electorate that the Greeks were able to secure the election of a Turk who could no longer be counted upon to support the Government. Though a man of straw, he nevertheless possessed in effect the casting vote of the Legislative Council. This completely upset the balance of power . . . The bill unanimously opposed by the Greek members, . . . and the little Turk—the thirteenth Greek— . . . voted with the traditional enemies of his race. The bill was thrown out, and once again the Governor was compelled in order to carry on the Government to invoke most reluctantly the assistance of an Order in Council." Storrs, *op. cit.,* pp. 531-532.

[75] Although the Tribute was abolished in 1927, it was not known to the Cypriots until the July, 1931 British statement that the money collected did not go to the Ottoman Sultan. The Chancellor of the Exchequer's statement explained that the money collected from the Cypriots went to the bond holders of an 1855 Ottoman Loan as a result of the Empire's default in 1877.

[76] Alastos, *op. cit.,* pp. 351-352.

[77] Pana, *op. cit.,* p. 104.

The Manifesto appealed directly to the emotions of the Greek Cypriots, and sparked the uprising:

> Hellenes:
> Fifty-three years of British occupation convinced us that:
> (a) Slaves do not become free by appealing to the good nature of their masters;
> (b) Masters disregard and frown on slaves who beg for favors;
> (c) Our only salvation is our National liberation; we must realize that our Masters are on our land for their own selfish interests.
> For all these reasons, we are determined to follow the only road which is open to us; the road that leads to our salvation. We shall raise the flag of Enosis and under its guidance we shall pursue our National Liberation, our Union with Greece. In the name of God, protector of Justice and Freedom; in the name of the Eternal Idea of our Hellenic heritage. Let us obey the Voice that guides us from the Sinai of our National Codes.
> Spiritually we are all citizens of Free Greece, and we condemn those among us who obey faithfully the Laws of our foreign masters. Let us show our civil disobedience against our oppressor, and let us make every effort to eliminate from our land, that which is called British Occupation of Cyprus.
> United, let us struggle together and He, who made man to be free not slave of others, shall guide our path.[78]

The Manifesto and the various speeches throughout the island by the Bishop of Kition and other inspired leaders, led to a spontaneous uprising. The Greek members of the Legislative Council resigned. In Nicosia, the Greek Cypriots staged a massive protest against the British. This protest ended in rioting and the burning of the Governor's house.[79]

The significance of this uprising is that the Church leadership was able to mobilize the whole Greek Cypriot community behind the *Enosis* cause.

---

[78] Kranidiotis, *op. cit.*, my free translation, pp. 47-48.

[79] The net results of the uprising were six killed and some three dozen wounded. There were no casualties on the Government side. This indicates that the uprising was not planned; but at the same time, there was no attempt on the part of the Church leadership to prevent it. For a detailed description of the uprising, see Storrs, *op. cit.*, pp. 538-544.

Within ten days, the uprising was suppressed. More than 2,000 persons were convicted for participating in the disturbances and the leadership was exiled.[80] The revolt was declared seditious, and the Legislative Council was abolished by Letters Patent on November 12, 1931. Power to legislate was now vested in the Governor.[81]

Laws were instituted prohibiting the flying of the Greek flag and meetings of more than five people without permission from the District Commissioner. The Governor became the central authority concerning all matters of the elementary schools, and students were "forbidden to sing the national anthem of Greece, to fly the Greek Flag, and to display any portraits of the heroes of the 1821 Greek Revolution." The teaching of Greek history and geography was also forbidden.[82] The Church leadership again reacted against the educational laws. In a memorandum sent to the Governor, the *locum tenens,*[83] the temporary head of the Church during the exile of the Archbishop, protested:

> Without considering the fact that in order to progress spiritually and morally our people would need more knowledge of Greek history and that to progress materially they would need . . . agricultural and other practical subjects in place of foreign languages; we are of the opinion that the results from the restrictions on Greek history and geography and the introduction of the English will be harmful to the education of the Greek Cypriots . . . Following the examples of all the Archbishops who . . . have kept the education of Cyprus under the protection of the Church, I consider it my duty to prove by this memorandum how harmful these educational changes will be and to ask that the people of Cyprus be allowed again to enjoy the rights and privileges in their educational affairs.[84]

---

[80] Among those banished from the island were Nicodemus, Bishop of Kition (who died in exile) and Makarios, Bishop of Kyrenia (who later became Archbishop Makarios II, 1947-1950). Makarios II returned to Cyprus in 1946 when the Labor Government withdrew the Order in October, 1946. See Alastos, *op. cit.,* p. 355.

[81] For a detailed description of the laws enacted in Cyprus after the disturbances of 1931, see Percy Arnold, *Cyprus Challenge* (London: The Hogarth Press, 1956), pp. 109-113.

[82] *Ibid.*

[83] "Locum Tenens" refers to a temporary substitute for the Archbishop while the Archiepiscopal See was vacant.

[84] Quoted in Weir, *op. cit.,* pp. 99-100.

The uprising having been suppressed and the restricted measures adopted, government was now carried on by the Governor and a hand-picked Advisory Council. There were five Cypriots selected to serve on the Advisory Council. They were only allowed to express their opinion on annual estimates and the possibility of re-establishing the Constitution. None of the clergy were invited to serve on the Advisory Council. Of the five members, four were Greek and one was a Turk. The Greek members were immediately branded as traitors.[85] As cooperation with the British was viewed as unpatriotic, the Church, which was not involved, maintained its dominant position.

Although the Church leadership was banished, the *Enosis* movement did not vanish. There were persistent efforts by Metropolitan Leontios of Paphos, who as *locum tenens* conducted the *Enosis* agitation during the vacancy of the Archiepiscopal See. He headed deputations to London and promoted *Enosis*. Thus, the hold of the Church on the Greek Cypriot people continued unabated.

In 1937, the Government passed three laws to curb the activities of the Church. *Law #25* gave the Government the authority to investigate the affairs and accounts of the Church. *Law #33, The Autocephalous Greek Orthodox Church of Cyprus Law,* provided for disqualification for Church office of anyone deported or convicted of sedition. Furthermore, *Law #34* permitted the Governor to invalidate, by veto, any election to the Orthodox See.[86]

The Church, although legally curbed, did not let any opportunity go by without dramatizing its martyrdom. The more the Church was curbed, the more it tightened its grip on the people.

This pattern of agitation and repression continued until the end of World War II when the *Enosis* movement entered a new phase.

---

[85] Hill, *op. cit.*, IV, p. 432.
[86] Arnold, *op. cit.*, p. 118.

2

ENOSIS AND BRITISH ATTEMPTS AT CONSTITUTIONAL SELF-GOVERNMENT IN THE POST-WORLD WAR II PERIOD

With the end of World War II, the political developments in Cyprus entered a new phase. On the one side, there was increased expectation by the Greek Cypriots and the Greek Cypriot Church leadership that Britain would accede to their *Enosis* demands. The Greek Cypriots felt that as a reward for the Greek efforts on the side of the Allies during the war, the British would grant them *Enosis*. On the other side, there was a changing British attitude toward granting a limited self-government to the Cypriots. This attitude can be attributed partly to the changing political opinion in Britain regarding British policy toward her colonies; partly to British attempts to satisfy the clamor of the Greek Cypriots and possibly to weaken their desire for *Enosis;* and finally to ensure British strategic needs in the Middle East.

Although the post-World War II British attitude toward Cyprus was to encourage limited self-government, this was not the Greek Cypriots' expectation. As a result, the respective positions of the British Colonial power and the Greek Cypriot leadership, remained, by and large, irreconciliable.

At this point, through an examination and an analysis of the major British constitutional proposals from the end of World War II to the Zurich and London Agreements, we shall endeavor to show how the positions of ruler and ruled affected the development of constitutional government in Cyprus.

The changing British policy in Cyprus appeared before the end of the war. In this context, the colonial government, in 1941, permitted the formation of political organizations in Cyprus.

The most important political organization emerging at this time was The Progressive Party of the Working People (AKEL), a left-wing organization.[1] It must be pointed out that the first Communist movement in Cyprus was organized in 1924 [2] under the name of The Communist Party of Cyprus (KKK). However, the predominantly agrarian nature of the Cypriot community, and the strong grip of the Church on its people had negative effects on the influence of Communism in Cyprus at that time. Therefore, the early Communist movement in Cyprus was forced to follow a purely nationalistic policy appealing to the sentiment of *Enosis*. With the 1931 nationalistic uprising in Cyprus and the restrictive measures imposed by the colonial government, the KKK was proscribed and some of its leaders were deported along with the Church leaders. When the party reappeared in 1941, it was closely interwoven with the labor union movement in Cyprus.[3] Since that time the labor union movement has been the major source of AKEL's strength.

The first test of the strength of the Communist movement in Cyprus came in the 1943 municipal elections, where AKEL, supported by the left-wing labor unions, won control of two out of six towns. The party's strength, which is presently estimated to be about 20 percent, has wavered all through the years depending on its position on the nationalistic issues of Cyprus and its relations with the Church leadership. By and large, AKEL's influence in the political spectrum of Cyprus has been nullified by the strong role of the Church.[4]

Besides allowing for the formation of political parties, the British, in Cyprus, began to show leniency toward the Church. Thus, on October 26, 1946, the Colonial government repealed the *1931 Deportation Law* and the 1937 restrictive laws on the Church. As a result, the Church was free to reassert its leadership in the *Enosis* movement.

The restoration of the Church to its traditional role coincides

---

[1] At the same time, two right-wing organizations emerged: The Cyprus National Party (KEK) and The Cyprus Farmers Union (PEK). However, the two right-wing groups were loosely organized and closely controlled by the Church of Cyprus. Therefore, their role as political factions was essentially absorbed by the Church leadership.

[2] Hill, *op. cit.,* fn. 3, p. 539.

[3] This was referred to as the Pancyprian Trade Union Committee (PTUC), which was essentially the forerunner of the present left-wing labor organization, The Pancyprian Federation of Labor (PEO).

[4] Their agreement to accept limited representation in the Makarios government in 1959 is a good example. *Infra* p. 74.

with the British attempts to promote limited self-government. In view of the fact, however, that the Church's sole political goal was *Enosis,* any attempts by the British for limited self-government were likely to be defeated. The Church, in fact, was able to consolidate the Greek Cypriot community under the banner of *Enosis* and to neutralize all possible opposition.

The most militant Church leader of the post-World War II *Enosis* movement was Makarios,[5] the Bishop of Kyrenia. Upon his return from exile on February 16, 1947, the Bishop addressed a large gathering in Nicosia, at which time he rejected any British plan for limited self-government and stressed that the only demand of the Greek Cypriots was *"Enosis* and only *Enosis."* Thus, the Bishop of Kyrenia set the stage for future Greek Cypriot political demands.

On June 21, 1947, the Church elected its first Archbishop since the 1931 uprising. Leontios, the new Archbishop, who served as *locum tenens* since 1931, was a strong Enotist. Leontios' early death, however, just over a month after his election, paved the way for the militant Enotist Bishop of Kyrenia to become Archbishop, Makarios II. Until his death in 1950, Makarios II refused to consider any British offer short of *Enosis.*

The Turkish Cypriot community opposed the new Greek Cypriot *Enosis* demands as they did in the past. More often, however, they abstained from taking direct action because they were usually assured by the Colonial Secretary that their interests as a minority would be safeguarded. An interesting point regarding the Turkish community's position at this time, may be seen in the statement by KATAK,[6] in January 1947. The Turkish Cypriots expressed their opinion that, if Britain were to leave, the island should go back to Turkey, its previous master and occupant.[7]

---

[5] Makarios the Bishop of Kyrenia should not be confused with the present Archbishop of Cyprus, Makarios III. The Bishop of Kyrenia was Archbishop Makarios II from 1947-1950.

[6] "KATAK" refers to *Cyprus Turkish Minority's Association* and was established in 1943. Dr. Fazil Kuchuk, the Vice President of Cyprus, joined the Association in 1943, but he later resigned and established the *Cyprus Turkish National Party* in 1945, and in 1955 he changed the name of his party to *Cyprus Is Turkish Party*.

[7] Hill, *op. cit.,* p. 564. Current Turkish Cypriot sources strongly indicate the Turkish Cypriot community's attachment to Turkey. "The Turks [of Cyprus] . . . never ceased to identify themselves with Turkey and expressed their

In 1950, Makarios III became Archbishop of Cyprus. Since then, he has been the dominant Greek Cypriot politico-religious leader.

Makarios was born in 1913 in a small village in the western part of Cyprus. At the age of 13, he became a novice at the twelfth-century Kykko Monastery. His early religious training was complemented with a strong Hellenic secondary education at the Pancyprian Gymnasium in Nicosia. There, at the Gymnasium, under the Church-directed curriculum, young Makarios was imbued with *Enosis* and Greek nationalism. In 1938, under a scholarship from the Church, Makarios attended the Schools of Theology and Law at the University of Athens—the center of Hellenism. In the same year, he was ordained a priest.

After graduating from the University of Athens in 1942, he remained in Greece throughout the German occupation. In 1946, upon receiving a World Council of Churches scholarship, he attended the School of Theology at Boston University. While a student in Boston, he was elected Bishop of Kition; and he returned to Cyprus in 1948 to undertake his duties as Bishop.[8]

Upon becoming Bishop of Kition, Makarios began to exercise a dominating role in both the religious and political life of Cyprus. In 1950, at the age of 37, he became the youngest Archbishop in the history of Cyprus. Since 1959, he has combined, in a Byzantine politico-religious marriage, his powerful role as leader of the Greek Orthodox Church with that of the Presidency of the Republic of Cyprus.

In his powerful position as Archbishop, Makarios was able to unite the Greek Cypriot community in the *Enosis* drive against the British; and later on, as Archbishop-President against Turkish and Turkish Cypriot opposition. However, because of the nature of his background and training, he was unable to cope effectively with British tactics. Moreover, he minimized Turkish and Turkish

---

will and their consciousness to remain part and parcel of Turkey." The Vice President, *et al, The Cypriot Turkish Case and Greek Atrocities in Cyprus* (Nicosia: Halkin Sesi Press, n.d.), p. 2.

[8] For a short biographical sketch of Archbishop Makarios; see, Cyprus, Public Information Office, *Short Biographies of the President and Vice President of the Republic of Cyprus* (Nicosia: Printing Office of the Republic, 1963) pp. 3-8.

Cypriot aims in Cyprus, thereby, inviting strong Turkish reaction and continued deadlocks. Thus, today, almost twenty years after he had played an instrumental role in defeating the 1948 British self-government plan, Makarios is still searching for a constitutional settlement, and in a sense, self-government of Cyprus from Greece and Turkey.

The 1948 British Constitutional Plan

The newly elected Labor Government in England announced its intention to create a more liberal regime in the internal affairs of Cyprus. This announcement was made by the Secretary of State for the Colonies in October, 1946.[9] Consequently, the Governor of Cyprus, Sir Charles Wolley, was to call for a Consultative Assembly representing the various factions in Cyprus. This Assembly's intent was to discuss the ways and means of creating a Council. The Council was intended to represent the people of Cyprus, and together with the British Governor, was to govern the internal affairs of the island.[10] Also, in an attempt to show its goodwill, the British Government was to propose a ten-year economic development plan.

When the new Governor, Lord Winster, addressed the people of Cyprus on April 6, 1947, he reiterated the British desire to grant a liberal Constitution. In July 1947 invitations were sent to organizations and individuals to meet in the Consultative Assembly for the purpose of drafting a Constitution for Cyprus.

The prospects of the Consultative Assembly, however, had been defeated from the start; the Church leadership of Cyprus was determined to ask for nothing less than "union with Greece." Therefore, the Church leadership boycotted the Assembly and refused to take part in the Consultative Assembly's proceedings.

Of the forty people invited, only eighteen attended the Assembly's opening meeting on November 1, 1947. Of the eighteen, seven were

---

[9] Mr. Creech-Jones, the Under-Secretary of State for the Colonies in answering a question stated in the House of Commons on October 23, 1946 that the Government intended to ask the Governor of Cyprus to call a Consultative Assembly "to consider . . . proposals for constitutional reforms . . . [and the] re-establishment of a Central Legislature." Great Britain, *Parliamentary Debates* (Commons), (London: Her Majesty's Stationery Office, 1946), Vol. 427, pp. 396-397. (Hereafter cited as: *Parliamentary Debates,* (year)).

[10] *Ibid.*

Turkish Cypriots, eight were left-wing Greek Cypriots, two were non-party affiliated Greek Cypriots and one was Maronite. Twenty-two rejected the invitation.[11] Heading the latter list was the newly elected Archbishop, Leontios. The reason for declining the invitation was that the Assembly's task precluded any discussion on union of Cyprus with Greece. During the Assembly's meeting on November 7, 1947, eight Greek members proposed discussion on full self-government for Cyprus. Sir Edward Jackson, Chief Justice of Cyprus and presiding officer of the Assembly, ruled that full self-government was not within the terms of reference of the Assembly.

Significantly, the eight Greek Cypriot members who proposed discussion on self-government were the left-wing Greek Cypriots. Although the left-wing leadership accepted participation in the Assembly, at no time were they willing to participate in a discussion where full self-government was ruled out. The Greek Cypriot Communists' participation in the Assembly must be viewed in the context of the Greek Civil War. In Greece, the Communists, although at first successful, suffered defeats in 1945 and 1946. The Cypriot Communists, therefore, viewed the Greek Government as "Monarcho-Fascist" and were cool to the idea of *Enosis* at that time. This may have been their basic reason for accepting participation in the Consultative Assembly. But, once the proceedings in the Assembly revealed that full self-government was not within its terms of reference, the Cypriot Communists objected to the British Plan.

By excluding any discussion on full self-government, the Assembly was unable to make any progress and adjourned. For the next six months, the Assembly remained inactive. Then, on May 7, 1948, the British Governor tried to break the deadlock by making "new Constitutional proposals." Since these new British proposals again excluded discussion of *Enosis* or full self-government, the Cypriot Church leadership urged their rejection.

The British proposals were made public in May 1948. They contained the following provisions: There was to be an elected Legislative Council consisting of twenty-two members, eighteen Greeks and four Turks; the Council was to include four official

---

[11] *Royal Institute of International Affairs, op. cit.*, p. 9.

members, the Colonial Secretary, the Attorney General, the Treasurer, and the Senior Commissioner.

The eighteen Greek members were to be elected on the general election register, and the four Turks on a separate Turkish communal register. Elections were to be based on universal adult male suffrage, which could be extended to women if the Assembly so decided. The presiding officer, a governor's appointee, could not be one of the members of the Council. Unlike the provision in the 1882 Constitution, the presiding officer would have no original vote. The matter of a casting vote was to be decided later on.[12]

In addition, the Governor was to be empowered to pass or reject any bill regardless of the decision of the Legislative Council. These powers were to be reserved for the Governor, to act "in the interest of public order, good faith, or good government." The Governor's consent was also required before any bill on defense, finance, external affairs, minorities and amendments to the Constitution were introduced for discussion.[13]

There was to be an Executive Council composed of three Greeks and one Turk appointed by the Governor from the Legislative Council. The Council's function was to assist the Governor in an advisory capacity. Finally, provisions were made for the appointment of Cypriot under-Secretaries in various departments.[14]

When the above proposals were officially presented to the Assembly on May 21, 1948, they were accepted by a vote of eleven to seven. The eleven votes consisted of six Turkish Cypriots,[15] one Maronite, and four independent Greek Cypriots.

---

[12] *Royal Institute of International Affairs, op. cit.*, pp. 9-10.

[13] *The Times* (London), May 12, 1948.

[14] *Ibid.*

[15] Current Turkish Cypriot literature indicates the Turkish Cypriot community's feelings vis-a-vis the Church leadership's position towards the 1948 British Constitutional Plan. "In 1948 Britain offered a form of restricted self-government to the island. The Greek Orthodox Church said 'No' because it declared 'our aim is *Enosis* . . . Any collaboration with the British is treason.' This threat and the threat of excommunication prevented the Greek people of Cyprus from testing the fruits of gradual self-government and lost the island the chance to grow into full self-government by a process of evolution." See, The Turkish Communal Chamber, *Looking Back: An Official Briefing* (Nicosia: Halkin Sesi Press, 1963), p. 6.

The opposing seven were Greek Cypriots.[16]

Since twenty-two Greek Cypriots had already declined to participate in the Assembly's work, and seven out of eleven of those participating voted against the proposals, it was evident that the overwhelming majority of the Greek Cypriots opposed the British proposals. Consequently, the Assembly was again forced to adjourn its meeting. Thereafter, the Governor was to consult London for future plans.

On August 12, 1948, Lord Winster, the Governor of Cyprus dissolved the Assembly, but he did not withdraw the May 7, 1948, proposals.[17] The proposals remained open for future reconsideration by the Cypriots. However, the Greek Cypriot leadership, under the aegis of the Church, persisted in its demands for *Enosis* and refused to reconsider the proposals. Finally, in July 1954, the British officially withdrew the offer.[18]

It is interesting to note that the 1948 British proposals provided for limited majority decisions in the Legislature, as long as they did not encroach upon the Governor's enumerated powers and did not conflict with principles of good government or prejudice the minority's rights. In this context, the eighteen Greek elected

---

[16] It is significant to note that the seven members voting against the proposals were the left-wing Greek Cypriots who originally accepted the invitation to participate in the Assembly.

[17] Lord Winster, the Governor of Cyprus, made the following statement: "The offer of a constitution of the nature outlined in the Secretary of State's dispatch of May 7 is not withdrawn. If at any time responsible and fully representative political leaders in Cyprus come forward to ask that those or comparable constitutional proposals may be re-examined and implemented, . . . His Majesty's Government will readily take the necessary steps to enable this to be done . . . I must repeat that no change in the sovereignty of the island is intended." *The Times* (London), August 13, 1948.

[18] On July 28, 1954, Mr. Hopkinson, the Minister of State for Colonial Affairs, stated in the House of Commons that the 1948 constitutional offer was being withdrawn, since it was not considered by "responsible . . . political leaders." At the same time, Mr. Hopkinson indicated that the British Government had intended to propose a new, modified Constitution. Under this new plan, there was to be created a single Legislature in which the official and nominated members would form a majority. However, immediate doubts were expressed in the House as to the prospect of such limited proposals. See, *Parliamentary Debates* (1954), Vol. 531, pp. 504-535.

Archbishop Makarios, in a statement regarding the new British Plan, described it as "unacceptable" and that the Greek Cypriots would continue to press for *Enosis.* The Turkish Cypriots, on the other hand, agreed to accept the new proposals provided their rights were safeguarded. *The Times* (London), August 2, 1954.

members could have carried the Legislature even if the four Turkish members and the four officially appointed members opposed them.

In retrospect, the 1948 British constitutional proposals could have become a basis for implanting limited constitutional government in Cyprus. That the Church leadership chose to oppose them, reflects its unwillingness to compromise the cause of *Enosis*.

The Church's uncompromising stand on *Enosis* had a two-fold effect: on the one hand, it succeeded in neutralizing the British Constitutional proposals; on the other, it meant that any British proposal had to be first accepted by the Church leadership. Since neither the British were willing to accede to the Church leadership's demands, nor was the Church willing to participate in the British limited self-government plans, prospects for implanting constitutional government in Cyprus remained on the theoretical level.

Church Leadership and the Intensification of the Enosis Movement

By 1954, when the original 1948 Plan was officially withdrawn, the *Enosis* movement was reaching new dimensions. The Church leadership had already initiated its courses of action to solidify its position over the Greek Cypriot community and to intensify the *Enosis* drive. In counteracting the British Plan, the Church leadership took the following steps: First, it initiated the *Enosis* plebiscite of January 1950; second, it increased pressure on the Greek Government for more active participation in the *Enosis* movement; third it encouraged the E.O.K.A.[19] underground movement.

The plebiscite of January 1950 was intended, on the one hand, to mobilize the Greek Cypriots behind the *Enosis* movement and, on the other hand, to counteract the British plan for limited self-government. It was proclaimed by Archbishop Makarios II. However, the real power instigating this plebiscite was the youthful Bishop of Kition, who later became Archbishop Makarios III and President of Cyprus. It is evident, therefore, that President

---

[19] E.O.K.A. stands for *National Organization of Cypriot Fighters.*

Makarios began to play a dominant role in Greek Cypriot politics as soon as he became Bishop of Kition in 1948.

As Bishop of Kition, Makarios began to exert his leadership by taking steps to reorganize and reform the Church machinery. In 1948, only one month after his enthronement, he began to reform the bureaucratic leadership of the Church—the Ethnarchy Council.[20] Membership in the Ethnarchy Council included religious and secular leaders. By the end of 1948, Bishop Makarios organized the Ethnarchy Bureau with himself as Director. The Bureau published an illustrated monthly magazine, *Helleniki Kypros (Greek Cyprus)* to promote the *Enosis* movement.[21] Makarios' youthfulness and administrative abilities, therefore, gave new impetus to *Enosis.*

In an encyclical issued on December 8, 1949, Archbishop Makarios II set the stage for the plebiscite. The Archbishop asked the people of Cyprus to vote for "*Enosis* and only *Enosis.*" All Greek Cypriots over eighteen, male and female, were given the right by the Church to take part in this plebiscite. The voting consisted of signing one's name on a sheet provided in the various polling places. The results showed that of the 244,747 entitled to vote, 215,108 or 95.7 percent, voted in favor of this plebiscite.[22]

The significance of the plebiscite can be viewed from two angles: First, the Church and the Greek Cypriots felt that the results were a clear indication of the overwhelming desire of the Greek Cypriots to unite with Mother Greece. In a sense, this was their answer to the constitutional proposals by the British Government; second, the predominance of the Church in the *Enosis* movement proved to be indisputable.[23] In addition, the plebiscite served as a pressure on Greece to take an active role in the *Enosis* movement, and it hampered British attempts toward limited self-government.[24]

---

[20] The Ethnarchy Council was the Church-controlled governing body of the Greek Cypriot community.

[21] The editor of *Helleniki Kypros* was Nikos Kranidiotis, a leading literary figure in Cyprus and presently the Cypriot Ambassador to Greece.

[22] *Royal Institute of International Affairs, op. cit.,* p. 11.

[23] After their attempt to participate in the Consultative Assembly, the left-wing organizations were now following a strong *Enosis* policy supporting the Church movement.

[24] The results of the plebiscite served as the cornerstone for new tactics in the *Enosis* drive. Delegations were dispatched to enlighten world opinion regarding the feelings of the Greek Cypriots.

As it was pointed out in Chapter I, Greece always had an interest in the *Enosis* movement. However, increasing involvement by Greece in the movement began in the post-World War II period, and it was intensified in the 1950's.

Already in 1948, King Paul of the Hellenes, in an interview in *The New York Times,* stated the following:

> Greece certainly desires and will continue to desire the union of Cyprus with the rest of Greece. It is difficult to understand why this has not yet been effected. The argument that this might interfere with the British security positions is not valid. Were Cyprus to be given to Greece, as the vast majority of its population desires, this would in no way interfere with any military or other bases Britain has established there. Furthermore, if it could be arranged under the United Nations, Greece would be prepared to offer further base facilities to Britain, or for the United States in Crete or elsewhere.[25]

The British representative in Athens delivered a strong protest against the encouragement of agitation in favor of union of Cyprus with Greece as not being in the best interest of Great Britain and Greece.

In 1950, following the *Enosis* plebiscite, the Greek Government debated the Cyprus question in Parliament. Two hundred members of the Greek Parliament signed a petition expressing their support for *Enosis.*[26]

In February 1951, when the British Minister of State, Kenneth Younger, in a statement in the House of Commons pointed out that no Greek Government ever had officially demanded *Enosis,* the then Prime Minister of Greece, Sophocles Venizelos, stated that every Greek Government since 1912 had in a sense made this request. To prove his point, Sophocles Venizelos stated in the Greek Parliament that his Government, there and then, demanded *"Enosis."*[27] The demand was not pressed, however,

[25] July 28, 1948; For a comprehensive analysis of Greece's involvement in Cyprus, see *Infra.,* Chapter 6.

[26] *The Cyprus Plebiscite and the Greek Parliament,* (London: The Cypriot National Delegation, 1950), p. 3.

[27] Prime Minister Venizelos's statement indicated that: "Since 1912 all Greek Governments have formulated this [*Enosis*] demand to His Brittanic Majesty's Government . . . I am pleased to avail myself of the opportunity of this official tribune to proclaim the Greek Government's demand for the union of Cyprus with Mother Greece." Quoted in *Manchester Guardian,* February 16, 1951.

for the Greek Government's attitude at that time, was to settle the question within the Anglo-Greek friendship.

However, pressures on the Greek Government continued. Pro-Greek Cypriot political activity was being carried out by the newly formed Pan-Hellenic Committee for Cyprus Struggle, headed by the Archbishop of Greece, Spyridon.[28] In addition, Archbishop Makarios III of Cyprus, during a visit to Greece, spoke over Radio Athens pressing for more active Greek participation in the *Enosis* campaign.

Following the November 1952 Greek elections, when Marshall Papagos and his Greek Rally party secured an absolute majority in the Greek Parliament, the Greek Government made plans to press Great Britain for *Enosis*. In September 1953, Papagos attempted to discuss the question of *Enosis* with Prime Minister Eden. Eden refused to discuss the question.[29] As a result of Eden's refusal, Marshall Papagos announced that Greece intended to bring the Cyprus issue before the United Nations. In August 1954, Greece requested that the issue of Cyprus be discussed by the United Nation's General Assembly.[30]

Reacting to the Greek Government's demands, Selwyn Lloyd, the British Minister of State, speaking in the United Nations General Committee on September 23, 1954, stated that in his view Greece was in effect, asking the United Nations to interfere in the domestic affairs of a foreign power.[31] Furthermore, the British stressed that agitation for *Enosis* could hamper progress toward self-government for the Greek and Turkish Cypriots alike.

The discussion in the United Nations Political Committee revealed Turkey's interest in Cyprus. The Turkish representative

---

[28] Alastos, *op. cit.*, p. 382.

[29] In February, 1955, Marshall Papagos made public his conversation with Anthony Eden. He was quoted as having stated that as far as the British Government was concerned, there was "no Cyprus question at the present time or in the future." Quoted in *The Times* (London), February 8, 1955.

[30] On August 20, 1954, the Greek Government asked the United Nations Secretary General to include on the agenda of the General Assembly's next session, the item, "Application under the auspices of the United Nations of the Principle of Equal Rights and Self-Determination of Peoples in the Case of the Population on the Island of Cyprus." United Nations, General Assembly, *Greece: Request for the Inclusion of a Supplementary Item in the Provisional agenda of the ninth Session* (A/2703, 20 August 1954) in General Assembly, *Official Records,* Ninth Session, Annexes, Agenda Item 62, pp. 1-3.

[31] United Nations, General Assembly, *Official Records,* Ninth Session, General Committee, 93rd Meeting, 23 September 1954, p. 8.

argued: ". . . [Greece's request] that the people of Cyprus were entitled to determine their own fate was probably linked to the assertion that Cyprus belonged to Greece." He added that "the people of Cyprus were no more Greek than the territory itself." [32]

The United Nations General Assembly adopted a New Zealand proposal "not to consider the problem further for the time being, because it does not appear appropriate to adopt a resolution on the question of Cyprus." [33]

The Greek setback in the United Nations had significant effects in Cyprus. Demonstrations and riots broke out on the island and a general strike was proclaimed. As a result, "a section of the Greek Cypriot population began to feel that only through force and armed resistance could the Colonial power be forced to grant freedom to the island."[34] Already in 1952, the E.O.K.A. plans were being made in Cyprus and Greece. The Cypriot Ethnarchy was playing a major role in the preparation for this armed struggle.[35] The Greek Government's official support, however, came after the defeat of the Greek appeal to the United Nations in 1954. The outbreak of the E.O.K.A. revolution came on April 1, 1955.

The 1955 Tripartite Conference and the Harding-Makarios Constitutional Negotiations

The outbreak of violence in Cyprus led to Britain's initiating the Tripartite Conference in August 1955. Greece and Turkey were officially invited to a London Conference to discuss "prob-

[32] United Nations, General Assembly, *Official Records,* Ninth Session, First Committee, 750th Meeting, 14 December 1954, p. 551; for a comprehensive analysis of Turkey's involvement in Cyprus, see *infra* Chapter 6.

[33] United Nations, General Assembly, *Application Under the Auspices of the United Nations, of the Principle of Equal Rights and Self-Determination of Peoples in the Case of the Population of the Island of Cyprus,* Resolution 814 (IX), 17 December 1954, in General Assembly, *Official Records,* Ninth Session, Supplement No. 21 (A/2890), p. 5.

[34] Kranidiotis, *op. cit.,* p. 95.

[35] According to General George Grivas, the leader of the E.O.K.A. underground movement, the first secret liberation committee held to prepare for an armed struggle in Cyprus, took place on July 2, 1952 in Athens. The Committee was "under the chairmanship of Archbishop Makarios with other members of the Cyprus Ethnarchy Council present. By November 1952 Andreas Azinas, the Secretary General of P.E.K., the Cyprus Farmers Union, became the liaison between Grivas and Archbishop Makarios. General George Grivas, *The Memoirs of General Grivas,* ed. Charles Foley (New York: Frederick A. Praeger, 1964), pp. 17-18.

lems of security in the Eastern Mediterranean including Cyprus." The Greek and Turkish Governments accepted the invitation.[36] The calling of the 1955 Tripartite Conference by the British was intended, on the one hand, to offset the Greek demands at the United Nations; and on the other, to emphasize the British strategic interests in Cyprus and the Middle East.[37]

Although the announcement for the Conference was made on June 30, 1955,[38] the Conference was not held until August 29, 1955. According to Stanley Mayes, this delaying tactic by the British was intended to pressure the Greeks to "postpone their demand for self-determination" and to "reassure" Turkish fears about Cypriot "self-government." [39]

The Tripartite Conference, however, failed to provide a basis for a compromise. Moreover, the multiplicity of vested interests tended to make the Cyprus issue more and more complicated. Any attempts to deal with the issue had to take into consideration the interests of Britain, Greece, and Turkey.[40]

The British Government had no intention of changing the status of the island, but it made attempts to prevent the collapse of the Tripartite Conference. Harold Macmillan, the Foreign Secretary and the presiding officer of the Conference, on Septem-

---

[36] *Royal Institute of International Affairs, op. cit.,* p. 17. Turkey accepted the invitation on July 2 and Greece on July 8, 1955. See *The Times* (London), July 3 and 9, 1955, respectively.

Charles Foley expresses the belief that the main purpose of the Tripartite Conference was to "introduce Turkey into the dispute"; Charles Foley, *Island in Revolt* (London: Longmans, 1962) p. 28. Stanley Mayes states that "Britain's aims in the Tripartite Conference was to gain time and get the Greeks to postpone their demand for self-determination." Mayes, *op cit.,* p. 209. Makarios, as soon as the British invitations went out, flew to Athens asking the Greek Government not to stop her appeal to the United Nations in spite of the Conference Foley, *op. cit.,* p. 29.

[37] For further analysis of British strategic interests in Cyprus see *infra,* pp. 139-141.

[38] The Prime Minister announced in the House of Commons that "Her Majesty's Government have been giving further considerations to the strategic and other problems affecting alike the United Kingdom, Greece and Turkey in the Eastern Mediterranean . . . Her Majesty's Government accordingly invite the Greek and Turkish Governments to send representatives to confer with them in London at an early date on political and defense questions which affect the Eastern Mediterranean, including Cyprus." *Parliamentary Debates* (1955), Vol. 543, p. 511.

[39] Mayes, *op. cit.,* pp. 208-209.

[40] The origin and nature of the interests of Britain, Greece and Turkey in Cyprus are discussed fully in, *infra,* chapter 6.

ber 6, 1955, put forth proposals for "a new liberal constitution." Macmillan's assumption was that, although there might have been basic disagreements among the "parties concerned," there could have been some general agreement on limited self-government. Therefore, the British proposed a limited self-government plan with appropriate guarantees for the minorities.

In this plan provisions were to be made for an assembly, with an elected majority and "a proportionate quota of seats reserved for the Turkish minority." No specific guarantees were given for a Greek majority in the Assembly. With reference to the Executive branch, it was proposed that, with the exception of the Department of Foreign Affairs, Defence and Public Security, all Departments were to be "progressively . . . transferred to Cypriot ministers responsible to the Assembly." A proportion of ministerial portfolios was to be reserved for the Turkish Cypriot community. In addition, the British Government proposed to set up a special tripartite conference in London, whose function was to draft a Constitution and to examine the problems which might arise in applying self-government on Cyprus. The question of the future status of Cyprus was shelved and no commitments were made, because of the existing disagreements of the "parties concerned." [41]

Greek Foreign Minister Stephanopoulos expressed his regrets that the proposals did not take into account the Greek Government's basic demand, namely: "the recognition, in favour of the people of Cyprus, of the right to choose the regime they prefer, as well as the creation of the conditions which would make it possible for them to exercise that right in a democratic manner and within a reasonable period of time.[42]

Turkish Foreign Minister Zorlu asked whether the British Government intended "for the present or for the future, to accept

---

[41] For Foreign Minister Macmillan's proposals at the Tripartite Conference, see Great Britain, *The Tripartite Conference on the Eastern Mediterranean and Cyprus* (London: Her Majesty's Stationery Office, 1955), Cmd. 9594, pp. 31-35.

[42] Furthermore, Mr. Stephanopoulos stated that "The Greek Delegation specially regret that, contrary to the invariable practice successfully pursued by the United Kingdom in dealing with its dependent peoples . . . the British Government have chosen to pursue a policy of discrimination towards the people of Cyprus by not admitting in the particular case of Cyprus, that internal self-government shall lead to self-determination." *Ibid.,* p. 36.

any principle of self-determination which might ultimately lead to the independence of the Island or to its accession to another country?" [43] The British Foreign Minister assured the Turkish delegation that "We do not accept the principle of self-determination as one of universal application. We think that exceptions must be made in view of geographical, traditional, historical, strategical and other considerations."[44] It should be stressed that at this time, the Macmillan proposals did not provide for partnership among Turkey, Greece, and Britain on Cyprus. However, the Tripartite Committee was to serve, as Mr. Macmillan put it, as a "partnership at the centre." [45]

The Tripartite Conference marks the beginning of Turkey's active participation, along with Greece and Britain, in finding a solution to the problem. The Tripartite Conference failed. The British press attributed the Conference's failure to Britain's lack of foresight, Greece's high emotions and the intransigeance shown by the Turkish Government.[46]

This Conference, however, aided British diplomacy in preventing United Nations action. At the Plenary Meeting of the Tenth Session of the General Assembly, Britain argued that constructive

---

[43] The Turkish Foreign Minister stated that "on the subject of Cyprus and its *Status Quo,* [the Turkish Government] feels that this *Status Quo* was created by an international treaty [the Treaty of Lausanne] to which we were all signatories, and it must be maintained. Furthermore, if any changes were to take place in the *Status Quo* of the Island, this Island should come back to Turkey. And my Government does not think that under present conditions self-government in the Island is possible.

This will not be possible until the Greek Government has given up its claims either for the annexation of the Island of Cyprus, its union with Greece, or for the application of the principle of the self-determination of peoples to the Island." *Ibid.,* p. 37, 40.

[44] *Ibid.*

[45] *Ibid* , p. 32.

[46] *The Manchester Guardian* pointed out that "the discussions on Cyprus have come, as was feared, to an inconclusive end. Indeed it is worse than inconclusive. The effort has been seriously to worsen relations between Greece and Turkey, while Britain's own position in Cyprus has not been in the least improved." *The Manchester Guardian,* September 8, 1955.

The Economist commented that "one most unfortunate by-product of the London meeting is the sad deterioration of Greco-Turkish relations. The Greek press, understandably incensed by the uncompromising attitude of the Turkish Government . . . insist on branding Britain as the nigger in the woodpile. There is not the slightest shred of justification for this. Turkey's firm opposition to Cypriot self-determination may at first sight seem diplomatically convenient for Britain. But the aggressive way in which the Turkish case has been pressed in London, has evoked new Greco-Turkish

proposals were being made in London, and there was no need for United Nations action.[47]

The failure of the Tripartite Conference, the intensification of the E.O.K.A. struggle, and the constant pressures on Great Britain by Greece and world opinion led to direct negotiations between the new Governor, Sir John Harding, and Archbishop Makarios.[48]

The new British attempts in Cyprus were facilitated by three developments: First, Makarios agreed to accept limited self-government for a certain period, after which the Cypriots would exercise the right of self-determination; second, Makarios agreed to Britain's retaining her bases and controlling foreign affairs and defense; third, the British admitted that self-determination could be a possibility if Makarios used his influence to end the E.O.K.A. violence.[49]

The Harding-Makarios negotiations appeared to have begun in a spirit of compromise. Behind this spirit of compromise, however, were some ominous signs of disagreement. When Mr. Macmillan was asked a question in Parliament to reveal the nature of the negotiations between Makarios and Harding, he pointed out

---

tension, added to the difficulties of finding a solution for Cyprus [and] threatened NATO's security arrangements in the Eastern Mediterranean." *The Economist,* September 10, 1955.

Tom Driberg of *The Tribune* pointed out that "the London Conference on Cyprus has ended in total failure. It was doomed to failure for two reasons —the presence of the Turks and the absence of the Cypriots. The Turks were intransigently determined not to concede a square inch of their former colony to their former subjects. The Cypriots—that is the Greek four-fifth's of them . . . were and are intransigently dedicated to integral union with their fellow Greeks of the Mainland; and were, moreover, affronted by the British Government's omission even to invite them to be present while their future was being discussed." *The Tribune* (London), September 16, 1955.

[47] United Nations, General Assembly, *Official Records,* Tenth Session, General Committee, 102nd Meeting, 23 September 1955, pp. 2-3. Furthermore, Mr. Nutting, the British Delegate, pointed out that "[Prime Minister Macmillan] proposed the introduction of a liberal constitution designed to lead to the fullest measure of self-government compatible with the strategic requirements of the present international situation." United Nations, General Assembly, *Official Records,* Tenth Session, Plenary Meetings, 521st Meeting, 23 September 1955, p. 56.

[48] Sir John Harding took over the Governorship of Cyprus on October 3, 1955. Before leaving London for Cyprus, he summarized his main objectives; "to establish and maintain law and order: . . . and to be prepared at any time to discuss constitutional developments towards self-government on the basis of the proposals put forward by Britain at the London [Tripartite] Conference." *The Times* (London), October 3, 1955.

[49] Foley, *op. cit.,* p. 60.

that "Turkish feelings should not be underestimated." He explained that if Cyprus goes to the wrong hands this would mean that it may be likened to a "pistol at her [Turkey's] heart."[50] Moreover, from the very beginning of the negotiations, Harding insisted that he should not be expected to "bargain with terrorism." He was alluding to the E.O.K.A. underground movement.

Some of the more sensitive points of disagreement centered around the nature of the Constitutional Plan. The British views were set forth by Governor Sir John Harding as follows:

> . . .
>
> (b) The constitution would enable the people of Cyprus through responsible Cypriot Ministers to assume control by a suitably phased process over the departments of Government except those relating to foreign affairs and defence which would be reserved to the Governor and to public security which would also be reserved to the Governor for as long as he deems necessary.
>
> (c) The constitution would provide for an Assembly with an elected majority.
>
> (d) A Cypriot Premier to head the new administration would be chosen by the Assembly with the approval of the Governor. Ministerial portfolios would be allocated by the Premier (subject to (e) below).
>
> (e) The constitution would provide for Turkish membership in the Council of Ministers.[51]

Archbishop Makarios demanded clarification of the Constitutional Plan in the following context:

> (a) It is not made clear that all powers, Executive (except those expressly reserved to the Governor in the spheres of defence and foreign affairs), Legislative and Judicial originate from the people and are exercised exclusively by them through their elected representatives and their other constitutional organs.
>
> (b) It is not made clear that the representation in the Assembly will be proportionate to the composition of the population.

---

[50] *Parliamentary Debates* (1956), Vol. 547, p. 39.

[51] Great Britain, *Cyprus: Correspondence Exchanged Between The Governor and Archbishop Makarios* (London: Her Majesty's Stationery Office, 1956), Cmd. 9708, p. 8.

(c) No assurance is afforded that the Governor's approval as to the person of the Prime Minister will be entirely formal.[52]

The inability to close the gap led to the collapse of the negotiations. The British Government blamed the breakdown on the unwillingness of Archbishop Makarios to renounce violence. Makarios' removal, the British felt, was necessary because of "his direct incitement to violence;" [53] on the other hand, Makarios blamed the breakdown on British bad faith.[54]

Following the collapse of the negotiations, the Governor of Cyprus lost no time in announcing a drive "with all our resources to restore law and order." [55] It was evident that Britain was determined to continue her control over Cyprus and to maintain her influence in the Middle East.

Turkey appeared to have welcomed the strong British stand on Cyprus. When Selwyn Lloyd visited Ankara, Premier Menderes praised him for his rebuke to Makarios "as a decisive step towards the maintenance of peace and stability in the area." Now Turkey appeared to be Britain's "most solid ally," [56] and a factor to be accounted for in determining any future course regarding Cyprus.

On March 9, 1956, the British Government sent Archbishop Makarios into exile; then Lord Radcliffe proceeded to draft his proposals for a new Constitution. The political climate, however,

---

[52] *Ibid.*, p. 11.

[53] *The Manchester Guardian,* March 13, 1956.

[54] Archbishop Makarios, in a press conference on March 5, 1956, summarized his differences with the Governor and his Colonial Secretary: "In short, the people of Cyprus were invited to accept a status under which it was doubtful if they would control their own Assembly and under which it was certain that the ruling Colonial power could interfere indefinitely in all phases of public life under the pretext of protecting 'public security' . . . The British camoflaged their stubborn intransigence behind vague sentences and pretexts that they could not, a priori, bind the hands of the framer's of the Constitution, who would be sent to Cyprus and who, in their opinion, ought to have free freedom to write the Constitution, the contribution of the inhabitants being exclusively advisory." Quoted in Royal Greek Embassy Information Service, *Statement of His Eminence Archbishop Makarios,* (Washington D. C., n.d.), p. 2.

[55] Foley, *op. cit.*, p. 63. Charles Foley, *Legacy of Strife: Cyprus from Rebellion to Civil War* (Baltimore: Penguin, 1964), p. 50-52.

[56] Foley, *Island in Revolt, op. cit.*, p. 68.

was not conducive to its success. The Greek Cypriots were not likely to negotiate with the British who, according to the Greek Cypriot view, "kidnapped our national leader."[57]

The Radcliffe Constitutional Plan

In the midst of increasing tension in Cyprus, attempts were made to give Lord Radcliffe an opportunity to sketch a new Constitution. Lord Radcliffe, himself, in his covering note to the constitutional proposals, expressed the belief that the proposals contemplated a situation whereby the existing emergency would be ended.[58] Thus, peace was a prerequisite to the success of the new constitutional plan.

Lord Radcliffe received his terms of reference from the Secretary of State for the Colonies on September 13, 1956. The terms of reference involved not a draft, as Radcliffe cautions the reader of the proposals, but rather "instructions to a draftsman."[59] The terms of reference included the following:

> (a) that during the period of the Constitution, Cyprus is to remain under British sovereignty;
>
> (b) that the use of Cyprus as a base is necessary for the fulfillment by Her Majesty's Government of their international obligations and for the defense of British interests in the Middle East and the interests of other powers allied or associated with the United Kingdom;
>
> (c) that all matters relating to external affairs, defence and internal security are retained in the hands of Her Majesty's

[57] Makarios was exiled on a day when he was preparing to leave on an "Enlightenment Crusade" to Athens and London. On the one hand, no Greek Cypriot would negotiate with the Governor during Makarios' exile; and on the other hand, the Turkish Cypriot leader, Dr. Kuchuk, was proposing a plan on behalf of the Turkish Cypriot community. Dr. Kuchuk's plan envisaged a legislature with a lower House with one elected member for every 10,000 Cypriots; and with an upper House of eight Greeks and eight Turks having a veto power over the lower House. In Dr. Kuchuk's plan, the general status of Cyprus was to be self-government under British control. *Enosis* through a plebiscite was to be ruled out. See *The Times* (London), June 28, 1956.

[58] Great Britain, *Constitutional Proposals for Cyprus: Report Submitted to the Secretary of State for the Colonies by the Right Hon. Lord Radcliffe, G.B.E.*, (London: Her Majesty's Stationery Office, 1956), Cmnd. 42, p. 5. (Hereafter cited as *Constitutional Proposals for Cyprus* (Radcliffe)).

[59] *Ibid.*, p. 6.

Government or the Governor;
(d) that, subject to this, the Constitution is to be based on the principles of liberal democracy and is to confer a wide measure of responsible self-government on elected representatives of the people of Cyprus, but is at the same time to contain such reservations, provisions and guarantees as may be necessary to give a just protection to the special interests of the various communities, religions and races in the island.[60]

Lord Radcliffe saw two fundamental problems in writing a constitution for Cyprus based on his terms of reference: first, the relationship between the Governor's reserved powers and the local legislature; and second, the restrictions on the local legislature in order to protect the local minorities.[61]

With regard to the first problem, Lord Radcliffe saw that the only way out was to provide for a system of "diarchy."[62] Radcliffe conceived the "diarchy" system to be as follows: first, the "Governor's matters," giving the Governor executive authority on external affairs, defence, and internal security;[63] second, the "self-governing matters," giving the Legislative Assembly authority over local matters, but excluding:

(a) the provisions of the Constitution which safeguard the special interests of the various communities, religions and races . . .
(b) the provisions of the Constitution which [exempt] . . . intercommunal education, and accord them special treatment in the interests of the different communities in Cyprus;
(c) the provisions of the Constitution which prescribe the Governor's duty to withhold or reserve assent to a Bill on the ground that it falls within a certain class or deals with certain matters, as later set out, or to make an Ordinance prevailing over other laws if he is of the opinion that the Ordinance is necessary in the interests of foreign affairs, defence or internal security;

[60] *Ibid.* For comments on Lord Radcliffe's mission, see *The Manchester Guardian* (London), July 3, 1956; *Spectator* (London), July 20, 1956; *The Observer* (London), July 15, 1956; *The Economist* July 26, 1956.
[61] *Constitutional Proposals for Cyprus* (Radcliffe), p. 7.
[62] This idea of two law-making authorities was similar to the general relationships in the history of the United Kingdom with its governed territories.
[63] Great Brtain, *Constitutional Proposals for Cyprus* (Radcliffe), p. 29.

(d) the provisions of the Constitution which allow for the making of Emergency Laws during a period of public emergency.[64]

These were significant restrictions on the Legislative Assembly. However, there was a wide range of matters left to the Assmbly.

With regard to local matters, Radcliffe provided for absolute control in the Assembly by the Greek majority. Of the thirty-six members in the Assembly, six were to be nominated by the Governor, six to be elected by the voters on a separate Turkish communal roll, and twenty-four to be elected on a Greek general roll.[65]

The Radcliffe plan did not provide for a high proportion of Turkish Cypriot representation in the Assembly. Moreover, Radcliffe discarded the ideas for a second House with equal Greek and Turkish Cypriot representation or separation along federal or functional lines. The Plan also provided for one Turkish Cypriot Ministry. The Turkish Cypriot Minister was to be appointed by the Governor to head the Office of Turkish Cypriot Affairs.[66]

The Radcliffe plan provided two methods for protecting the rights of the Turkish minority: first, through the Ministry of Turkish Affairs, intended to control religious, educational and other matters; second, through legal and constitutional restraints on the Assembly to prevent its encroachment on the affairs of the Turkish Ministry. Any changes along these lines would have required the consent of two-thirds of the Turkish Cypriot members of the Assembly.[67]

Provisions were also made for a Supreme Court to be composed of three judges, one Greek, one Turk, and the Chief Justice, a non-Cypriot.[68] There were provisions for a "Tribunal of Guarantees" with the power to investigate complaints of discrimination and violation of fundamental rights. This Tribunal of Guarantees was to consist of three members, one Greek, one Turk and one neutral, the Chairman.[69]

---

[64] *Ibid.*, pp. 29-30.
[65] *Ibid.*, p. 31.
[66] *Ibid.*, p. 35.
[67] *Ibid.*, p. 14.
[68] *Ibid.*, p. 39.
[69] *Ibid.*, p. 43-44.

The conclusion can be drawn from the Radcliffe proposals that limited majority government was provided with adequate safeguards for the Turkish community. Radcliffe's proposals, therefore, were intended to provide for a working Constitution without compartmentalizing the two major Cypriot communities.

The Turkish Cypriots accepted the Constitution as a basis for discussion. This acceptance was probably due to the fact that British presence in Cyprus would have continued. It should be noted that though the Radcliffe proposals provided for majority rule and a possibility for future self-determination, the Greek Cypriots rejected them. The Greek Cypriots were unwilling to discuss the proposals while Makarios was in exile.

The British Government did convey the proposals to Makarios. Makarios, however, made it clear to the British, that he could not discuss constitutional proposals while in exile in the Seychelles. Thus, the nature of the political climate was such that all the Greek Cypriot leadership failed to take advantage of the Radcliffe proposals. This in itself prevented the implanting of constitutional government in Cyprus.

The Macmillan Plan and the Zurich Agreement

The intransigence of the Greek Cypriot position led to a change of British tactics. In discussing the Radcliffe Constitution in the British Parliament, Lennox-Boyd proposed that if the Greek Cypriot demands for self-determination continued to be identified with union with Greece, the Turks of Cyprus would also have the right to "union with Turkey." Lennox-Boyd was alluding to the idea of partition.[70] Thus, the idea of partitioning the island between Greeks and Turks was officially born.

The parties to the Cyprus dispute solidified their position behind irreconciliable slogans. The Greek Cypriots wanted *Enosis* with

---

[70] Lennox-Boyd expressed his views in the House of Commons on December 13, 1956. "When the international and strategic situation permits . . . Her Majesty's Government will be ready to review the question of the application of self-determination . . . [but] the Turkish Cypriot community, no less than the Greek Cypriot community shall, in the special circumstance of Cyprus be given freedom to decide for themselves their future status . . . [this the Government recognizes] that the exercise of self-determination in such a mixed population must include partition among the eventual options." *Parliamentary Debates* (1957), Vol. 562, pp. 1267-1268.

Greece; the British wanted continued control of Cyprus, and the Turkish Cypriots now wanted partition or double *Enosis*. Thus, by the time Makarios was released from exile in March 1957, the political climate had changed considerably. On the one side, the Turkish Cypriots were demanding *taxim* (partition).[71] On the other, the British insisted that any negotiations concerning Cyprus must include Greece and Turkey.

The British made new attempts to pacify the island. On December 1, 1957, Sir Hugh Foot became the new Governor of Cyprus. Foot's reputation as a "liberal" was viewed as a welcome change. Within one month after his appointment, Foot came up with proposals for a solution. The essence of the Foot proposals was to provide for a five to seven-year limited self-government intended to cool off tempers. Then Cyprus was to be given an opportunity to decide her own future. If the Greek Cypriots still wanted *Enosis*, Turkey had to agree to it.[72]

Turkey and the Turkish Cypriots rejected the idea. In turn, the British Cabinet cautioned "that Turkey was a cardinal factor in the defence of the West; and if Turkey was offended, it might lapse into neutrality."[73] Thus, the Foot proposal was put aside.

The last British constitutional proposal, before the Zurich and London Agreements, was announced in Parliament on June 19, 1958, by Prime Minister Macmillan.[74] This proposal is known as

---

[71] The Cyprus is Turkish Party, *Intercommunal Strife in Cyprus* (Nicosia, 1958), *passim*. See also, Doros Alastos, *Cyprus Guerilla: Grivas, Makarios and The British* (London: Heinemann, 1960), p. 182; Mayes, *op. cit.*, p. 179; Present Turkish Cypriot literature explains their position on *taxim* at that time as follows: "[When] Makarios was back in Athens [from exile] still insisting on *Enosis* . . . using a more useful cliche 'self-determination for the people of Cyprus' [the] Turks immediately retorted that there were two peoples in Cyprus: Turks and Greeks. If Greeks have to have self-determination (which they would clearly use for *Enosis*) then Turks would also have self-determination, the result being partition." The Turkish Communal Chamber, *Looking Back: An Official Briefing, op. cit.*, p. 10.

[72] The *Foot Plan*, which the Governor presented to the Cabinet was based on the theory that the best way out was to try to reduce tension, leaving the ultimate political solution open. Foot's idea was that a five to seven year self-government under colonial rule would help cool off tempers. Then Cyprus would be given an opportunity to decide her own future, but if the Greek Cypriots still wanted *Enosis*, they could only get it if Turkey agreed to it. Sir Hugh Foot, *A Start in Freedom* (New York: Harper and Row, 1964), p. 159. See also, Foley, *Island in Revolt, op. cit.*, p. 173.

[73] Foley, *Island in Revolt, op. cit.*, p. 173; Foot, *op. cit.*, p. 164.

[74] Great Britain, *Cyprus: Statement of Policy* (London: Her Majesty's Stationery Office, 1958), Cmnd. 455.

the Seven-Year Partnership Plan or the Macmillan Plan.[75]

According to the Macmillan Plan, the Greek and Turkish Governments were invited to appoint representatives in Cyprus to assist the Governor in achieving peace, progress and prosperity in the island. The major features of this Plan were:

> Authority for internal administration other than communal affairs and internal security would be undertaken by a Council presided over by the Governor and including the representatives of the Greek and Turkish Governments and six elected ministers . . . four being Greek Cypriot and two Turkish Cypriots.[76]

The Departments of Defence, Foreign Affairs, and Internal Security were to be reserved for the Governor.[77] Also, there were provisions for two separate Houses of Representatives, one for each community, and separate municipalities.

In August 1958, Macmillan flew to Athens and Ankara to sell his Plan. The Greek Government, together with Makarios, who attacked the Plan as aiming at "partition," rejected it. Turkey accepted it; Britain tried to implement the Plan, but without success.

The most significant effect of the Macmillan Plan, however, was the birth of the idea of independence. NATO contributed to this idea through its Secretary General, Paul-Henri Spaak, who suggested that the Macmillan Plan be withdrawn and a new plan be proposed.[78]

In Paris, on December 28, 1958, the three interested parties, Britain, Greece and Turkey, began to discuss the idea of an independent Cyprus.[79] This was also facilitated by Makarios's willing-

[75] *The London Times,* under the heading "Tridominium" commented as follows: "Many details of the Plan are left to be worked out in conjunction with Greece and Turkey. Like all 'fancy Constitutions' it may be hard to work. It involves what is virtually a system of non-territorial partition. The presence of the Greek and Turkish representatives in the Governor's Council could make for serious difficulties. Without goodwill, it would be virtually unworkable. And there are the obvious and serious difficulties of applying the communal system to a population which is not geographically segregated." *The Times* (London), June 20, 1958. For a detailed description of the Macmillan Plan see *Parliamentary Debates* (1958) Vol. 589, pp. 1315-1320.

[76] Great Britain, Colonial Office, *Cyprus Report For The Year 1958,* (Nicosia: Cyprus Government Printing Office, 1959), pp. 106-110.

[77] *Ibid.*

[78] *Ibid.*, pp. 6-8.

[79] Great Britain, Colonial Office, *Cyprus Report For The Year 1959* (London: Her Majesty's Stationery Office, 1961), p. 3.

ness to discuss independence.[80] Hope prevailed when the Prime Ministers and Foreign Ministers of Greece and Turkey initiated negotiations in Zurich on February 5, 1959. On the eleventh of February, it was agreed that Cyprus should become an independent Republic. Thus, the Zurich Agreement became the foundation for the Cyprus Republic.[81] The London Conference, which eventually ratified the Zurich Agreement, included, in addition to Greece and Turkey, the United Kingdom and the representatives of the Greek and Turkish Cypriot communities.

However, at the London Conference, Makarios raised major objections to the Zurich Agreement. Some of the major points he objected to were: the stationing of troops in Cyprus by Greece and Turkey; the 30 per cent representation of Turkish Cypriots in the Legislature in the Public Service and the Council of Ministers; the separate majority vote in the House of Representatives; and the final veto of the President and Vice President.[82]

The Greek Government was not willing to support Makarios's objections, since it had already agreed to the Zurich document. Makarios, therefore, had to either accept or reject the Zurich Agreement unchanged. He chose to accept it. The London and Zurich

---

[80] Great Britain, Colonial Office, *Cyprus Report For The Year 1958, op. cit.*, p. 6. It seems that Makarios was so alarmed over the possibilities of a Macmillan "partition" that he attempted to convey his idea of independent Cyprus even before October 1, 1958, the date when the *Macmillan Plan* was to go into effect. In a letter received by General Grivas on September 28, 1958, Makarios stated that "as you will have read in the newspapers, I yesterday made a statement to Mrs. Barbara Castle, the MP, by which I virtually created a new situation. I declared that if the British Government abandoned the Macmillan—Foot Plan, I would be willing, after a fixed period of self-government, to accept a regime of independence which could not be transformed except by the U.N. Although this new line could possibly be described as a retreat, it is what the situation, if coldly appraised, requires . . . The imposition of the British Plan, no matter how bold and determined the resistance of the Greek people in Cyprus, would inevitably lead to partition." Grivas strongly rejected this idea. "After three and a half years of unprecedented sufferings, death and disaster, and acts of heroism we are turning the people over to a slavery more oppressive than the one which they now suffer, a slavery to two masters instead of one. . . . Which of us among the leaders will dare to face the Cypriot people? . . . At all events, I declare that my opposition to the overall policy which is being followed on the Cyprus question is final." General George Grivas, *The Memoirs of General Grivas, op. cit.*, pp. 162-164.

[81] Great Britain, Colonial Office, *Report For The Year 1959, op. cit.*, pp. 3, 106-108. For the provisions of the Zurich Agreement see Appendix A *Infra.* pp. 171-177.

[82] *The New York Times,* February 19, 1959.

Agreements[83] were finally ratified on February 19 at Lancaster House.[84] The Greek Cypriots took them with caution. They were disappointed because *Enosis* was not attained. On the other hand, the Turkish Cypriots welcomed the "Agreements."[85]

Following the signing of the Agreements, a machinery was established for the transference of government. A Joint Constitutional Commission was created to draft the Constitution of the Republic based on the Zurich document;[86] A Transitional Committee was established to prepare the transferring of the governmental power to the Republic; finally, a Joint Committee in London, was established to prepare final treaties, including the treaty regarding British sovereign bases.[87]

The general tenor of the Agreements was compromising. The Greek and Turkish Cypriots, along with Greece and Turkey, respectively, gave up their original demands: *Enosis* and partition were put aside. The British on the other hand, ensured their strategic interests.

In retrospect, a question could have been asked at this early stage: Could the compromise be looked upon as a practical solution, or was it the only way out? Could a solution of this kind formulate a theoretical basis for a constitutional framework in bicommunal Cyprus, or would the entrenched interests of the "interested parties" [88] reassert themselves? Questions concerning the viability of the Cyprus constitutional framework will be examined in the remaining chapters of this study.

---

[83] Hereafter referred to as "Agreements" or Zurich and London Agreements.

[84] Great Britain, *Conference on Cyprus: Documents signed and initialled at Lancaster House on February 19, 1959* (London: Her Majesty's Stationery Office, 1959), Cmnd. 679.

[85] Dr. Fazil Kuchuk, the Turkish Cypriot Vice President, indicates this feeling in the following statement: "[The Zurich Agreement provided for Cyprus] to be a State where the fear by the Turks of *Enosis* or complete Greek domination would be eliminated; a State in which the Greek and Turk would work in full cooperation as partners in a joint venture." Fazil Kuchuk, *Cyprus: Turkish Reply to Archbishop Makarios' Proposals* (Nicosia; n.d.), p. 10.

[86] Great Britain, Colonial Office, *Cyprus: Report For The Year 1959, op. cit.,* p. 5.

[87] *Ibid.,* p. 6.

[88] Great Britain, Greece and Turkey; the entrenchment of the interests of these "interested parties" in the affairs of Cyprus, are fully discussed in, *infra.* Chapter six.

3

MAJOR FEATURES OF THE 1960 CONSTITUTION

The Zurich and London Agreements laid the foundation for the constitutional structure of the Republic of Cyprus. It will be the purpose of this Chapter to present and evaluate the major features of the Republic's constitutional framework resulting from these Agreements. The major features of the Constitution reflect, on the one hand, the various compromises arrived at by the interested parties at Zurich and London; and on the other, they shed light on the inability and unwillingness of the Greek and Turkish Cypriot communities to function within the Republic's 1960 constitutional framework.

The inability and unwillingness of the two Cypriot communities to function under the 1960 Constitution will be examined in the light of the major compromises reached at Zurich and London. In effect, these compromises can be seen from two viewpoints: first, within the context of the three principal treaties; specifically, the *Treaty of Establishment Concerning the Republic of Cyprus,* the *Treaty of Guarantee,* as well as the *Treaty of Alliance;* and second, within the context of the Cypriot Constitution of 1960.

The Nature of the Treaties

The *Draft Treaty Concerning the Establishment of the Republic of Cyprus,* in effect safeguards British strategic interests in Cyprus:

> The territory of the Republic of Cyprus shall comprise the Island of Cyprus, together with the islands lying off its coast, with the exception of the two areas defined in Annex A to this Treaty, which areas shall remain under the sovereignty of the United Kingdom.[1]

[1] Great Britain, *Cyprus* (London: Her Majesty's Stationery Office, 1960), Cmnd. 1093, p. 13. The two areas defined in Annex A of the above *Treaty* are the Akrotiri Sovereign Base Area and the Dhekelia Sovereign Base Area, see *Ibid.*, pp. 16-17.

Thus, Britain recognized the independence of Cyprus only after British military interests were guaranteed. This, in essence, secured British influence in the Middle East. British military interests are entrenched through the above *Establishment Treaty,* providing for two sovereign military bases in Cyprus of approximately ninety square miles.

The *Treaty of Alliance* is a defense treaty between Cyprus, Greece and Turkey. Its major provisions are:

> . . .
> The High Contracting Parties undertake to resist any attack or aggression direct or indirect, directed against the independence or the territorial integrity of the Republic of Cyprus.
> For the purpose of this alliance, and in order to achieve the object mentioned above, a Tripartite Headquarters shall be established on the territory of the Republic of Cyprus.
> Greece and Turkey shall participate in the Tripartite Headquarters so established with . . . military contingents . . .
> The Command of the Tripartite Headquarters shall be assumed in rotation, for a period of one year each, by a Cypriot, Greek and Turkish General Officer, who shall be appointed respectively by the Governments of Greece and Turkey and by the President and the Vice-President of the Republic of Cyprus.
> . . .
> The Greek and Turkish contingents which are to participate in the Tripartite Headquarters shall comprise respectively 950 Greek officers, non-commissioned officers and men, and 650 Turkish officers, non-commissioned officers and men.[2]

The Treaty's provision for permanent stationing of Greek and Turkish troops on Cyprus is the result of Greek and Turkish involvement in drafting the compromised constitutional framework for Cyprus. The presence of Greek and Turkish armed forces on Cyprus reflect, moreover, the unwillingness of Greece and Turkey to allow the development of a Cypriot political consciousness.

The *Treaty of Guarantee* is a pact between Cyprus, Greece, Turkey and the United Kingdom. Its major provisions are:

---

[2] *Ibid.*, pp. 88-89.

> . . .
> The Republic of Cyprus undertakes to ensure the maintenance of its independence, territorial integrity and security, as well as respect for its Constitution.
> It undertakes not to participate, in whole or in part, in any political or economic union with any State whatsoever . . .
> . . . Greece, Turkey and the United Kingdom likewise undertake to prohibit, so far as concerns them, any activity aimed at promoting, directly or indirectly, either union of Cyprus with any other State or partition of the Island . . .
> In the event of a breach of the provisions of the present Treaty, Greece, Turkey and the United Kingdom undertake to consult together with respect to the representations or measures necessary to ensure observance of those provisions. In so far as common or concerted action may not prove possible, each of the three guaranteeing Powers reserves the right to take action with the sole aim of reestablishing the state of affairs created by the present Treaty.[3]

These provisions give the three Guarantor powers the constitutional right to act as "philosopher kings" in the constitutional development of the Republic. Any developments in Cyprus interpreted as detrimental to the interests of the three Guarantors could lead to collective or individual action directed toward "reestablishing the state of affairs created by the present Treaty." Implied in this provision is that each Guarantor could give its own interpretation and terms of "reestablishing the state of affairs." The effect of this provision within the constitutional framework of the Republic of Cyprus is negative because it links British, Greek, and Turkish interests to the constitutional developments of the Republic of Cyprus.

The Nature of the Constitution

An analysis of the Cypriot Constitution of 1960 reveals a strong bi-communal character. Its major provisions are directed toward

[3] *Ibid.*, pp. 86-87. It should be noted that both the above *Treaty of Guarantee* as well as the *Treaty of Alliance* form part of the Constitution of Cyprus as provided in Article 181: "The Treaty guaranteeing the independence, territorial integrity and Constitution of the Republic concluded between the Republic, the Kingdom of Greece, the Republic of Turkey and the United Kingdom of Great Britain and Northern Ireland, and the Treaty of Military Alliance concluded between the Republic, the Kingdom of Greece and the Republic of Turkey, . . . shall have constitutional force."

establishing and regulating bi-communal interests. The Constitution recognizes and legitimizes bi-communalism; at the same time, it guarantees community interests through an intricate system of constitutional devices. These constitutional devices and provisions are additional elements revealing the compromising nature of the constitutional framework.

The recognition of the two existing Cypriot communities is indicated in Article 2 of the Constitution:

> For the purposes of this Constitution—
> (1) the Greek Community comprises all citizens of the Republic who are of Greek origin and whose mother tongue is Greek or who share the Greek Cultural traditions or who are members of the Greek-Orthodox Church;
> (2) the Turkish Community comprises all citizens of the Republic who are of Turkish origin and whose mother tongue is Turkish or who share the Turkish cultural traditions or who are Moslems.[4]

The languages of the two communities are accorded equal recognition as the official languages of the Republic.[5] In addition, Article 5 gives the two communities "the right to celebrate . . . the Greek and Turkish national holidays" and Article 4(4) the right to fly the Greek or Turkish flag:

> Any citizen of the Republic or any body, corporate or unincorporate other than public, whose members are citizens of the Republic, shall have the right to fly on their premises the flag of the Republic or the Greek or Turkish flag without any restriction.

With the two ethnic communities institutionalized and given respective communal recognition, the framework of the 1960 Constitution ensures bi-communal participation in all spheres and levels

---

[4] Great Britain, *Cyprus, op. cit.*, Cmnd. 1093, p. 91. (Hereafter the Constitution will be cited by Article.)

[5] Article 3(1) provides that "the official languages of the Republic are Greek and Turkish." Article 180(1) provides that "The Greek and the Turkish texts of this Constitution shall both be originals and shall have the same authenticity and the same legal force."

of government. In this context, the Constitution attempts to create a balance of interests by securing fixed minority community participation in Government. In part this balance is ensured through fixed numerical ratios. These fixed ratios, however, do not reflect the proportional strength of the majority and minority communities of Cyprus.

According to Article 62, for example, a ratio of "seventy per centum" Greeks and "thirty per centum" Turks is provided for communal representation in the House. Article 46 provides for the same ratio in the Council of Ministers; and Article 123 provides similar communal participation in the Public Service. Article 129 fixes the ratio of "sixty per centum" Greeks and "forty per centum" Turks in the Army; Article 130 fixes the same ratio transitionally to the police and gendarmerie.

The character of the 1960 Constitution, although seemingly encompassing the features of majority rule, incorporated a strong voice in government for the minority community. It appears that in all spheres of government, regardless of whether the character is national or local, the Constitution recognizes the Turks and Greeks of Cyprus primarily as members of their respective communities with political and constitutional rights, that is, not as citizens of Cyprus but as members of one or the other community. This constitutional bi-communalism becomes more evident in the analysis of communal participation in the Executive, Legislative, and Judicial branches.

THE EXECUTIVE BRANCH

Article 1 of the Constitution describes the nature of the political system and Articles 36 through 60, as enumerated in Part III of the Constitution, describe the functions and powers of the Executive branch.

According to Article 1:

> The State of Cyprus is an independent and sovereign Republic with a presidential regime, the President being Greek and the Vice-President being Turk elected by the Greek and the Turkish Communities of Cyprus respectively as hereinafter in the Constitution provided.

The Constitution, therefore, provides for a Presidential system: The President must be Greek and the Vice President must be Turk, both directly elected by universal suffrage by their respective communities for an identical term of five years.[6] The President is elected separately by the Greek Cypriot community, and the Vice President separately by the Turkish Cypriot community.[7]

The separate election of the President and Vice President by the Greek and Turkish communities, respectively, implies a constitutional and political principle of bi-communal authority and by implication of bi-communal responsibility and accountability. In a sense, this provision makes the President and Vice President of the Republic *par excellence* political leaders of their respective communities.

For the President, the main source of political authority is the Greek Cypriot community, and for the Vice President, the main source of political authority is the Turkish Cypriot community. Thus, the two sources of authority for the President and Vice President of the Republic give the Executive branch strong bi-communal features.

In analyzing the relationship of the Vice President to the President of the Republic, we find that this relationship is not similar to the traditional presidential systems, as for example in the United States, where the Vice President succeeds the President in case of death or incapacity. The Cypriot Constitution provides that in the event of temporary absence or incapacity, the position and duties of the President and the Vice President of the Republic shall be carried out by the President and Vice President of the House of Representatives, respectively, as follows:

> In the event of a temporary absence or a temporary incapacity to perform the duties of the President or of the Vice-President of the Republic, the President or the Vice-President of the House of Representatives . . . shall act for the President or the Vice-President of the Republic respectively during such temporary absence or temporary incapacity.[8]

[6] Article 43.
[7] Article 39(1) provides that: "The election of the President and the Vice-President of the Republic shall be direct, by universal suffrage and secret ballot, and shall . . . take place on the same day but separately."
[8] Article 36(2).

So, for purposes of deputizing and replacing the President of the Republic, the Vice President is not the second in line as is generally accepted in presidential systems. The Vice President is automatically disqualified from assuming the presidential responsibilities because he is a Turk.

In ceremonial matters, the Constitution goes to great extent to recognize the President as Head of the State and the Vice President as Vice-Head of the Republic.[9] This leading recognition of the President in ceremonial matters does not offset the bi-communal distinction granted to the President and Vice President under the Constitution.

The character of the roles and the executive powers of the President and Vice President are exhaustively defined in the Constitution. In Article 47 there is a long enumeration of areas where both the President and Vice President can exercise executive power conjointly. Article 48 specifically refers to the executive powers exercised by the President, and Article 49 refers to the specific areas of executive powers exercised by the Vice President. Furthermore, Articles 48(d) and 49(d) give the President and Vice President, respectively, the right of final veto on decisions of the Council of Ministers concerning foreign affairs, defence or security.

The executive right of final veto is also extended to matters stemming from decisions of the House of Representatives. This executive veto in the Legislative branch is provided in Article 50:

> 1. The President and the Vice-President of the Republic, separately or conjointly shall have the right of final veto on any law or decision of the House of Representatives or any part thereof concerning—
>
> (a) foreign affairs, except the participation of the Republic in international organizations and pacts of alliance in which the Kingdom of Greece and the Republic of Turkey both participate . . .
>
> (b) the following questions of defence:—
>
> (i) composition and size of the armed forces and credits for them

[9] See Articles 37 and 38.

> . . .
>
> (iii) importation of war materials and also explosives of all kinds;
>
> (iv) cession of bases and other facilities to allied countries;
>
> (c) the following questions of security:—
>
> . . .
>
> (ii) distribution and stationing of forces;
>
> (iii) emergency measures and martial law;
>
> (iv) police laws.
>
> It is specified that the right of veto under subparagraph (c) above shall cover all emergency measures or decisions, but not those which concern the normal functioning of the police and the gendarmerie.
>
> 2. The above right of veto may be exercised either against the whole of a law or decision or against any part thereof, and in the latter case such law or decision shall be returned to the House of Representatives for a decision whether the remaining part thereof will be submitted, under the relevant provisions of the Constitution, for promulgation.

What emerges from the enumeration of the powers of the President and Vice President is that the Constitution of Cyprus introduces a strong Vice President. Justification for this must be viewed in the context of the political climate during the Zurich and London Agreements and the involvement of the interested parties. The constitutional framers of Cyprus, therefore, sought to provide and secure a balance between the two major communities, which necessitated in their view such constitutional provisions intended to prevent the Greek majority from overpowering the Turkish minority. The final and unqualified veto provided in Articles 48, 49, and 50 is indeed the culmination of such constitutional guarantees. In essence, we must view the Vice President as representing the interests of the Turkish Cypriot community, and his powers must be viewed as constituting the safeguards for the Turkish Cypriot minority.

Although the Constitution does not expressly provide for a dual presidency, it is evident that the unique and powerful positions ascribed to the President and Vice President alike imply that the functioning of the Executive branch depends on the absolute cooperation of the leaders of the two communities. Thus, there is an inherent provision of *bona fide* cooperation between the two leaders, which, in essence, places a heavy burden of responsibility on the President and Vice President. When *bona fide* cooperation between the President and the Vice President does not materialize, decision-making in the Executive branch can be hampered. This can increase tension in the other branches of government.

The bi-communal nature of the Executive branch is crowned by the provisions of Article 46:

> The executive power is ensured by the President and the Vice-President of the Republic.
> The President and the Vice-President of the Republic in order to ensure the executive power shall have a Council of Ministers composed of seven Greek Ministers and three Turkish Ministers. The Ministers shall be designated respectively by the President and the Vice-President of the Republic who shall appoint them by an instrument signed by them both. The Ministers may be chosen from outside the House of Representatives.

The executive responsibilities of the President and Vice President are elusively ensured by the Council of Ministers, composed of seven Greek Ministers and three Turkish Ministers. The seven Greek Ministers and the three Turkish Ministers are designated respectively by the President and Vice President of the Republic.[10] Thus, the seventy-thirty ratio and bi-communalism pervade the whole Executive branch. In this sense, the President and the Vice President have a respective authority in choosing their Ministers representing their respective communities.

Subject to certain restrictions, the Council of Ministers is entrusted with a great deal of executive power as provided in Article 54:

> Subject to the executive power expressly reserved under Articles 47, 48 and 49, to the President and the Vice-President of the Republic, acting either separately or conjointly, the Council of Ministers shall exercise executive power in

[10] Articles 48(a) and 49(a).

> all other matters other than those which, under the express provisions of this Constitution, are within the competence of a Communal Chamber, including the following:
> (a) the general direction and control of the government of the Republic and the direction of general policy;
> (b) foreign affairs as in Article 50 set out;
> (c) defence and security, including questions thereof as in Article 50 set out;
> (d) the co-ordination and supervision of all public services;
> (e) the supervision and disposition of property belonging to the Republic in accordance with the provisions of this Constitution and the law;
> (f) consideration of Bills to be introduced to the House of Representatives by a Minister;
> (g) making of any order or regulation for the carrying into effect of any law as provided by such law;
> (h) consideration of the Budget of the Republic to be introduced to the House of Representatives.

The decisions in the Council of Ministers are based on absolute majority,[11] except on matters concerning foreign affairs, defense and security, where the final veto of the President or Vice President can be exercised.[12]

It appears from these provisions that the Council of Ministers is entrusted with substantial executive authority and responsibility. If this were so, it seems strange for a non-elective body to be entrusted with such preponderance of executive powers. However, since the Council's meetings are convened by the President and Vice President[13] and the agenda of the meetings is prepared by the President and suggested by the Vice President,[14] coupled with the final veto of the President and Vice President on foreign affairs, defense and security, in practice there emerges a different power structure in the Council of Ministers. In this context, Article 59(3) reveals the real source of authority and responsibility of the Council:

> The Ministers shall hold office in the case of the Greek Ministers until their appointment is terminated by the Presi-

[11] Article 46.
[12] Article 57(3).
[13] Article 55.
[14] Article 56.

> dent of the Republic and in the case of the Turkish Ministers until their appointment is terminated by the Vice-President of the Republic.

In effect, the Council has no collective responsibility because its general source of authority does not seem to be ministerial, but rather clearly identified with the President and Vice President of the Republic. The Greek Ministers must show their allegiance to the President and through the President to the Greek community; the Turkish Ministers to the Turkish Vice President and through the Vice President to the Turkish community. In essence, the Council's character is strictly bi-communal.

The presidential system, therefore, as envisaged by the Zurich and London Agreements and incorporated in the 1960 Constitution of Cyprus implies a limited dual Executive system reflecting the bi-communal nature of the Cypriot society.

THE LEGISLATIVE BRANCH

Article 61 of the Constitution of Cyprus provides that the legislative powers shall reside in a single House of Representatives, but inherent in this Article are some additional features:

> The legislative power of the Republic shall be exercised by the House of Representatives in all matters except those expressly reserved to the Communal Chambers under this Constitution.

Article 61 establishes a single Legislative Chamber. However, the same Article extends legislative powers to the two Communal Chambers over certain legislative matters. The legislative authority of the Communal Chambers is limited to communal affairs of the two communities of Cyprus. In the broader context, however, the Communal Chambers can be viewed as two additional Houses.

The House of Representatives reflects the following features: first, bi-communalism in its composition; second, bi-communalism in its functions.

The bi-communal composition of the House is based on a fixed ratio of seventy-thirty and is strengthened by the electoral method, providing that the Greek and Turkish representatives shall be elected separately by the Greek and Turkish communities respectively:

> 1. The number of Representatives shall be fifty:
>
> . . .
>
> 2. Out of the number of Representatives provided in paragraph 1 of this Article seventy per centum shall be elected by the Greek Community and thirty per centum by the Turkish Community separately from amongst their members respectively, and in the case of a contested election, by universal suffrage and by direct and secret ballot held on the same day.[15]

In its committee organization, the House again reflects the bicommunal character of the Constitution. The responsibility for selecting the members of each committee lies within the Committee of Selection, which is considered to be the Committee on Committees. The procedures followed by this Committee, as well as the rules for its composition, are described in Article 73(2).

> There shall be a Committee to be known as the Committee of Selection consisting of the President of the House as Chairman, the Vice-President of the House as Vice-Chairman and eight other members elected by the House of Representatives at its meeting after the election of the President and the Vice-President of the House, six from amongst the Representatives elected by the Greek Community and two from amongst the Representatives elected by the Turkish Community.

Thus, the composition of this Committee is drawn on bi-communal lines institutionalized along the general pattern of organization in the House. It is needless to state that the same proportion of representation was transferred to the composition of all the Committees.[16]

---

[15] Article 62. Furthermore, the same Article provides that the proportional ratio of the Greek and Turkish Representatives shall remain unchanged, irrespective of any population changes: "The proportion of Representatives . . . shall be independent of any statistical data."

[16] According to Article 73(4), "The Greek and Turkish Communal groups . . . in the House of Representatives shall be adequately represented on each

The presiding officers of the House represent the interests of both communities: The President of the House must always be Greek; the Vice President of the House must be Turkish.

> 1. The President of the House of Representatives shall be a Greek, and shall be elected by the Representatives elected by the Greek Community, and the Vice-President shall be a Turk and shall be elected by the Representatives elected by the Turkish Community. Each shall be elected separately as above at the same meeting at the beginning and for the whole period of the term of office of the House of Representatives.
>
> . . .
>
> 3. In case of temporary absence or pending the filling of a vacancy . . . in either of the offices of the President or the Vice-President of the House, their functions shall be performed by the eldest Representative of the respective Community unless the Representatives of such Community should otherwise decide.[17]

It should be recalled that the President and the Vice President of the House are also authorized to deputize for the President and Vice President of the Republic.[18]

The Constitution recognizes the independence of the House by not granting the power to dissolve it to either the President or the Vice President. However, the President or the Vice President can summon the House, independently, to extraordinary sessions provided there is a request of ten Representatives addressed to both the President and Vice President.[19] Moreover, the absolute veto power of the President and Vice President in foreign affairs, defense, and security, prescribes executive limitations on the House.

There are classes of legislation which require specific procedures for their introduction. The Constitution specifies that in financial

---

of the Standing, and of any other temporary, *ad hoc* or special, Committee of the House: Provided that the total number of the seats on such Committees distributed respectively to the Representatives elected by the Greek and the Turkish Communities shall be in the same proportion as that in which the seats in the House are distributed to the Representatives elected by the Greek and the Turkish Communities respectively."

[17] Article 72.

[18] See Article 36 quoted, *supra,* p. 58.

[19] Article 74(3).

matters "No Bill relating to an increase in budgetary expenditure can be introduced by any Representative.[20] This provision reserves the right to increase budgetary bills to the Executive branch. The preparation and introduction of the budget is also reserved to the Executive branch.[21] However, the House is afforded an opportunity to discuss it.[22]

Most decisions of the House require a simple majority.[23] In certain key areas of legislation, the two communities are accorded separate communal majority votes:

> Any modification of the Electoral Law and the adoption of any law relating to the municipalities and of any law imposing duties or taxes shall require a separate simple majority of the Representatives elected by the Greek and the Turkish Communities respectively taking part in the vote.[24]

The inherent difficulty of such a legislative veto is that it can hamper the legislative process. The intent of the framers of the Constitution was to secure and guarantee minority community participation in legislation. However, the separate majority vote was, in essence, a legislative veto power entrusted to the minority community to offset majoritarian dominance. In a sense, communal minority rights in the framework of Article 78(2), if misused, can be just as detrimental to constitutional government as an unchallenged majority.

The Communal Chambers' most important features are that they represent the institutionalization of the two ethnic Cypriot communities:

> The Greek and the Turkish Communities respectively shall elect from amongst their own members a Communal Chamber which shall have the competence expressly reserved for it under the provisions of this Constitution.[25]

The "competence" reserved to the Communal Chambers is enumerated in Article 87 and mainly constitutes the following:

---

[20] Article 80(2).
[21] Article 54(h).
[22] Article 81.
[23] Article 78(1).
[24] Article 78(2).
[25] Article 86.

> . . .
> (a) all religious matters;
> (b) all educational, cultural and teaching matters;
> (c) personal status;
> (d) the composition and instances . . . of courts dealing with civil disputes relating to personal status and to religious matters;
> . . .
> (f) imposition of personal taxes and fees on members of their respective Community in order to provide for their respective needs and for the needs of bodies and institutions under their control as in Article 88 provided;
> (g) in matters where subsidiary legislation in the form of regulations or bye-laws within the framework of the laws relating to municipalities will be necessary to enable a Communal Chamber to promote the aims pursued by municipalities composed solely of members of its respective Community;
> (h) in matters relating to the exercise of the authority of control of producers' and consumers' co-operatives and credit establishments and of supervision in their functions of municipalities consisting solely of their respective Community, vested in them by this Constitution.

The significance of these provisions is that through their very existence and nature the Communal Chambers serve to fragment the political allegiance of the two communities. Moreover, this is strengthened by the fact that the Communal Chambers are given independent judicial power in all matters reserved to them under Article 87(d). To carry out their judicial functions, the Communal Chambers are authorized to establish separate Communal Courts.[26]

A further important area under the control of the Communal Chambers is education. The two distinct cultures of Cyprus are further strengthened by the provisions in Article 108:

> (1) The Greek and the Turkish Communities shall have the right to receive subsidies from the Greek or the Turkish Government respectively for institutions of education, culture, athletics and charity belonging to the Greek or the Turkish Community respectively.

[26] Article 152(2).

> (2) Also where either the Greek or the Turkish Community considers that it has not the necessary number of schoolmasters, professors or clergymen . . . the functioning of its institutions, such Community shall have the right to obtain and employ such personnel to the extent strictly necessary to meet its needs as the Greek or the Turkish Government respectively may provide.

The constitutional power to conduct such cultural and educational exchanges with Greece and Turkey perpetuates the attachment of the Communal Chambers to these two countries. Moreover, the ability of each Communal Chamber to receive direct assistance from Greece and Turkey respectively, on the one hand, tended to strengthen the ties of the two communities to these two countries and, on the other hand, to undermine the authority of the government of the Republic. Thus, these factors tend to prevent the development of a Cypriot political consciousness.

What emerges from the analysis of the Communal Chambers and the House of Representatives is: strong bi-communalism, fixed numerical representations, and fragmentation of functions and legislative powers all the way down to the grass-roots.

THE JUDICIAL BRANCH

The Judicial branch institutionalizes the separation of the two communities in the administration of justice. At the apex of the judicial system is the Supreme Constitutional Court; it is authorized to decide constitutional bi-communal disputes and to serve as a guardian of the Constitution.

Article 133(1) provides that the Court shall be composed of three members—a Greek Cypriot, a Turkish Cypriot, and a neutral judge appointed jointly by both the President and Vice President of the Republic. In the event of a single vacancy in the Court, and when no agreement could be reached on the vacancy, the President is authorized to appoint a candidate if the vacancy is that of the Greek judge, and the Vice President to appoint the candidate if the vacancy is that of the Turkish judge. While the two Cypriot judges are to be permanent members of the judiciary of the Republic of Cyprus, the third member, the President, is not.[27] The neutral

[27] Article 133(6)(1), (7)(1).

judge, the President of the Court, is to be appointed by a joint decision of the President and Vice President of the Republic for a period of six years. The President of the Court cannot be a citizen of the Republic of Cyprus, Greece, Turkey, the United Kingdom or any of its colonies.[28]

The Court has exclusive jurisdiction and final authority over two broad areas: on the allocation of powers in the different organs of the Republic and on the constitutionality of legislation.

The Constitution recognizes the right of recourse to the Court by the President and Vice President of the Republic, either separately or conjointly, on matters where a law discriminates against either of the two communities.[29] This actually means that the provision gives a constitutional right to the President and Vice President to defend their respective communities before the Court.

Recourse to the Supreme Constitutional Court can be made by the President and Vice President on the adoption of the budget:

> 1. Where on the adoption of the Budget by the House of Representatives the President and the Vice-President of the Republic, either separately or conjointly, has or have exercised his or their right to return it to the House of Representatives on the ground that in his or their judgment there is a discrimination and the House has persisted in its decision, the President and the Vice-President of the Republic, either separately or conjointly, as the case may be, shall have a right of recourse to the Supreme Constitutional Court on such ground.
>
> . . .
>
> 3. Upon such a recourse the Court may annul or confirm the Budget or return it to the House of Representatives, in whole or in part.[30]

Moreover, recourse by the President and Vice President can be made on "any matter relating to any conflict or contest of power or competence arising between the House of Representatives and the Communal Chambers or any one of them and between any

[28] Article 133(3).
[29] Article 137(1).
[30] Article 138.

organ of, or authorities in, the Republic." [31] Recourse to the Court in the above context can also be effected by the House of Representatives, by the Communal Chambers or by any other organ involved in such a conflict.[32]

In addition to the Supreme Constitutional Court, the Constitution provides for another major judicial tribunal, the High Court of Justice. The High Court is composed of two Greek judges, one Turkish judge and a neutral judge. The neutral judge is the President of the Court with the authority of casting two votes in each decision.[33]

The main function of the High Court is to hear and decide cases appealed from the lower tribunals. Furthermore, the High Court has original jurisdiction in trying two classes of offences:

> . . .
> (a) treason and other offences against the security of the Republic;
> (b) offences against the Constitution and the constitutional order.[34]

Although the High Court has original jurisdiction over two important types of criminal offences against the State, its major jurisdiction is primarily appellate in civil and criminal offences.[35]

The composition of the lower courts depends on the communal membership of disputants. When the disputants are members of the same community, the courts are to be composed of judges exclusively of the same community:

> 1. A court exercising civil jurisdiction in cases where the plaintiff and the defendant belong to the same Community shall be composed solely of a judge or judges belonging to that Community.
> 2. A court exercising jurisdiction in a case where the accused and the person injured belong to the same Community, or where there is no person injured, shall be composed of a judge or judges belonging to that Community.[36]

---

[31] Article 139(1).
[32] Article 139(3).
[33] Article 153(1).
[34] Article 156.
[35] Articles 157 through 164.
[36] Article 159(1)(2).

Where the parties to a dispute are members of the two Cypriot communities, the courts are to be composed of judges belonging to both communities.[37] Moreover, in communal offences the composition of the courts and the nature of the law applied, is to be determined by the Greek and Turkish Communal Chambers, respectively.[38]

In this chapter we have discussed the major features of the 1960 Constitution in order to place constitutional government in Cyprus in its proper perspective.[39] It must be added that these major features of the Constitution are permanently fixed by the provision in Article 182:

> 1. Articles or parts of Articles of this Constitution set out in Annex III hereto which have been incorporated from the Zurich Agreement dated 11th February, 1959, are the basic Articles of this Constitution and cannot, in any way be amended, whether by way of variation, addition or repeal.

Annex III,[40] as incorporated in Article 182, enumerates some forty-eight provisions classified as "basic Articles," and which are to remain unalterable in perpetuity. These basic Articles include, among others, the provisions relating to the executive final veto, the separate majority vote in the House of Representatives, the seventy-thirty ratio in the House of Representatives and the Public Service, the sixty-forty ratio in the Army, and the *Treaty of Alliance,* as well as the *Treaty of Guarantee.* In essence, the basic Articles reflect the compromising spirit of the Zurich and London agreements and are intended to ensure bicommunal balance. However, the unalterable nature of the basic Articles, made the constitutional life of the Republic extremely rigid. In part, this is reflected in the constitutional deadlocks discussed in the following chapter.

[37] Article 159(3)(4).
[38] Article 160.
[39] Some major provisions which have not been dealt with in this chapter are extensively analyzed in case study form in Chapter 4. They are the provisions on Separate Municipalities, the Public Service and the Army.
[40] For the enumerations of the provisions in Annex III, see Great Britain, *Cyprus, op. cit.,* Cmnd. 1093, pp. 171-172.

4

MAJOR CONSTITUTIONAL TENSION AREAS

In this chapter, through a case study presentation, we shall examine how the Constitution became a basis for constant friction between the two ethnic communities. We shall endeavor to show that the tension resulting from the basic provisions of the Constitution had a two-fold effect: first, it tended to place the two communities into two major opposing camps in all spheres of government; second, it meant that the Greek and Turkish Cypriots were either unwilling or unable to function under the constitutional government established by the 1960 Constitution.

From the very inception of the Republic, the two communities solidified into two opposing groups with fixed positions toward the constitutional framework. In fact, the process of bi-communal grouping began with the Zurich and London Agreements, which established the Cyprus Republic. Thus, the two Cypriot communities, which had already been polarized in the past, now found themselves grouped against each other in order to guard their respective communal interests within the framework of the new Constitution.

The process of solidification was more difficult to attain among the Greek Cypriots, due to the fact that from the very start, there were strong voices of dissent regarding the nature of the "Agreements." The Turkish Cypriots were able to solidify their position much more easily in order to safeguard their interests against the powerful Greek majority.

The major opposition among the Greek Cypriots came from General George Grivas [1] and the staunch supporters of *Enosis*,[2] who attacked Makarios for having betrayed *Enosis* and the "na-

---

[1] Interview with General George Grivas, ex-leader of E.O.K.A., Nicosia, August 11, 1965. During my interview, General Grivas implied that his position since 1959 has not been altered. At the time of the "Agreements," Grivas issued a statement purporting that they were "harmful attempts to enslave the Cypriot people." *The New York Times*, July 30, 1959.

[2] Interview with Dr. Themistocles Dervis, leader of the pro-*Enosis Democratic Union*, Nicosia, July 31, 1965.

tional cause." Opposition also came from the Communists, who attacked the provisions which allowed for British bases and the stationing of Greek and Turkish troops on the island.[3]

The rift within the Greek Cypriot community was evident during the December 1959 presidential elections. The Communists, clothed in an elusive alliance with the staunch Enotists, supported John Clerides for the Presidency. The Left did not support Makarios for the presidency because of his refusal to issue a statement that he would follow an "independent and neutral foreign policy."[4] The fact, however, that Makarios did, from the very beginning, follow a neutral foreign policy, makes the leftist explanation unsatisfactory.

The 1959 presidential election must have presented the Communists with the opportunity to test their popular strength for the first time since 1953. It must be pointed out that in 1953 they won three out of six town municipalities. Their opposition to E.O.K.A. in 1955, however, harmed their image, and the Communist popular support dwindled. The 1959 presidential election must have clarified some of the questions in the minds of the leftist leadership regarding their popular strength.[5]

Although Makarios was able to weather the challenge by receiving about two-thirds of the total vote,[6] the election itself had some significant effects. The results indicated that a large number of Greek Cypriots were strongly opposed to the Agreements. This, in effect, meant that Makarios needed to consolidate the Greek Cypriot community in order to strengthen his position. Since many Greek Cypriots who supported Makarios also expressed doubt about the Agreements, this put pressure on President Makarios to take a much more inflexible position toward the Turkish Cypriot community.

Makarios' attempts to rally the Greek Cypriots under his leader-

[3] Interviews with Ezekias Papaioannou, leader of the *Progressive Party of the Working People* (AKEL), Nicosia, August 19, 1965; and Andreas Ziartides, leader of the *Pancyprian Federation of Labor,* (PEO), Nicosia, August 21, 1965. Both groups are leftist organizations.

[4] *Ibid.*

[5] Since the opposition to Makarios, which was about 32 percent, included the right-wing group of staunch pro-Enotists and a substantial number of Greek Cypriots opposed to the Zurich Agreements, we may conclude that the communists' support did not exceed 20 percent.

[6] Makarios received 144,501 votes compared to John Clerides, who received 71,773 votes. See *Eleftheria* (Nicosia), December 15, 1959.

ship as President of the new Republic were successful. First he was able to nullify Grivas' and the Enotists' opposition by including four ex-E.O.K.A. members in his first cabinet.[7] Second, Makarios was able to avoid a second electoral confrontation during the mid-1960 elections for the House of Representatives, convincing the Communists to agree to have five out of thirty-five Greek seats allotted to the Greek community in the House by the Constitution.

The Communists accepted Makarios' invitation to cooperate with his administration for the following reasons: first, AKEL and PEO realized that the electoral system in Cyprus practically eliminated their chances of gaining any seats in Parliament, since they could not expect to carry a majority in any of the six electoral districts; second, their cooperation with Makarios would give them a voice in Parliament; their position in government, however, was not influential, since they were given no participation in the Cabinet; third, they considered a Greek-Cypriot common front as absolutely paramount, in view of the expected strong Turkish Cypriot opposition on most key constitutional issues; finally, they may have realized that a challenge to the dominant position of the Church leadership would be fruitless.[8]

By the time the Republic's independence was proclaimed on August 16, 1960, the Greek Cypriot community found itself almost completely unified under the leadership of the Archbishop—President Makarios.[9] Makarios' appointments of key E.O.K.A. men and rapproachement with the Communists nullified the opposition. With the additional thirty Greek members in the House, forming a loose confederation under the umbrella of Makarios' Patriotic Front,[10] Makarios secured complete control in the House. Any

[7] Of those included in Makarios' first cabinet, the most important E.O.K.A. men were: Polycarpos Georgadjis, the Minister of Interior, a leading member of E.O.K.A. and Tassos Papadopoulos, the Minister of Labor, a leading member in the E.O.K.A. propaganda machine.

[8] The fact that after the 1963 crisis Makarios sought Soviet support against possible Turkish invasion, should not be interpreted as resulting from Cypriot communists' influence; rather, Makarios sought support from the Soviets, because he could not get it from the West and because he mistrusted NATO plans for Cyprus. See, *infra* pp. 159, 160.

[9] It was possible for the Church leadership to unify both left and right wing Cypriots, because both factions opposed the "unjust and undemocratic Zurich Constitution."

[10] The *Patriotic Front* has been serving as a convenient way of incorporating under its loose confederation the pro-Makarios forces. All Greek Cypriot

disagreement with the Turkish Cypriot community on the basic provisions of the Constitution tended to further solidify the Greek Cypriots.

The Turkish Cypriot community's solidification was not difficult to attain. The *Enosis* drive and the E.O.K.A. underground movement necessitated strong Turkish Cypriot opposition to the Greek Cypriot demands. The Agreements, which brought about the Turkish Cypriot community's effective participation in Government, were an added factor for greater solidification. Thus, from the very beginning, the Turkish Cypriot's objective was to protect their constitutional safeguards.[11]

Characteristic of the Turkish Cypriot solidarity was the fact that Dr. Fazil Kuchuk was unopposed at the primary for the Vice Presidency on December 3, 1959, and Rauf Denktash was elected President of the Turkish Communal Chamber without any opposition. In all spheres of government, the Turkish community's representation was mainly directed toward securing the interests of the Turkish community under the leadership of the Vice President, Dr. Fazil Kuchuk, and the President of the Turkish Communal Chamber, Mr. Rauf Denktash.

The persistent bi-communal groupings reflected the attitude of the two communities toward the 1960 Constitution. On the one hand, the Greek Cypriots felt that the Constitution established a "privileged position" for the Turkish Cypriot community[12] and from the start challenged the Constitution's basic provisions. On the other hand, the Turkish Cypriots viewed the Constitution as securing absolutely minimum guarantees for their effective participation in Government.[13]

---

representatives in the House, with the exception of the five leftists, are members of the *Patriotic Front*.

[11] Rather than involving themselves in internal factional differences, the Turkish Cypriots, Stanley Mayes observes, "were too busy entrenching in their new privileged positions under the Zurich and London Agreements." See Mayes, *op. cit.*, p. 56.

[12] Interviews with Tassos Papadopoulos, Minister of Labor, Nicosia, September 2, 1965, and with Andreas Papadopoulos, Minister of Public Works, Nicosia, July 13, 1965. The Minister of Public Works described the Constitution's basic weakness as producing an "unbalanced equilibrium."

[13] Kuchuk, *Cyprus: Turkish Reply to Archbishop Makarios' Proposals, op. cit.*, pp. 16-17.

Some of the major Constitutional provisions regarded by the Greek Cypriots as "unjust" and "unworkable" were the final veto power of the Vice President, the Separate Majority Right in the House of Representatives, the Separate Municipalities in the five largest towns, and the seventy-thirty communal ratio in government, especially the composition of the Public Service. These same provisions, the Turkish community felt, not only were not "unjust" but were absolutely necessary to ensure Turkish Cypriot participation in government and to prevent complete domination by the Greek Cypriot majority.[14]

The disagreement on the validity of the basic provisions of the Constitution had negative results. There was no willingness on the part of the Greek Cypriot community to preserve the Constitution, which they felt did not reflect the composition of the Cypriot society. On the other hand, the Turkish Cypriots clung to the Constitution as the only means of preserving their distinct communal identity. The net result of this constitutional factionalism was to prevent the Constitution from becoming a common symbol. In addition, this bi-communal factionalism constantly threatened the Constitution's preservation.

It follows, therefore, that the friction regarding the Constitution did not revolve around traditional lines of executive-legislative relations, but it was bi-communal in all spheres of governmental activity; namely, Executive, Legislative, Judicial and Administrative. Each friction tended to become an obstacle to compromise. Thus, there developed an intricate system of frictional crises, which set the two communities in constitutional factionalism.

The Turkish Cypriots further state: "The two communities were put on par [under the Constitution]: distinct communities, as they in fact were, were to have equal rights . . . A partnership Government was formed. The ratio of 7:3 was fixed as a proportion in which the Turks and Greeks should contribute to the running of the Government machinery. In a country which had two official languages and had to serve two communities this was a reasonable [arrangement]." The Turkish Communal Chamber, *Looking Back: An Official Briefing, op. cit.*, p. 11.

[14] Halit Ali Riza, *The House of Representatives: The Separate Majority Right* (Nicosia: The Turkish Communal Chamber, 1963), pp. 6-9; The Turkish Communal Chamber, *The Turkish Case: 70:30 and The Greek Tactics* (Nicosia, 1963), pp. 3-5; Turkish Communal Chamber, *A Report on Cyprus, op. cit.*, pp. 13-16.

In the following pages we shall endeavor to present, through four case studies, the major areas of friction which resulted in bi-communal constitutional deadlock. The tension areas presented here are the seventy-thirty ratio in the Public Service, the Income Tax Legislation, the Army and the Municipalities. We shall analyze these tension provisions as they evolved in the Executive branch, in the House of Representatives, in the two Communal Chambers and in the Supreme Constitutional Court, in order to show the process of constitutional breakdown.

The Seventy-Thirty Constitutional Provision and the Tension in the Public Service

The seventy-thirty tension reflects the friction in the Public Service. According to Article 123 of the Constitution, the Public Service is to be composed of "seventy per centum Greeks and thirty per centum Turks." To implement the provision, a Public Service Commission was established under Article 124.[15]

The seventy-thirty provision regarding the Public Service became a basis of tension even before independence. On the one hand, the Turkish Cypriots looked upon its implementation as essential to "secure for the Turkish community adequate representation in all spheres of [government] activity . . ."[16] On the other hand, the Greek Cypriots looked upon this provision as causing the Greek Cypriot community a "loss of jobs;" and furthermore, causing "hardship to the Greek Public Servants . . . in a discriminatory way."[17]

In April 1960, Mr. Denktash, the President of the Turkish Communal Chamber, warned that if the Turkish rights in the Public Service were not forthcoming, this would be the beginning of bring-

[15] According to Article 124(2) "Seven members of the Commission shall be Greeks and three members shall be Turks."

[16] The Turkish Communal Chamber, *The Turkish Case: 70:30 and the Greek Tactics, op. cit.*, p. 5.

[17] "The Problem of the 70 to 30 Ratio in the Participation of the Two Communities in the Civil Service of the Republic." Pamphlet issued by the Office of the Director of the House of Representatives, Nicosia, n.d., p. 1. (Mimeographed.) This pamphlet, which was issued after the December 1963 Crisis, reflects the Greek Cypriot point of view. (Hereinafter cited as "The Problem of the 70 to 30 Ratio: The Greek Cypriot Case").

ing to the surface old hatred and mistrust. At the same time, the Greek Public Servants Association called for mass protests and demonstrations to express their opposition to these provisions.

The Turkish Cypriot position was expressed along the following lines. They argued that the Greek Cypriots during the British occupation "managed to maneuver themselves into high administrative and executive posts . . . and by 1959 many key posts had been occupied by Greeks and almost all Selection Boards had become Greek-dominated.[18] Therefore, the Turkish Cypriots felt they were left behind. They believed that the Constitution restored equity and thereby helped promote dignity for the Turkish Cypriot community and that anything less than thirty percent in the Public Service "indicated that the Turkish community would be ill-served and discriminated against."[19]

The Greek Cypriots believed that the provision was not only discriminatory, but it meant that the person's ethnic origin and religion rather than his ability was to be the basis for appointment in the Public Service. Furthermore, the Greeks felt that it failed to protect the experienced public servants already in government service.[20]

Attempts to come to grips with this constitutional provision were made by the President and Vice President of the Republic, who asked the Joint Consultative Committee to study the problem of how this ratio should be implemented.[21] A detailed report followed which was to become the guideline for applying the seventy-thirty ratio to the Public Service.[22] However, differences in interpreting some of the terms of the report prevented its full implementation.

One of the difficult points of the report was the phrase that called for full implementation of the ratio "within five months from

[18] The Turkish Communal Chamber, *The Turkish Case: 70:30, op. cit.*, p. 3.

[19] *Ibid.*, p. 5.

[20] "The Problem of the 70 to 30 Ratio: The Greek Cypriot Case," p. 2. (Mimeographed.)

[21] The Committee was made up of the under-Secretary to the President, the under-Secretary to the Vice-President, the Chief Establishment Officer, the Administrative Officer to the Ministry of Finance, three representatives of the Greek Civil Service Association, and three representatives of the Society of Turkish Civil Servants.

[22] The Joint Consultative Committee, *Recommendations for the Implementation of the 70:30 Ratio in the Civil Service,* quoted in The Turkish Communal Chamber, *The Turkish Case: 70:30 and the Greek Tactics*, *op. cit.*,

the date of the establishment of the Republic."[23] This phrase was taken literally by the Turkish Cypriots. The Vice President, on October 14, 1960, pointed out to President Makarios that the Republic was already in existence for more than two months, and no "appreciable progress had been made by the Public Service Commission."[24] Also, the Turkish Cypriot press considered the implementation of seventy-thirty ratio in the Public Service as a "[Turkish] national" problem.

Further difficulties in interpreting the terms of the report were suggested in the phrase that "care should be taken not to prejudice as far as possible the right of promotion of the existing members of the Public Service."[25] The question arose how the statement "as far as possible" should be interpreted by those directly concerned. The Turkish Cypriots did not feel that this meant a delay in the implementation of the seventy-thirty provision. The Greek Cypriots, on the other hand, interpreted the phrase "care should be taken not to prejudice . . ." to mean not to displace or prevent from promotions the experienced civil servants.

The seventy-thirty problem indicates that the tension was much deeper than the argument of "fair participation in government." The Greek Cypriot community argued that the realities within the Republic proved that the fixed ratio of seventy-thirty was unjust and arbitrary:

> The Greek Community resents this provision of the Constitution because it considers it unjust and that it tantamounts to discrimination against persons on the basis of their ethnic

Appendix "A." According to the July, 1960 report of the Committee, the Turkish Cypriot ratio in the various grades of the Public Service were as follows:

Grade	*Percent*
Supergrade	26.0
Grade I	18.6
Grade II	20.5
Grade III	18.5
Grade IV	17.0
Grade V	25.4

[23] *Ibid.*, Appendix "A."

[24] The Turkish Communal Chamber, *The Turkish Case: 70:30 and the Greek Tactics, op. cit.*, p. 3.

[25] The Joint Consultative Committee, *Recommendations for the Implementation of the 70:30 Ratio in the Civil Service,* quoted in The Turkish Communal Chamber, *The Turkish Case: 70:30 and the Greek Tactics, op. cit.*, Appendix "A."

> origin or religious beliefs. The following facts will show how unjust a provision is which arbitrarily fixes participation of the Greek community in the Civil Service at seventy percent and of the Turkish community at thirty percent.
> . . . The population of the Republic consists of 82 percent Greeks and 18 percent Turks.
> . . . It creates a discrimination against citizens of the Republic on the basis of their community or religion which is contrary to the spirit of the Charter of the United Nations and the Convention on Human Rights. A citizen of the Republic, whether Greek or Turkish, possessing all the qualification to be employed in the Civil Service can be rejected on the ground that his community has the seventy or the thirty percent participation in the Civil Service fixed by the Constitution.[26]

In spite of this, the Greek Cypriots argued that a great amount of progress had been made in implementing the seventy-thirty provision reflecting the good intent of the Greek Cypriot community.[27] The fact that the full seventy-thirty implementation could not come about, the Greeks argued, should be viewed within the context of the following realities:

> No Greek civil servant could be dismissed in order to make room for Turkish civil servants. That this is so, it is clear from the provision of the Constitution which safeguards the rights of civil servants who were serving in the service of the Republic at the time of Independence.
> . . .
> No unnecessary appointment should be made to vacant posts in the civil service and thus burden the taxpayer with the

[26] "The Problem of the 70 to 30 Ratio: The Greek Cypriot Case," p. 2. (Mimeographed.)

[27] According to the Greek Cypriots the "composition of the Government Service as of February 26, 1963," was as follows:

Grade	*Greeks* (in per cent)	*Turks*
Supergrade	66 2/3.0	33 1/3.0
Grade I	72.5	27.5
Grade II	73.6	26.4
Grade III	77.0	23.0
Grade IV	82.2	17.8
Grade V	73.0	27.0

See, "The Problem of the 70 to 30 Ratio: The Greek Cypriot Case," p. 5. (Mimeographed.)

> cost of maintaining an excessively heavy Civil Service simply for the purpose of giving effect to the ratio of seventy to thirty.
>
> No lowering of the standards and the qualifications required to enter the Civil Service should take place for the purpose of implementing the seventy to thirty ratio.[28]

In this context, the Public Service Commission dominated by the Greeks emphasized that it was practically impossible to apply the seventy to thirty ratio in a short time for there were many problems to be considered, including the fact that:

> The Commission had to draw from a population forming the 18 percent of the population which was poorly educated in order to fill 30 percent of the Civil Service (and) made it difficult to find qualified Turks for many posts.[29]

Consequently, the Turkish Cypriot complaints were directed against the Public Service Commission, which by virtue of the Constitution, Article 125(1), was the sole appointing authority for the Public Service. In the Commission, the Turkish Cypriots found constant arbitrary decisions. Numerous cases are cited to show their dissatisfaction with the Commission's work:

> On the 16th October, 1961, the Commission agreed to fill 17 vacancies in the post of Clerical Assistant at the ratio of 2 Turks to one Greek. It was further agreed that the vacancies which would occur in the future were to be allocated at the ratio of 3 Turks to one Greek until the 70:30 ratio was applied in the post of Clerical Assistant. But soon after the first 17 vacancies were so filled, the Greek members refused to abide by the second part of the agreement, which was recorded in the minutes as a decision of the Commission, on the grounds that there was no need for Clerical Assistants. Yet 60 vacancies existed in 1961 Estimates and provision for 38 more Clerical Assistants was made in 1962 Estimates.[30]

---

[28] *Ibid.*, pp. 5-6.
[29] *Ibid.*, p. 7.
[30] The Turkish Communal Chamber, *The Turkish Case: 70:30 and the Greek Tactics, op. cit.*, p. 13.

In another case the Turkish Cypriots indicate the following:

> On the 9/7/63 the Commission proceeded to fill 22 vacancies in the post of "Land Clerk, Grade I" in the Department of Lands and Surveys. Turks were deficient in their share of the post, so the Turkish members proposed the promotion of four experienced and qualified Turkish candidates who were due for promotion. But the Greek head of the Lands and Surveys department had used the usual extra nice words about 21 Greek candidates who were also being considered. The Greek members of the Commission refused to allocate the vacancies and promoted the 21 Greeks and one Turk, leaving out three Turkish candidates on the grounds that the Greeks had better reports.[31]

Although arguments were oriented toward supporting the respective positions of the two communities, it seems that the dichotomy and the polarized position of the two communities seemed to be irreconcilable. The constitutional provision of seventy-thirty seemed to help increase tension. The only avenue open to find some kind of a compromise "solution" was the Supreme Constitutional Court.

The Court succeeded in hearing the legal issues on only five of the twenty-seven cases filed by the Public Service Commission, but no ruling was given on any.[32] With the resignation of the Supreme Constitutional Court President in May, 1963, the tension resulting from the seventy-thirty was never alleviated by the Court.[33] In contrast, the referral of cases to the Court resulted in friction within the Public Service Commission itself. The Turkish Cypriots accused the Greek Cypriots of using delaying tactics, and the Greeks argued that there was no universal rule which bound the Public Service Commission to refer cases to the Court. The significant point to be

---

[31] *Ibid.*, p. 15.

[32] *Ibid.*, p. 21; *Eleftheria* (Nicosia), April 26, 1962. It should also be pointed out that in the three short years of the Republic's life, more than two thousand civil service appointments were contested on communal grounds and were appealed to the Supreme Constitutional Court. "If all [these appointments] had been declared invalid, it would have meant the collapse of the island's administration." Robert Stephens, *Cyprus: A Place of Arms* (London: Pall Mall Press, 1966), p. 175.

[33] *Eleftheria* (Nicosia), May 24, 1963.

made here is that neither the Court nor the Commission was able to provide a formula to satisfy both sides. The Court avoided entering this politically-loaded tension area of the seventy-thirty provision, and the Public Service Commission, where the Greek Cypriots had a majority, expressed its opinion by following strictly bi-communal lines. In the end, the seventy-thirty provision remained a point of continuous friction and a tension-producing area.

The Separate Majority Vote and the Income Tax Legislation Crisis

Article 78(2), of the Constitution provides that "any law imposing duties or taxes shall require a separate simple majority of the representatives elected by the Greek and Turkish communities respectively taking part in the vote."

To the Greek Cypriots, this provision was considered to be a powerful weapon enabling the minority to obstruct the legislative process. The Greek Cypriots felt that this power gave the Turkish community "a privileged position" in the affairs of Government far exceeding their proportional strength in the Cypriot society.[34] The Turkish Cypriots argued, on the other hand, that the "separate majority right" was one of the very few constitutional provisions where "equal rights of the Turkish community were preserved."[35] The Turkish community felt, therefore, that only through provisions such as the "separate majority right" could they resist complete domination by the powerful Greek Cypriot majority.[36] The effects of Article 78(2) will be analyzed in the context of the failure of the two communities to agree on tax legislation. The inability to agree on the tax legislation left the Government without legal authorization to collect taxes and contributed to the Constitutional breakdown and the crisis.

When the Republic came into being, there was no agreement on a new tax law. Therefore, Article 188(2), of the Constitution provided that ". . . any law imposing duties or taxes may continue to

[34] Greek Communal Chamber, *Cyprus: A Handbook on the Island's Past and Present* (Nicosia, 1964), pp. 155-157.

[35] Halit Ali Riza, *The House of Representatives: The Separate Majority Right, op. cit.*, p. 4.

[36] Kuchuk, *Cyprus: Turkish Reply to Archbishop Makarios' Proposals, op. cit., passim.*

be enforced until December 31, 1960." Thus, the existing colonial law was extended in order to give the two communities time to reach a compromise solution on a new tax law.

The inability of the two communities to reach an agreement over tax legislation by the time limit set by Article 188(2), necessitated the introduction of a bill in the House entitled "Laws Imposing Duties or Taxes (Continuation of Provisions) Law of 1960," which provided for an extension of the existing law for three more months up to March 31, 1961.[37] The extension was obviously intended to give more time for a more representative law reflecting the new constitutional provisions of the newly established state and to see that the new Law reflected the new economic conditions in Cyprus.

The Turkish Cypriot community agreed, but questioned the constitutionality of such an extension. They stated that: "The bill was clearly unconstitutional [and it was only] . . . in accordance with an agreement reached between the Turkish and Greek representatives that the continuation in force of the laws imposing duties or taxes until March 31, 1961, was approved, with the understanding that the required new laws would be passed in the meantime."[38]

The tax extension period granted by the House in December 1960 produced no tax law acceptable to both sides. Therefore, the Council of Ministers asked the House for passage of a bill extending the tax law, already extended once, for another three months. This Council of Minister's proposal for a new extension was intended to give time to the Executive branch to prepare an acceptable tax law.

The Turkish Cypriot community was opposed to the Council of Minister's proposals in principle but was willing to accept a two-month extension. The two-month extension was proposed by Representative Halit Ali Riza during the House meeting on March 31, 1961:

> Five or at least four members of the Turkish Group wish to give a period of two months for the operation of the bill

[37] *Eleftheria* (Nicosia), January 1, 1961. Halit Ali Riza, *The House of Representatives: The Separate Majority Right, op. cit.*, p. 11.

[38] Halit Ali Riza, *The House of Representatives: The Separate Majority Right, op. cit.*, p. 11.

> under debate. Although the majority of the Group is against any extension, they will not vote against the proposal of the four or five colleagues I mentioned. I hope that my Greek colleagues also will appreciate the seriousness of the situation and will not vote against this proposal.
>
> . . .
>
> This period of two months is enough for doing plenty of work. Every effort should be exerted to submit these bills to the House as early as possible. Therefore, an extension of two months is sufficient. . . . If the period of two months is not accepted our Group or the majority of our Group will vote against the bill and responsibility will lie with the Greek Representatives.[39]

The Greek Cypriot representatives were opposed to a shorter extension, because they felt that three months were absolutely the minimum time needed to prepare a well-structured tax law. They refused to accept a shorter extension, which they felt would give the Turkish Cypriots an opportunity to bring pressures upon the solution of the other existing tension problems.[40]

The unwillingness on the part of the two communities to agree to an extension as asked by the Council of Ministers meant that the Republic was stripped of its right to collect taxes. The vote on the three-month extension in the March 31, 1961, meeting of the House was twenty-five Greek Cypriot members in favor, eleven Turkish Cypriot members against, and two Turkish Cypriot abstentions. The bill, therefore, failed to obtain the separate majority vote needed and was defeated.[41]

The House debates reveal that all the issues of disagreement and tension were tied very closely together with the tax bill. A statement made by the Turkish Cypriot representative, Jemil Ramadan, shows that a solution of the tax law was related to other unresolved constitutional issues:

---

[39] Quoted in Halit Ali Riza, *The House of Representatives: The Separate Majority Right, op. cit.,* pp. 11-12.

[40] Namely, the seventy-thirty problem in the Public Service and the Municipalities problem.

[41] Cyprus, House of Representatives, *Minutes,* (in Greek, my free translation) "Laws Imposing Duties or Taxes (Continuation of Provisions) Law of 1961," March 31, 1961, p. 24. (Typewritten.)

> Let us suppose that the proposed extension of the tax laws is not approved. Then the operation of government will be extremely hampered . . . for the government will not be in a position to collect taxes . . . Parallel to this, there are, according to the basic provisions of the Constitution, certain rights for the Turkish community like the seventy:thirty and the geographical separation of the municipalities, which must not remain perpetually in abeyance . . . When the three-month extension was granted, we were given the promise from those directly concerned that these problems would be solved . . . therefore, with this promise we voted for the extension. Unfortunately the same situation exists today. In spite of these bitter truths, I am in favor of extending [the tax laws] for two months. This we are doing for the *last time* in order to show our good faith . . . to give time to those directly concerned to solve the pending problems. If during this extension no progress is made and another extension is asked, I will be one of the first to vote against such an extension. [my emphasis] [42]

Mehmet Kemal Deniz, another Turkish Cypriot representative emphasized that:

> The day we entered this House, we took an oath, and we remember it very well. [Through this oath] we promised to respect the territorial integrity, the Constitution and the laws of the Republic of Cyprus. One of the basic provisions is the seventy:thirty provision in which, unfortunately, no progress has been made. We have been waiting to see that this provision be implemented by March 31, 1961; unfortunately we saw no results . . . but again we would like to show our good intent for the last time.
>
> Thus we will not find ourselves in difficulty giving an explanation to our people when the next elections take place . . . For there is one fundamental subject for which we are all responsible and that is the duty of this House . . . to see that *the Constitution . . . must be implemented to the letter;* . . . and if with this extension these basic provisions are not implemented, our duty shall end . . . [my emphasis].[43]

[42] *Ibid.*, pp. 2-3.
[43] *Ibid.*, p. 7.

The Turkish Cypriot representatives made it clear that the delay in solving other constitutional issues, specifically the seventy-thirty and the Municipalities,[44] affected their general outlook toward tax legislation. It is clear that one issue was tied together with the other, and all placed together, tended to show that the provisions helped increase tension and mistrust.

The Greek Cypriots felt that they were being blackmailed by the Turkish Cypriots. Characteristic of this feeling is the statement of the President of the House, who emphasized that the Turkish Cypriot representatives have extensively tried to "tie together the tax extension matter with the subject of the seventy-thirty." Mr. Clerides summarized the Greek Cypriot position as follows:

> Honorable colleagues, at 12 midnight today the laws on import duties and income tax expire, and the Republic of Cyprus will remain without such laws . . . I see with pleasure that those of the Honorable Turkish members who spoke stressed the fact that they are willing . . . to vote an extension for two months, but they are not willing to vote for a three-month extension; and I ask . . . is it right to see anyone endangering the state to remain without tax laws for there is a conviction that extension must be limited to two months? I fail to see how anyone who is looking at this matter objectively . . . could claim that two months extension is sufficient . . . Some of the Honorable Turkish members demanded to parallel the matter of the tax extension with that of the seventy-thirty . . . But I fail to see the connection between the seventy-thirty and the extension of the tax law. If there is a belief that some departments of Government do not abide by the Constitution surely there is the proper mechanism in the Constitution through which the Vice President and those whose interests and rights are violated to ask the Supreme Constitutional Court to decide about these matters. It is a misguided policy for a political organ like the House to refuse to pass a bill absolutely essential for the State, because according to the belief of the Honorable Turkish members there is no full implementation of the Constitution by some other political organ . . . We are prepared to appoint a committee to study the whole matter. [seventy-thirty] This

[44] For the bi-communal tension on the Municipalities, see *infra* pp. 94-103.

> committee will make proposals, but we are not prepared without any investigation of specific recommendations on the subject to succumb to any kind of blackmail on this subject.[45]

The defeat of the tax law brought strong reaction from the President. President Makarios regarded the Turkish Cypriot stand as "regrettable" pointing out that "the Constitution exists for the benefit of the State and not the State for the benefit of the Constitution."[46] The President then issued the following Executive Order: "With the present [Order] all the public officials are ordered to continue the collection of taxes and import duties as usual."[47]

The Vice President and the three Turkish ministers disputed the President's action.[48] Immediately after the President's order, the Turkish merchants and businessmen claimed that they would appeal the presidential action to the Constitutional Court. At the same time, the Turkish press asked for the resignation of Makarios and demanded the intervention of Turkey, Greece, and Britain to carry out the Constitution.

Beginning with March 31, 1961, the Republic was left without income tax legislation. The complete breakdown, however, came in a House debate on December 18, 1961, when an attempt was made to enact new income tax legislation.

The Greek Cypriot representatives supported a tax bill submitted by the Executive branch intending to give the government power to tax. The Turkish Cypriot representatives, however, proposed that the House be authorized to review the tax rates on a yearly basis. The debates in the House, therefore, centered on the following difference. The Turkish Cypriots wanted to exercise yearly control over the tax rates, while the Greek Cypriots felt that this provision was dangerous. The Greek Cypriots felt that if the House for any reason was unable to agree on the tax rates before the yearly ex-

---

[45] Cyprus, House of Representatives, *Minutes,* (in Greek, my free translation) "Laws Imposing Duties or Taxes (Continuation of Provisions) Law of 1961," March 31, 1961, pp. 9-12. (Typewritten.)

[46] Interview with Archbishop Makarios, President of the Republic of Cyprus, Nicosia, September 4, 1965.

[47] *Eleftheria* (Nicosia), April 2, 1961. It should be noted that at the same time the Greek Cypriot press criticized the Separate Majority Right as a "crippling" power in the hands of the Turkish minority and as "detrimental to the functioning of the State."

[48] Kuchuk, *Cyprus: Turkish Reply to Archbishop Makarios' Proposals, op. cit.*, pp. 21-22.

piration, the government would essentially remain without the power to tax.

The House debate of December 18, 1961, centered around the Turkish proposal of yearly restrictions by the House on the tax schedule of rates. The Turkish representatives were not against a tax law *per se.* They wanted to keep a constant check on tax legislation.

The two communal positions are exemplified in the following dialogues:

Halit Ali Riza: (Turkish Cypriot representative)

> Our proposal is this: There shall not be any restrictions on the operation of the body of the law. But the rates and provisions contained in the second schedule [the tax rates] shall before the end of each year be submitted to the House for approval; and naturally if they are not approved, they will cease to be in force . . . The schedule of rates will expire on December 31, 1962 unless it is approved by the House before that date . . . If it is not approved by the end of the following year, it will expire and this method will follow next year.[49]

Glafcos Clerides: (President of the House of Representatives)

> This House is being asked to bind itself by law not to have the right to renew the tax schedule of rates for more than one year at a time . . . For the House to be able to renew [the schedule of rates] more than a year, there must be a revision of the basic law. Is this the meaning of your proposals? . . . [Such an adoption would] prevent the House from renewing the schedule of rates for longer than one year without revising the basic [tax] law . . .[50]

The Greek Cypriot position was further amplified by Representative Vassos Lyssarides:

---

[49] Quoted in Halit Ali Riza, *The House of Representatives: The Separate Majority Right, op. cit.,* p. 15.

[50] Cyprus, The House of Representatives, *Minutes,* (in Greek, my free translation) "Income Tax Law of 1961," December 18, 1961, pp. 1-2. (Typewritten.)

> We find ourselves with a fantastic proposal by the Turkish members . . . The sole purpose for the proposal was to use this as a weapon through which the Greek members would be under constant surveillance by the Turkish Group and be forced to obey like undisciplined children . . . Honorable Turkish colleagues, if you really believe in the interests of this country, there is no other way but to withdraw this monstrous proposal which in itself degrades this House. This will be the clear proof of your good intention, and the first step towards real cooperation.[51]

Halit Ali Riza, Floor Leader of the Turkish Group of the House of Representatives, further clarified the position of the Turkish Cypriot representatives:

> . . . In countries where the state functions normally . . . the income tax rates are revised every year. But, no one may claim that in Cyprus the state is functioning normally. Still the Constitutional Order has not been applied. The greatest factor which will cultivate trust in a foreigner as well as in a citizen, is action in accordance with the Constitution . . . It is useless to argue that some affairs may be adversely affected by this or other conditions as if affairs in every field are conducted normally. We believe that every responsible Turkish representative and all colleagues realize their responsibility. Never will they use their votes solely to create difficulty for the government. For this reason, in re-considering the rates at the end of each year, the Turkish representatives, with the realization of their responsibility both to their Community and to all citizens, will do what is best.[52]

The character of the debate is exemplified by the statement and opinions of the President of the House, Glafcos Clerides, who questioned the Turkish Cypriot intent in the following manner:

> There are serious reasons why the proposal of the Turkish colleagues is unacceptable [to us]. Let us suppose that the

[51] *Ibid.*, pp. 3-4.
[52] *Ibid.*, pp. 13-15; Halit Ali Riza, *The House of Representatives: The Separate Majority Right, op. cit.*, p. 16.

> Ministry of Economics and the Executive branch are responsible for preparing the budget for the Republic, which this House must approve or reject. If on December 31, 1962, it is not known what the tax law will be . . . it would be impossible for the responsible Ministry to prepare the budget. Certainly it will not know the income of the State although it will know the expenses . . . The Honorable Halit Ali Riza assured the Greek members that the Honorable Turkish members have no other purpose but to protect the rights of their community . . . If these rights really need protection, we call upon them to join us in protecting the rights of the Cypriot people *as a whole* by voting for the income tax law. Surely the income from this tax, which comes mainly from the well-to-do Cypriot classes, will be used to cover the expenses of the five year plan, which plan will benefit not only the Greeks or the Turks but *Cyprus as a whole* . . . I hope that the House which consists of representatives of the Greek community and of the Turkish community will not permit the State to remain without an income tax law for a second time. [my emphasis] [53]

The emphasis in Mr. Clerides' statement is on the benefit of Cyprus *as a whole*. This indicates the psychological fears of partition on the part of the Greek Cypriot community. The Turkish Cypriot position, on the other hand, was directed toward safeguarding the rights of the Turkish community against complete domination by the powerful Greek Cypriot majority.

No income tax law was passed, for neither bill secured a separate majority vote. The Executive-proposed bill, which was supported by the Greek Cypriots, received thirty votes, all Greek. There were eleven Turkish Cypriot votes opposed to it, with three Turkish Cypriot votes abstaining. The Turkish proposal received fourteen votes in favor—all the Turkish members—and thirty votes against—all Greek members.[54] Thus, an attempt to institute a new tax bill was defeated.

Both communities reverted to their Communal Chambers in

[53] Cyprus, The House of Representatives, *Minutes*, (in Greek, my free translation) "Income Tax Law of 1961," December 18, 1961, pp. 16-23. (Typewritten.)

[54] *Ibid*., pp. 33-34.

order to fill the gap. On December 20, 1961, the Greek Communal Chamber, following President Makarios' statement, voted for a bill imposing a "Personal Contribution" on the members of the Greek Community. This "Personal Contribution" law covered the amount included in the defeated personal income tax bill in the House of Representatives.[55] At the same time, the Greek Communal Chamber abolished the communal taxation, originally implemented in December 1960. The Turkish Communal Chamber also passed its own income tax law. Therefore, income taxation became the function of the Communal Chambers. Characteristically, this action dramatized the importance of the Communal Chambers. Thus, the Chambers played an increasingly active role in the affairs of the Republic and contributed to further separation.

Regarding the constitutionality of the Communal Chambers' actions, the Supreme Constitutional Court upheld both Communal Chambers.[56] But the effect of having to revert to the Communal Chambers for the income tax legislation placed the two communities further apart, thereby limiting the prospects of constitutional government.

The Constitutional Provision of the Final Veto and the Army Deadlock

The deadlock in the Army is related to the basic structure and provisions of the Constitution. It emanates from the provision of the final veto granted to the President and Vice President according to Article 50. This constitutional provision was applicable to the formation of the Army as indicated in Article 129:

> 1. The Republic shall have an army of two thousand men of whom sixty per centum shall be Greeks and forty per centum shall be Turks.
> 2. Compulsory military service shall not be instituted except by common agreement of the President and the Vice-President of the Republic.

---

[55] *Eleftheria* (Nicosia), December 19, 1961.

[56] The Court's position with reference to the legality of the actions of both Communal Chambers is reflected in the following case involving the Greek Communal Chamber. "In the Matter of the Tax Collection Law No. 31 of 1962, and Hji Kyriacos and Sons Ltd. of Famagusta," (Case No. 298/62), in *Reports of Cases of the Supreme Constitutional Court of Cyprus* (Cyprus: The Printing Office of the Republic, 1963), Vol. 5, pp. 22-23.

The provisions for the establishment of the Army were clearly indicated in the Constitution. The Ministry of Defense as early as March 2, 1961, issued a proclamation stating it was ready to accept the first enlistees.[57] From the very beginning, some major questions developed with regard to the formation of the Army. The outstanding issue between the Greeks and the Turks of Cyprus was whether the Army would be formed on a separate or a mixed basis. The Council of Ministers, on the one hand, decided to form the Army on a mixed basis; the Vice President, on the other, insisted on separation. He returned the decision of the Council of Ministers for "reconsideration."[58] The Council reiterated its decision for a mixed Army.[59]

The Turkish views were further expressed by the Defense Minister, Osman Orek, who projected the view that the Turkish Cypriots did not actually want two separate armies. He proposed that both communities agree that an army of five battalions be formed; each battalion should consist of three companies, and each company of three platoons. The Turkish Cypriot position was that the battalions could be mixed. However, on the company level, separation on a bi-communal basis was necessary. The Turkish Cypriots argued that owing to the linguistic and religious differences, it would be difficult for soldiers of Greek and Turkish ethnic backgrounds to be quartered together. Furthermore, this argument was tied in with the projected disciplinary problems.[60]

In line with the Turkish Cypriot position, the Turkish Vice President used his final veto power according to Article 50 of the Constitution and vetoed the Council of Minister's decision for a completely mixed Army.[61] The President's reaction to the Vice President's veto was that he considered the reasons for the veto unacceptable, and questioned the constitutional right of the Vice President to

[57] During the first day of enlistment, 59 Turkish Cypriots and 51 Greek Cypriots went to the enlistment centers. See *Eleftheria* (Nicosia), March 3, 1961.

[58] Kuchuk, *Cyprus: Turkish Reply to Archbishop Makarios' Proposals, op. cit.*, p. 22.

[59] Interview with Polycarpos Georgadjis, Minister of the Interior, Nicosia, September 8, 1965.

[60] Interview with Ahmet Akyamac, Special Adviser to the United Nations Turkish Delegation, New York, July 14, 1966.

[61] Kuchuk, *Cyprus: Turkish Reply to Archbishop Makarios' Proposals, op. cit.*, p. 22.

exercise a veto on the separation of the armies. Consequently, President Makarios indicated that there was no reason, under the existing circumstances, to form an Army of two thousand men as provided for in the Constitution. The Army deadlock was never solved. It has remained a dormant source of tension and testifies to the inability of the leadership of the two communities to agree on basic constitutional provisions.

The Separate Municipalities Provision in the Constitution and the Municipalities Crisis

The Municipalities provision was probably the greatest source of trouble in the 1960 Constitution. The focal point of friction regarding the Municipalities was in the headlines of the Greek Cypriot press even before the Republic was born.[62] The Municipalities crisis continued throughout the life of the Republic. It continued to be a thorn in the relations of the two communities; indeed, it was never solved.

According to the 1960 Constitution:

> Separate municipalities shall be created in the five largest towns in the Republic, that is to say, Nicosia, Limassol, Famagusta, Larnaca and Paphos by the Turkish inhabitants thereof.
> . . .
> The council of the Greek municipality in any such town shall be elected by the Greek electors of the town and the council of the Turkish municipality in such town shall be elected by the Turkish electors of the town . . .[63]

Up to 1958, there existed in Cyprus unified Municipalities under CAP 240; this Municipal Corporations Law was originally enacted in June, 1930. During the emergency of the E.O.K.A. rebellion, the Turkish Cypriots established, in 1958, separate Municipalities. In 1959, the British Colonial Administration gave *de jure* recogni-

[62] The provision of separate Municipalities implanted in the Greek Cypriot community the fear of partition. On April 4, 1959, the Mayor of Paphos, Mr. Jakovos Jakovides stated that he would oppose all attempts to establish separate Municipalities. Dr. Themistocles Dervis, the Mayor of Nicosia, on April 11, 1959, similarly expressed strong opposition to the separate Municipalities provision. *Phileleftheros* (Nicosia), April 5, 12, 1959.

[63] Article 173(1)(2).

tion to the Turkish Cypriot Municipalities, by enacting Law No. 33/1959 known as The Turkish Municipal Committees (Temporary Provision) Law.

When the Republic of Cyprus came into being, therefore, the Greek Cypriot Municipalities were functioning under CAP 240 and the Turkish Cypriot Municipalities under Law 33/1959. Under the 1960 Constitution, Article 188 (2) provided for the existing laws to be effective for six more months after the independence of Cyprus on August 16, 1960, to enable the President and the Vice President to come to a compromise solution.

As the compromise solution was not forthcoming, a "Municipalities Laws (Continuation) Law No. 10/1961,"[64] was passed by the House. This Law extended the provisions of Article 188(2) for three additional months. This extension was repeated eight times in total up to December 1962[65] when, finally, unable to find a solution, a complete breakdown of negotiations occurred. However, during these extensions of the law, the Turkish Cypriots called for full implementation of the constitutional provisions as provided in Article 173. The Greek Cypriots, fearing separation as a step toward partition, objected to the Turkish demands.

From the very beginning, the Greek Cypriots criticized the provision of separate Municipalities.[66] Vice President Kuchuk attacked the Greek press for preventing cooperation. He emphasized that the implementation of separate Municipalities would not be difficult because of the fact that the Turkish Cypriot community in the large cities was already separated from the Greek sector.[67]

On behalf of the Greek Cypriot community, the first major proposal regarding the Municipalities came from the President. On March 19, 1962, President Makarios issued the following statement:

---

[64] Cyprus, *Annual Report 1961* (Nicosia: Printing Office of the Republic of Cyprus, 1962), p. 85.

[65] Interview with Constantinos Fanos, member of the House of Representatives, Nicosia, August 24, 1965.

[66] On January 17, 1961, the Mayor of Paphos, Mr. Jakovos Jakovides, stated that "all the Greek Mayors of the cities follow a common policy and support his Beatitude in his efforts for the just solution of the Municipalities, i.e., the establishing of unified Municipalities." Quoted in *Eleftheria* (Nicosia), January 18, 1961. Similar statements were made by other Greek Cypriot Mayors at the time.

[67] Kuchuk, *Cyprus: Turkish Reply to Archbishop Makarios' Proposals, op. cit.*, pp. 22-23.

> In his Beatitude's view, the geographical separation of the Municipalities, irrespective of its financial repercussions, is difficult to materialize without affecting the interests of the Greek and Turkish citizens. His Beatitude suggested the maintenance of a united municipal authority and the proportional representation of Greeks and Turks thereon in accordance with the proportion of the population in each town.[68]

The Vice President's answer stated that geographical partiton of the Municipalities could be brought about.[69]

Continued negotiations failed to reconcile the two views. Moreover, the Greek Cypriot side made it clear that it would not accept another three-month extension in the House of Representatives beyond December 1962. The Greek conviction was that the Turkish side would not accept anything less than absolute separation. In addition, the Greeks believed that the Turkish Cypriots utilized the Municipalities crisis to extract more concessions from the Greeks on the other tension areas.

Last-minute attempts to prevent a collapse of negotiations were made by the President and Vice President before the December deadline. At a meeting held on December 17, 1962, the President and the Vice President agreed that the President of the House, Glafcos Clerides, and the President of the Turkish Communal Chamber, Rauf Denktash, be invited to express their opinions.

The President of the House, Clerides, together with the Attorney General, Kriton Tornarides, who was acting as Legal Adviser of the Government, drafted the following set of proposals on December 22, 1962. These proposals were intended to become the basis of a new "experiment:"

> 1. The Municipal Corporation Law (CAP. 240) will be re-enacted subject to the necessary drafting amendments.

---

[68] Communique issued by President Makarios to Vice President Kuchuk, March 19, 1962. In "Outline of the Negotiations Regarding the Question of the Municipalities in the Five Towns" (Nicosia: The Office of the Director of the House of Representatives, n.d.), Appendix "A." (Mimeographed.) This is an unpublished collection of documents accompanied by a text, prepared by the Director of the House of Representatives concerning the negotiations between the leadership of the two Cypriot communities on the question of the Municipalities. The arguments within the text reflect the Greek Cypriot point of view. For the Turkish Cypriot point of view, see Kuchuk, *Cyprus: Turkish Reply to Archbishop Makarios' Proposals, op. cit.*, pp. 22-23.

[69] *Ibid.*

> Provided that such Law in its application to the towns of Nicosia, Limassol, Famagusta, Larnaca and Paphos shall be subject to the following modification, that is to say, instead of the existing municipal councils in each such town there will be a Joint Committee composed as in paragraph 2 hereof provided to perform all the functions performed by a council of a municipal corporation under the provisions of the afore-cited Law subject to the modification provided in paragraph 3 hereof.
> 2. (1) The members of the Joint Committee will be appointed by the President and the Vice President of the Republic.
> (2) Each Joint Committee shall consist of Greek and Turkish members proportionately to the Greek and Turkish population of each town . . .[70]

In essence, the above proposals provided for unified Municipalities. Vice President, Dr. Kuchuk, opposed the above proposals on the following grounds:

> The proposals drafted by Messrs. Clerides and Tornarides have been very carefully and exhaustively considered today at a general meeting attended by the Turkish Ministers, the Turkish members of the House of Representatives, the President and members of the Executive Committee of the Turkish Communal Chamber and certain other Turkish leaders.
> . . .
> that the time was yet premature either for examining the question whether or not the separation of Municipalities should continue, or for considering any change in our Constitution,
> . . .
> that the proposals drafted by Messrs. Clerides and Tornarides envisaged departure from, or alteration of, the Constitutional provisions, . . .
> that once joined it would be unconstitutional and illegal to separate again the Municipalities should the proposed experiment fail, . . .
> that separate Greek and Turkish Municipalities should continue to function for services prescribed in the Constitution,

[70] "Draft prepared by the President of the House of Representatives and the Attorney General Regarding the Solution of the Problem of the Municipalities," in "Outline of the Negotiations Regarding the Question of the Municipalities in the Five Towns," *op. cit.*, Appendix "C." (Mimeographed.)

> . . .
> that the Municipal Law should be so amended as to be consistent with the Constitutional provisions and the amended Law should be extended for a period of at least one year.[71]

Efforts to salvage the talks and to help prevent a breakdown failed.

President Makarios' reaction to the Turkish position was to reject the geographical partition and to suggest that an extension of Law No. 10/1961 would not facilitate a compromise solution:

> The Constitutional provision for separate Municipalities in the five main towns is wholly inapplicable . . . During the past two years, the Municipalities law was extended eight times with the hope that a compromise solution could be found. During my last meeting with the Turkish leadership, I discovered that there is no hope [for solution]. Therefore, I see no reason for any further extension of the Municipalities Law.
> Neither at present nor in the future will we ever accept geographical partition [of the Municipalities].[72]

The friction concerning the Municipalities reflects a bi-communal ideological warfare and can be explained from two angles. The Turkish Cypriots believed in and demanded a strict carrying out of the Constitutional provisions in order to guarantee their rights and to eliminate any possibility of complete domination by the powerful Greek majority. Furthermore, they identified separate Municipalities as a sign of separation from the Greek Cypriot community. The Greek Cypriots, on the other hand, saw Municipal separation, even on a small scale, as a step toward partition—a word that was anathema to them.

The final failure on the question of the Municipalities in the Executive branch brought the matter before the House. As expected, the Turkish position in the House reflected the general views of the Turkish Cypriot community. At the House meeting of December 31, 1962, Representative Halit Ali Riza made the following proposal:

---

[71] Letter by Vice President Kuchuk to President Makarios on the Municipalities, December 22, 1962 in *Ibid.*, Appendix "D." (Mimeographed.)
[72] Quoted in *Eleftheria* (Nicosia) (my free translation), December 31, 1962.

> We believe that, taking into consideration the complexity of the question not only politically but also technically, much more time should be allowed for such discussions to continue, which we hope and expect would be with an open mind and elasticity within the framework and provisions of the Constitution and not based on fixed, unchangeable ideas and assumptions;
> . . . With every good will and intention . . . we have submitted this bill of which the effect, if approved, by the House, would be to prolong the operation of the existing Municipal Corporation Laws for a certain period of time; we suggest a year but will accept any reasonable period.[73]

To the Greek members of the House, this Turkish proposal was intended to evade the issue. To them, continuation of the existing law meant an acceptance of separate Municipalities created under the Turkish Municipal Committee Law of 1959.

The Greek Cypriot counter position to the Turkish statement is clearly reflected by the position expressed by Representative Constantinos Fanos:

> Honourable colleagues, the real object of the Constitutional provisions for separate Municipalities is not to create difficulties, complications and tension in the relations between Greeks and Turks, but simply to safeguard the reasonable lawful rights of the Turkish community against any excesses or unjust decisions of the majority, resulting in discrimination against Turkish citizens.
> Since, however, for the reasons set out by His Beatitude and repeated by us today, i.e. inapplicability in practice, the above object cannot be achieved through separate Municipalities, the Greek leadership has submitted the well known proposals about unified Municipalities, which can, through a proper legislative act, best satisfy any reasonable interests of the Turkish community . . . What is therefore the purpose of the new extension of the Municipal Corporations Law sought by the present Bill? Since eight previous extensions have not in any way helped find a satisfactory solution but on the contrary

[73] Cyprus, The House of Representatives, *Minutes,* "A Law to Amend the Municipalities Laws (Continuation) Law 1962," December 31, 1962, p. 2. (Typewritten.)

> have through recent developments shown that there is no common ground to bring dissenting views close together, we can see no sufficient reason or expediency why we should vote for this Bill. On the contrary if we vote this time too for an extension, we shall perpetuate a bad suspense which does not and cannot in any way serve the well-meant interests of the Cypriot people as a whole. For these reasons I suggest that we should vote against the Bill.
> Concluding, I should like to express the hope that the Turkish leadership will revise its whole attitude so that the realization of the unification of Municipalities may become possible with full safeguards of the reasonable lawful rights and interests of the Turkish community which the Greek side has never and will never seek to trample upon.[74]

The above Fanos statement places the Greek position in its proper perspective. In no circumstances would the Greek Cypriots accept geographical partition.

Both sides, Greek and Turkish Cypriots alike, seemed to have had some reasonable proposals, but it seems that neither side ever listened to the other. Their positions were fixed and no amount of reasoning could change each view. It followed, therefore, that when the Municipalities issue was voted upon in the House, the result was as expected. It took a definite bi-communal course, where all Greek representatives voted against the projected Turkish Bill and the Turkish representatives voted for it. Thus, the attempt to find a solution to the Municipalities problem in the House failed.

The breakdown in the Executive and Legislative branches led to the attempt by the two communities to establish municipal bi-communal legitimacy. On December 31, 1962, the Turkish Cypriots acted through their Communal Chamber. The law passed, known as the "Turkish Communal Chamber's Turkish Municipal Corporations Law,"[75] attempted to legitimize the separate status of the Turkish Municipalities. It was intended to become effective on January 1, 1963—the day after the breakdown of the Municipalities crisis in the House.

---

[74] *Ibid.*, pp. 4-5.

[75] Turkish Communal Chamber, Official Gazette, Number 1, January 3, 1963 in "Opinion by the President of the House of Representatives, on the Turkish Municipal Corporation Law," (Nicosia, n.d.), Appendix "A." (Mimeographed.)

The Greek Cypriot action was initiated by the Council of Ministers. On January 2, 1963, the Council of Ministers issued the following:

> During a special meeting under the Chairmanship of the President of the Republic, Archbishop Makarios, the Council of Ministers decided on the basis of an existing law, to issue an order under which all municipal territories would come under the "Administration and Improvement Law." Under this order it is intended to establish Municipal Councils to carry out all the powers and authority of said Law [The Village Administration and Improvement Law, CAP 243].[76]

The action of the Council of Ministers intended to reinstate the law originally passed on June 2, 1950, and amended in 1953 and 1955. In accordance with this law the objective was to create Improvement Areas and to appoint Improvement Boards under the "Villages Administration and Improvement Law (CAP 243)," which included the five largest towns. By appointing Improvement Boards, the Government attempted to create Municipal Councils, in order to fill the gap left by the lapse of the "Municipalities Law, No. 10/1961," which expired on December 31, 1962. The Government, in this case the Greek Cypriots who controlled the voting in the Council of Ministers, intended by this action to bring both Greek and Turkish sections of the Municipalities under unified control.

The Greek and Turkish Cypriot actions on the Municipalities were contested in the Supreme Constitutional Court. For its part, the Turkish community wanted to show that the Turkish Communal Chamber had the legal power to extend the 1959 Law which established the "Turkish Municipal Committees (Temporary Provisions)." On the other hand, the Greek Cypriots emphasized the legality of the old "Villages Improvement Law." The Greek Cypriots felt that the Council of Ministers was justified in reenacting the existing law, thereby establishing complete control over Municipalities.

The Supreme Constitutional Court's decisions, handed down on April 25, 1963, stated that both communal actions were unconsti-

[76] Quoted in *Eleftheria* (Nicosia), (my free translation), January 3, 1963.

tutional. It is also important to note here that the Court's decisions were both issued not unanimously but by majority opinion within the Court.

In the one case where the Court ruled that action of the Council of Ministers was unconstitutional, the Greek Supreme Constitutional Court Justice, Michalakis Triantafyllides, dissented. The decision was delivered on April 25, 1963, by the Supreme Constitutional Court President, Ernst Forsthoff, with the Turkish Supreme Court Justice Mehmet Munir, concurring:

> The Order made by the Council of Ministers on the 2nd January, 1963, and published under Notification No. 4 in Supplement No. 3 to the official Gazette of the Republic of the 10th January, 1963, is void *ab initio* and without any legal effect whatsoever.[77]

On the other hand, in the case regarding the action by the Turkish Communal Chamber, again the Court decided by majority opinion. The Supreme Constitutional Court President Forsthoff, with Justice Triantafyllides concurring and Justice Munir dissenting, decided on April 25, 1963, the following:

> *By majority* (2) the making of the said Law [The Turkish Municipal Corporations Law passed by the Turkish Communal Chamber on December 29, 1962] was not within the power or competence of the Turkish Communal Chamber.[78]

Thus bi-communalism was extended within the Supreme Constitutional Court.

The Constitutional Court called the acts of the two communities unconstitutional, but it had no power to solve the thorny political issue.

The Municipalities breakdown represents the culmination of persistent bi-communal deadlocks. The Greek and Turkish Cypriots,

[77] "The Turkish Communal Chamber, And/Through Its Social and Municipal Office v. The Council of Ministers," (Case No. 10/63), in *Reports of Cases of the Supreme Constitutional Court of Cyprus,* (Nicosia: Printing Office of the Republic of Cyprus, 1963) Vol. 5, p. 64.

[78] "The House of Representatives v. The Turkish Communal Chamber And/Or The Executive Committee of the Turkish Communal Chamber," (Case No. 12/63), in *Ibid.,* p. 125.

having solidified themselves into two opposing groups with fixed positions toward the 1960 Constitution, were unable to function within its constitutional framework.

Following the Supreme Constitutional Court's decision on the Municipalities, the Greek Cypriots increasingly pressed for amendments to the basic structure of the Constitution. The Turkish Cypriots, on the other hand, insisted on the full implementation of the 1960 constitutional provisions.

The Greek Cypriots were determined to amend the Constitution, and in November 1963, President Makarios submitted his thirteen proposals. However, the political climate was not conducive to their success. The increasing communal deadlocks and mistrust, coupled with Makarios' proposals,[79] led to the December, 1963 crisis.

[79] For Makarios' thirteen proposed amendments to the Constitution, see *infra*. pp. 105, 106.

5

CRISIS IN CONSTITUTION AND GOVERNMENT

Our purpose at this point is to examine and analyze, first, President Makarios' constitutional proposals and the reaction of the Turkish Cypriot community; second, the constitutional breakdown and the resulting intercommunal violence; third, the nature of government in crisis; and fourth, the evaluation of bi-communal attitudes toward the crisis.

The Makarios Constitutional Proposals

The Makarios proposals to amend the Constitution represent the culmination of persistent Greek Cypriot demands to removing what the Greek Cypriots referred to as the "negative elements" of the Constitution. The Greek Cypriot leadership felt that the removal of the negative elements in the Constitution was a prerequisite to the "smooth functioning of the state." In essence, these proposals were intended to establish a more unified state.[1]

The Turkish Cypriots, on the other hand, strongly opposed the Greek Cypriot attempt to establish a more unified state. They believed that any proposals to change the basic structure of the 1960 Constitution were directed to removing the Turkish Cypriot community's constitutional safeguards.[2]

---

[1] Interviews with Archbishop Makarios, President of the Republic of Cyprus; Ezekias Papaioannou, member of the House of Representatives and Secretary General of *The Progressive Party of the Working People* (AKEL); Panayiotis Orphanos, Secretary General of the *Cyprus Farmers Union* (PEK), *op. cit.;* Spyros Kyprianou, Foreign Minister, Nicosia, July 16, 1965; Riginos Theocharous, President of the Bank of Cyprus and formerly Minister of Finance, Nicosia, August 27, 1965.

[2] The Turkish Cypriots "defend the Constitution and refuse to amend any of its provisions because all amendments requested by the Greeks are directed at those parts of the Constitution which recognize the existence of the Turkish community as a *community* in Cyprus." The Turkish Communal Chamber, *Looking Back: An Official Briefing, op. cit.,* p. 17.

President Makarios felt that the proposals to amend the Constitution were the result of the persistent bi-communal deadlock on outstanding constitutional issues; namely, the tax legislation, the seventy-thirty provision in the Public Service, the Municipalities, and the Army.

On November 31, 1963, Makarios submitted his proposals to the Turkish Vice President, Dr. Kuchuk, for consideration. At the same time, he informed the three Guarantor powers, Britain, Greece, and Turkey of his intentions.[3] Makarios' message stated the reasons for his proposed amendments to the Constitution:

> The three years' experience since the coming into operation of the Constitution, which was based on the Zurich and London Agreements, has made clear the necessity for revision of at least some of those provisions which impede the smooth functioning and development of the state . . . One of the consequences of the difficulties created by certain constitutional provisions is to prevent the Greeks and Turks of Cyprus from cooperating in a spirit of understanding and friendship, to undermine the relations between them and cause them to draw further apart instead of close together, to the detriment of the well being of the people of Cyprus as a whole.
> This situation caused me as President of the State, great concern. It is necessary to resolve certain of the difficulties by the removal of the obstacles to the smooth functioning and development of the state . . .[4]

Thus, Makarios proposed the following thirteen points:

1. The right of veto of the President and the Vice-President of the Republic to be abandoned.
2. The Vice-President of the Republic to deputise for the President of the Republic in case of his temporary absence or incapacity to perform his duties.
3. The Greek President of the House of Representatives and

[3] Makarios had no intention to discuss his constitutional proposals with the three Guarantor powers. *Eleftheria* (Nicosia), December 6, 1963; Foley, *Legacy of Strife, op. cit.*, p. 165.
[4] See, "President Makarios' Proposals to Amend the Cyprus Constitution," in the Greek Communal Chamber (Cyprus), *Cyprus Today* (Nicosia: November-December, 1963), p. 1.

the Turkish Vice-President to be elected by the House as a whole and not as at present the President by the Greek Members of the House and the Vice-President by the Turkish Members of the House.

4. The Vice-President of the House of Representatives to deputise for the President of the House in case of his temporary absence or incapacity to perform his duties.

5. The constitutional provisions regarding separate majorities for enactment of certain laws by the House of Representatives to be abolished.

6. Unified Municipalities to be established.

7. The administration of Justice to be unified.

8. The division of the Security Forces into Police and Gendarmerie to be abolished.

9. The numerical strength of the Security Forces and the Defence Forces to be determined by Law.

10. The proportion of the participation of Greek and Turkish Cypriots in the composition of the Public Service and the Forces of the Republic to be modified in proportion to the ratio of the population of Greek and Turkish Cypriots.

11. The number of the Members of the Public Service Commission to be reduced from ten to five.

12. All decisions of the Public Service Commission to be taken by simple majority.

13. The Greek Communal Chamber to be abolished.[5]

In essence, seven of thirteen of the President's proposals were aimed at rectifying those constitutional provisions which led to the bi-communal deadlocks as discussed in Chapter four; proposals one and nine were intended to amend those constitutional provisions which led to the army deadlock; proposal five intended to amend the constitutional provision which caused the tax legislation deadlock; proposal six was intended to unify the Municipalities; proposals ten, eleven, and twelve were intended to amend those provisions which led to the friction in the Public Service. The remaining proposals were intended to establish a more unified state, thus abolishing what the Greek Cypriots called "Separatist Constitutional Provisions." [6]

---

[5] Ibid., pp. 1-8.

[6] Interview with Tassos Papadopoulos, Minister of Labor.

On December 16, 1963, the Turkish Government rejected Makarios' proposals.[7] Shortly thereafter the Turkish Cypriot leadership also rejected the proposals. In the meantime, the Turkish Cypriots challenged Makarios' proposals as intended to promote *Enosis*.[8] The Turkish Cypriot Press demanded that if the President insisted on his proposals, Greece and Turkey should take over the administration of the Greek and Turkish Cypriots, respectively.

The Turkish Cypriot position is indicated in Vice President Kuchuk's answer to President Makarios. The Vice President pointed out that the proposed amendments represented the Greek Cypriot community's "preconceived intention to abrogate the Constitution and the Agreements and to undermine the present regime when it suited them."[9] He stressed that the experience of the constitutional life of the Republic did not prove that the Constitution was unworkable; rather it proved the Greek Cypriot's bad faith toward the constitutional rights of the Turkish Cypriot community:

> Whenever the Turks tried to make use of any of their constitutional rights, they were met with the same pre-conceived intention to undermine the relevant constitutional provisions with a view to rendering the Constitution inoperative. The argument that the three years' experience has made it clear that it is necessary to revise the Constitution is nothing but a pretext to take away the just rights of the Turks.
>
> In short, whenever a crisis arose as regards the implementation of the Constitution and the Turks were forced to rely on their constitutional rights, the Greek side came out with a counter claim to rescind that part of the Constitution which provided

---

[7] For a detailed analysis of Turkey's role in the affairs of Cyprus, see *infra*, chapter six.

[8] Current Turkish Cypriot literature describes the Turkish Cypriot feelings: "By December 1963 the Greek Cypriot leadership, which was supposed to cooperate with the Turkish Cypriot leadership as its 'partner' in the Constitutional regime of the island, had worked itself into . . . a frenzy of fanaticism and had become . . . eager to destroy the independent Republic in order to achieve *Enosis*." The Turkish Communal Chamber, *A Report on Cyprus, op. cit.*, p. 16.

[9] Kuchuk, *Cyprus: Turkish Reply to Archbishop Makarios' Proposals, op. cit.*, p. 21.

> for the Turkish community some powers to make their views heard in the general administration of the Republic's affairs.[10]

Thus, the Turkish Vice President attributed the causes of the deadlock to the Greek Cypriots' unwillingness to cooperate with the Turkish Cypriot community within the framework of the 1960 Constitution. To the Turkish Cypriot leadership, constitutional revisions had to be viewed within the framework of bi-communal Cyprus. Any proposals intended to weaken the distinct identity of the Turkish Cypriot community, were regarded as an attempt to suppress it.

The Vice President, in counteracting Makarios' proposals, stated that the only way to establish mutual trust and cooperation between the two communities was strict adherence to the Constitution based on the following principles:

> (a) that all subversive activity and propaganda directed against the regime and the abrogation of the Agreements is stopped.
> (b) that all activity and propaganda directed for Union of Cyprus with any other country be made a punishable offence;
> (c) that the institutions which were created by the Constitution such as the Public Service Commission be backed up by proper legislation in order to enable them to function smoothly and properly;
> (d) that legislation for the municipalities as envisaged by the Constitution be enacted;
> (e) that the Election Law proper be enacted;
> (f) that the President removes all causes of friction between

[10] Vice President Kuchuk gives the following examples: "When in April 1961 the Greeks and Turks in the House of Representatives could not agree whether the Colonial taxation legislation should be extended for a further period of three months or two months, Government was faced with a serious situation. The Turkish members of the Council of Ministers almost begged the President to re-introduce the extension proposition to the House and try to bring both sides together on an agreed extension period instead of leaving the country without taxation legislation. The Turkish Ministers hoped that in this way it would be possible to settle the dispute within constitutional provisions but the President categorically refused even to discuss the matter and, by assuming he had supra-constitutional powers, directed personally that Law or no Law taxes shall be collected . . .
When in October 1961, there was a difference of opinion between myself and the President and Greek Members of the Council, on the composition of the

his office and mine by consenting to take my views on matters of foreign affairs, defence and security and the Turkish Ministers be treated as necessary parts of this government and not as opposition to it;

(g) that adequate subsidies be given to the Communal Chambers at least to the extent of services which they have taken over from the British Administration, thereby treating them as autonomous public bodies which are running services essential for the country and not treating them as undesirable anti-government institutions, the function of which are alien to the government's policy.

(h) that the seventy to thirty ratio is applied on the basis of our original Agreement which bears our signature so that no injustice is done to any serving officer.[11]

It seems that the Turkish Cypriot leadership, as well as the Greek Cypriot leadership, was concerned with the "smooth functioning" of the Republic. However, their views as to how this "smooth functioning" would be accomplished were diametrically opposed. On the one hand, the Greek Cypriot leadership insisted that "smooth functioning" could be achieved through basic revisions of the 1960 constitutional framework; on the other hand, the Turkish Cypriot leadership insisted that "smooth functioning" could be accomplished through strict implementation of the 1960 Constitution.

The irreconcilable attitudes of the two communities over the applicability of the 1960 Constitution created mutual suspicion and mistrust. The magnitude of this mistrust is reflected in the intercommunal fighting of December 1963.

---

units of the Cyprus Army, I had to rely on my power of veto, in order to prevent the Council from taking an administrative decision which would not work but would present a constant danger and constitute a breeding place for the spread of intercommunal friction . . . The President's handling of the question of municipalities is another example of the Greek attitude and determination not to implement constitutional provisions relating to Turkish rights. The President clearly stated that he would not allow any legislation providing for the creation of separate municipalities. Later, after he had tried his hand to set up un-constitutional Governmental agencies instead of municipalities and the matter was referred by us to the Supreme Constitutional Court, he clearly stated that he would not listen to any judgment of the Constitutional Court . . ." *Ibid.*, pp. 21-23.

[11] *Ibid.*, pp. 24-25.

Constitutional Breakdown and Intercommunal Violence

The December 1963 intercommunal fighting was the culmination of many negative forces. In this sense, the constitutional difficulties and the inability of the leadership of the two communities to promote any genuine basis for cooperation brought to the surface dormant fears and mistrust.

Makarios failed to gain the confidence of the Turkish Cypriot community. Archbishop Makarios could not have been regarded as President of all the Cypriots. As a symbol of the Greek Orthodox Church, he could not gain the allegiance of the Moslem Turkish Cypriot community. Moreover, the President-Archbishop took every opportunity to express the attachment of the Greek Cypriots to the "Hellenic ideals." [12]

As Chief Executive, Makarios showed an inability to promote genuine cooperation with the Turkish Cypriot Ministers. In cabinet meetings, for example, the Turkish Cypriot Ministers felt that Makarios and his Greek Cypriot Ministers constantly bypassed them on every important question.[13] Thus, when the President presented his constitutional proposals, the Turkish Cypriots interpreted them as an attempt by the Greek Cypriots to dominate them.

On the other hand, the Turkish Cypriot leadership showed an inability to understand the Greek Cypriot sensitivity toward major provisions of the Constitution. The Greek Cypriot community felt that the Zurich and London Agreements were undemocratic and unjust. In particular, the Greek Cypriots objected to the separate majority vote in the House, the Vice President's final veto power, the seventy-thirty provision in the Public Service, and the separate Municipalities provision.[14] Turkish demand for full imple-

[12] On October 3, 1960, in commemorating one of the E.O.K.A. heroes, Makarios stated: "In these mountainous caves of the Machaera Monastery, the glory of Greece, has once more been immortalized." *Eleftheria* (Nicosia) (my free translation), October 4, 1960. On September 28, 1962, during a visit to Greece, Makarios addressed King Paul of the Hellenes: "I am a Greek leader of a Greek island whose great majority is always attached to Greece." *Eleftheria* (Nicosia) (my free translation), September 29, 1962.

[13] Stephens, *op. cit.,* p. 173; see also, Kuchuk, *Cyprus: Turkish Reply to Archbishop Makarios' Proposals; op. cit.,* p. 25.

[14] Interviews with Antonios Anastassiades, member of the House of Representatives; Polycarpos Georgadjis, Minister of the Interior; Renos Solomides, Minister of Finance; Panayiotis Orphanos, Secretary General of the *Cyprus Farmer's Union* (P.E.K.), *op. cit.*

mentation of the rights granted to it by the Constitution and the Turkish Vice President's reminding the Greek community of the Turkish Cypriots' love for "Mother Turkey," [15] alienated the Greek Cypriots.

The persistent polarization of positions and the resulting bi-communal constitutional deadlocks gave every opportunity to extremist groups to exert increasing influence. While former E.O.K.A. men were applying pressure for radical solutions to the deadlock and were demanding *Enosis,* the Turkish Cypriot organization, *Turk Mudafaa Teskilati* (T.M.T.[16]), was demanding partition.[17]

In the midst of the Republic's difficulties, the extremist groups were able to thrive. Within each community "secret armies" were organized by the extremists. The Turkish Cypriots were determined to prevent any Greek Cypriot attempts to bring about extra-constitutional solutions to the deadlocks. The Greek Cypriots were preparing to forestall partitioning of the island and eventual intervention by Turkey.[18] By Christmas 1963, the two communities confronted each other as two opposing armed camps. Thus, the resulting intercommunal violence aroused bitterness and hatred between the two communities; thus, exacerbating historical animosity. The violence led to physical and psychological communal separation.

The most evident physical separation was the "green line" [19] in Nicosia, where most of the intercommunal fighting took place. The green line separated the Greek from the Turkish sectors of the town, thus clearly demonstrating the dimensions of the breakdown. All Turkish Cypriot civil servants remained in the Turkish quarter of Nicosia, and neither the Vice President, nor the Ministers, nor the House members could participate in the Government.

[15] Dr. Kuchuk speaking in a ceremony in the town of Lefka on January 22, 1962 stated: "We must remain united as we were [united] during the days of the struggle [during the time of E.O.K.A.]. The London and Zurich Agreements were not given to us as gift. They represent our victory which we won through the sacrifice of our children . . . Our mother nation [Turkey] stands always by our side." Quoted in *Eleftheria* (Nicosia) (my free translation), January 23, 1962.

[16] T.M.T. refers to *Turkish Resistance Organization.*

[17] Stephens, *op. cit.,* p. 181; Foley, *Legacy of Strife, op. cit.,* p. 167.

[18] Stephens, *op. cit.,* pp. 181-183; Foley, *Legacy of Strife, op. cit.,* pp. 167-169. See also *infra,* chapter six.

[19] The "green line" refers to the demarcation line which separates the Greek and Turkish quarters in Nicosia.

The physical separation had psychological repercussions. While the Turkish Cypriots felt that they could not live with the Greeks unless physically separated, the Greeks believed that the Turks were purposely trying to promote partition through physical separation of the two communities. The United Nations was finally invited to maintain peace in Cyprus.[20]

Parallel to the physical separation, the Greek and Turkish Cypriots hold diametrically opposed views concerning the intercommunal conflict. The Greek Cypriots, controlling the government and 98 percent of the territory of the Republic,[21] regard the Turkish Cypriots as rebels and their actions as an insurrection against the state.[22] The Turkish Cypriots consider the Greek Cypriot-controlled government illegal and unconstitutional [23] and administer their affairs under the authority of the Vice President.

The Turkish Cypriot-controlled territory is scattered in areas all over the island. The most important is the northern section of Nicosia and the region extending beyond it. These Turkish-controlled areas, referred to as "enclaves," cover an area of about 2 percent of the territory of the Republic. The total population in these Turkish Cypriot enclaves is about 59,000 or about fifty percent of the total Turkish Cypriot population.[24] It should be noted the remaining Turkish Cypriots live in mixed villages and recognize the local Greek Cypriot administration. However, the wholly Turkish Cypriot villages lying in Greek Cypriot controlled areas have little contact with the government.[25]

[20] For the role of the United Nations in Cyprus, see *infra,* pp. 150-157.

[21] United Nations, Security Council, *Report by the Secretary-General on the United Nations Operation in Cyprus (For the Period 10 September to 12 December 1964),* (S/6102, 12 December 1964), p. 19.

[22] Interviews with Archbishop Makarios, President of the Republic of Cyprus; and Andreas Araouzos, Minister of Commerce and Industry, *op. cit.*

[23] Statement by Mr. Rauf Denktash, first President of the Turkish Communal Chamber before the Security Council, United Nations, Security Council, *Official Records,* Nineteenth Year, 1099th Meeting, 28 February 1964, pp. 8 and 21.

[24] Some 25,000 Turkish Cypriots from 94 Turkish Cypriot villages and suburbs have concentrated in predominantly Turkish villages and towns. Of these, about 21,000 found accommodations in larger Turkish Cypriot communities; approximately 4,000 live in refugee camps. See, United Nations, Security Council, *Report by the Secretary-General on the United Nations Operation in Cyprus (For the Period 10 September to 12 December 1964),* (S/6102, 12 December 1964), p. 19.

[25] *Ibid.,* pp. 62-63. Before the crisis of December, 1963 the 104,000 Turkish Cypriots lived in 235 villages and towns either purely Turkish Cypriot or

Government in Crisis

Crisis government in Cyprus operates at two distinct levels of authority. On the one hand, the Greek Cypriots conduct their affairs through the established governmental machinery; and on the other, the Turkish Cypriots conduct their affairs under the office of the Vice President.

The Greek Cypriots, having secured absolute control over the government, enacted legislation which incorporated most of Makarios' thirteen proposed amendments to the 1960 Constitution.

On February 3, 1964, the Greek Cypriot-controlled House of Representatives gave a vote of confidence to Makarios' government:

> It [the House] expresses its full support to the Government of the Republic, for its policy during the crisis, which is directed to secure a unitary, independent and democratic state, without any interference from outside forces.[26]

On May 28, 1964, the House enacted legislation placing the Police and Gendarmerie under a single command.[27] On June 1, 1964, the House passed a Conscription Law creating the National Guard and calling under arms more than 10,000 men.

On July 9, 1964, the House enacted legislation establishing the Supreme Court of Cyprus. The Supreme Court took jurisdiction over the areas previously under the Supreme Constitutional Court and the High Court of Justice. Thus, the supreme judicial authority was incorporated in a single body, the Supreme Court.[28]

On November 28, 1964, a new Municipalities Law was enacted to fill the gap resulting from "the expiration of the Municipalities

---

mixed. In spite of the great movement of Turkish Cypriots, the Secretary-General, in his Report indicated that "the largest segment of the Turkish Cypriot population . . . remained where it was [before the crisis]." *Ibid.*, p. 19.

[26] Cyprus, House of Representatives, *Minutes,* (in Greek, my free translation), "Resolution," February 3, 1964, pp. 1-2. (Typewritten.)

[27] Cyprus, House of Representative, *Minutes,* (in Greek, my free translation), "The Police Force (Amended) Law of 1964," May 28, 1964, pp. 9-10. (Typewritten.)

[28] Cyprus, House of Representatives, *Minutes,* (in Greek, my free translation), "The Administration of Justice (Various Provisions) Law of 1964," July 9, 1964, pp. 2-9. (Typewritten.)

Law on December 31, 1962." [29] The Law gave the power to the Council of Ministers to appoint Municipal Councils, but no elections were to be held, owing to "the existing circumstances." The Greek Cypriot justification for this enactment is expressed in Representative Georghios Djirkotis' statement:

> Today's [House] meeting will become a significant station in the history of Hellenic Cyprus. Today we are called upon to practically prove the invalid nature of the shameful Zurich and London Agreements, which had been imposed on the Greek Cypriot people in 1959. The passage of this Law is a clear proof that we consider the Agreements which provide for separate municipalities, as dead letter.[30]

On March 31, 1965, the House abolished the Greek Communal Chamber and replaced it with a Ministry of Education.[31] Furthermore, it abolished the Communal Courts and transferred their jurisdiction to the "regular Courts of the Republic." [32]

On July 23, 1965, two important laws were enacted. The first extended the term of the President and the members of the House until elections were to be held "but not for a period of more than twelve months." [33] The second law was the electoral law which provided for the:

---

[29] Cyprus, House of Representatives, *Minutes,* (in Greek, my free translation), "The Municipalities Law of 1964," November 11, 1964, pp. 6-25. (Typewritten.)

[30] *Ibid.,* p. 12.

[31] Cyprus, House of Representatives, *Minutes,* (in Greek, my free translation), "The Transfer of the Jurisdiction of the Greek Communal Chamber and the Ministry of Education Law of 1965," March 31, 1965, pp. 2 and 14. (Typewritten.)

[32] *Ibid.,* p. 3.

[33] Cyprus, The House of Representatives, *Minutes,* (in Greek, my free translation), "The President of the Republic and the Members of the House of Representatives (Extension of Term of Office) Law of 1965," July 23, 1965, pp. 8 and 11. (Typewritten.) It is interesting to point out that the two committees which prepared this Law parallelled the extension of the term of office of the House of Representatives to the extension of the term of office of the House of Commons of the United Kingdom from 1940 to 1944, *Ibid.,* p. 8. Until February 25, 1968, no elections were held since the Extension of Term of Office Law of 1965. Makarios' reason for holding presidential elections may be explained as a tactical move to strengthen his position regarding any future constitutional settlement in Cyprus. The nature of his landslide victory (over 95 percent of the total vote), indicates that the Greek Cypriots support his Independence move at home, and his policy of

> . . . abolition of separate electoral lists of Greek and Turkish [Cypriots] as well as the abolition of Separate Greek and Turkish electoral districts; in their place it projected unified electoral lists and unified electoral districts for the election of the President of the Republic as well as the Members of the House of Representatives.[34]

Along with the enactment of legislation in the House of Representatives, the Greek Cypriots have taken complete control of the Executive branch and the Public Service. Owing to the "absence" of the Vice President and the three Turkish Cypriot Ministers, all executive decisions have been carried out by the Greek Cypriots under the leadership of President Makarios. The President, in turn, has transferred the functions of the three Turkish Cypriot Ministers to Greek Cypriot Ministers.

The structural and functional changes of the 1960 Constitution by the Greek Cypriot leadership have been directed toward establishing a unified state with "unfettered" independence. The Greek Cypriot leadership believes that the Turkish Cypriots have abandoned the government in order to undertake a rebellion against the Republic. To the Greeks, therefore, all actions and laws enacted by the government, without the consent of the Turkish Cypriots, are binding. If the Turkish Cypriots wish to "return" and cooperate with the government, they must first accept the legality of the laws enacted during their "absence."

It is evident that there is no intention on the part of the Greek Cypriots to revert to the conditions existing before the December 1963 crisis. They consider the present government as the only lawfully constituted authority in Cyprus. Accordingly, in answering a Turkish Cypriot request that a Turkish Cypriot Minister be included in the Cyprus delegation to the Afro-Asian Conference in the Summer of 1965, they emphasized this point:

---

independence from Greece. The poor showing of the opposition by the strong enotists in the candidacy of Dr. Takis Evdokas (3.71 percent) indicates Makarios' strong position at home, and at the same time, the strong Greek Cypriot opposition to any *Enosis* moves under the present political conditions in Greece.

[34] Cyprus, The House of Representatives, *Minutes,* (in Greek, my free translation), "The Electoral (Transistional Provisions) Law of 1965," July 23, 1965, p. 12. (Typewritten.). The above Law has been renewed yearly.

> The government of the Republic does not recognize Dr. Kuchuk as Vice-President as he, having abandoned the office of Vice-President since December, 1963, has been leading a rebellion against the State and has repeatedly stated that there is no Cyprus State and that the Cyprus Republic is dead . . . Neither Dr. Kuchuk nor the three former Turkish Ministers who have themselves played an undermining role against the State, are considered as holding or being able to hold positions in the Government . . .[35]

The Turkish Cypriot community has been functioning under the leadership of the Vice President, Dr. Kuchuk, "who for the purposes of the Turkish Communal Chamber, performs the functions of a Head of State [but] who is the Deputy Head of State."[36] The Vice President, the three Turkish Cypriot Ministers, the fifteen Turkish Cypriot members of the House of Representatives and the Turkish Communal Chamber perform the political and administrative functions of the Turkish Cypriot community.

The Turkish Cypriot leadership believes that this arrangement is a temporary one necessitated by the crisis. There is no claim that this represents a Turkish Cypriot government in crisis; every effort is made to give assurances that the administration of the Turkish Cypriot community is conducted, as far as possible, according to the 1960 Constitution.[37]

All necessary services in the Turkish Cypriot enclaves are performed under the authority of the Vice President. The Turkish Cypriot civil servants in the Republic before the crisis, now perform the Turkish Cypriot administrative functions. For example, under this arrangement, the highest Turkish Cypriot Police official under

[35] United Nations, Security Council, *Letter Dated 23 June 1965 from the Permanent Representative of Cyprus Addressed to the Secretary-General,* (S/6473, 24 June 1965). This supplies the text of the statement issued by a spokesman of the Government of Cyprus.

[36] Turkish Communal Chamber, "Text in English of the Official Gazette No. 1 dated 27th July, 1965, published in Turkish Under the Authority of the Vice-President of the Republic of Cyprus," Nicosia, n.d.

[37] Interview with Ahmet Akyamac, Special Adviser, United Nations Turkish Delegations, *op. cit.* Although the Turkish Cypriot leadership stressed its allegiance to the 1960 Constitution, after the November 1967 crisis, and with the strong support of Turkey, they have established there own "Transitional Administration." This move may be interpreted as an attempt to put pressure on Makarios for a quick constitutional settlement. *The New York Times,* December 30, 1967.

the Republic, now serves as the chief of police for the Turkish Cypriot community. This pattern is applied in the financial, postal, and all other services in the Turkish Cypriot enclaves.[38]

Unlike the Greek Cypriots, the Turkish Cypriot leadership insists that the 1960 Constitution is still binding.[39] They further stress that all Greek Cypriot laws passed without the participation of the Turkish Cypriot community are unconstitutional and, therefore, invalid.

Rauf Denktash, the first President of the Turkish Communal Chamber summarized the Turkish Cypriot views:

> There can only be a Cyprus government as long as the Turkish side of the administrators is incorporated in that government and the constitutional setup is maintained—not otherwise. Therefore, if this unlawful organization of Greek administrators tries to impose its will on us, then we shall react . . .[40]

Thus, the Turkish Cypriot leadership claims allegiance to the 1960 Constitution and protests all Greek Cypriot actions directed at changing its basic structure. This pattern of protests is reflected in Dr. Kuchuk's letter to the United Nations Secretary General regarding the Greek Cypriot enactment of a new Judicial Law:

> The Greeks in Cyprus have destroyed yet another pillar of the Constitution by abolishing the Supreme Constitutional

[38] Interview with Ahmet Akyamac, *op. cit.*

[39] Vice President Kuchuk in a cable addressed to the United Nations Secretary General, expressed this feeling: "It is common knowledge that certain offices in the government vested in the Turkish community continue to be held by Turks in accordance with the Constitution. But in an abortive attempt to deprive the Turkish Community of their governmental authorities and to dictate to them their terms, the Greeks have prevented them by force or threats from exercising their full functions . . . This state of affairs can not in any way be taken to mean that, in the Republic of Cyprus, the government authority can only be exercised by the members of the Greek communty in complete disregard of the existing consitutional and international guaranteed rights of the Turkish community." United Nations, Security Council, *Letter Dated 2 May 1964 from the Permanent Representative of Turkey Addressed to the Secretary General,* (S/5680, 4 May 1964). This submits the cable of Dr. Fazil Kuchuk, Vice President of Cyprus, to the Secretary General.

[40] Statement by Mr. Denktash; United Nations, Security Council, *Provisional Verbatim Records of the Twelve Hundred and Thirty-Fifth Meeting, 5 August 1965,* (S/PV.1235, 5 August 1965), p. 52.

> Court and by introducing such drastic changes in the Administration of Justice as to destroy the existing judicial system and to replace it by an entirely new and unconstitutional one with the sinister object of depriving the Turks of the judicial safeguards given to them by the Zurich and London Agreements and the Constitution . . . The Cyprus Constitution is based on the Zurich and London Agreements, the provisions of which constituted the basic articles of the Constitution. The basic articles can only be changed or replaced with the agreement of the Guaranteeing Powers who are the signatories of these international agreements. All the provisions of the Constitution which are violated by the new Administration of Justice Law are the basic articles of the Constitution.[41]

Following the extension of the term of office of the President and the members of the House and the enactment of a new electoral law by the Greek Cypriots, the Turkish Cypriots protested,[42] and they proceeded to extend the term of office of the Vice President, the Turkish Cypriot members of the House, and the Turkish Communal Chamber. These Turkish Cypriot laws [43] are intended to

---

[41]United Nations, Security Council, *Letter Dated 14 July 1964 From the Permanent Representative of Turkey Addressed to the Secretary-General,* (S/5818, 14 July 1964). This submits the above cable by Vice-President Kuchuk addressed to the Secretary-General. For additional views of Vice President Kuchuk, see Appendix "B" *infra.* pp. 177-180.

[42] "The Greek Cypriots, having forcibly prevented the Turkish Members of the Cyprus House of Representatives from attending the meeting of the House, have purported to pass a law extending the term of office of the President and the Greek Members of the House for a period not exceeding one year. At the same meeting they purported to pass an election law which for the life of them they will never be able to apply after their own heart . . . Admittedly what they have purported to do has removed the remaining props of the Constitution and is tantamount to opening the doors wide open to lawlessness.

. . . Like all the laws passed by the Greek Members of the House of Representatives since the 21st December, 1963, the latest laws are unconstitutional and legally invalid and worthless. The Turkish Cypriots are not bound to comply with illegal and unconstitutional laws especially when such laws have not received the sanction of their elected representatives. It follows, therefore, that these laws, like all the other invalid ones, will not be binding on the Turkish Cypriots and will not be enforced in sectors where Turkish Cypriots are living."

The Turkish Communal Chamber, *Special News Bulletin,* August 4, 1965. (Hereafter cited as *Special News Bulletin).*

[43] The Turkish Cypriots passed the following two Laws; "Law No. 1/1965: A Law Making Temporary Provisions Regarding the Election of Vice-President of the Republic and Turkish Members of the House of Repre-

facilitate the constitutional functioning of the Turkish Cypriot community and to reiterate that "the fundamental rights of the Turkish community as provided by the Constitution are in force." [44] There still has been no attempt by the Turkish Cypriot leadership to create a separate state. Dr. Kuchuk emphasizes this point:

> These Turkish resolutions and laws are, as far as possible, in conformity with the Constitution of the country and are not intended to lead to the creation of a Separate Turkish state. I continue to be the Vice President of the Republic of Cyprus.[45]

The Crisis and Bi-Communal Attitudes

THE TURKISH CYPRIOT ATTITUDES

The persistence of the crisis and the continued physical separation have hardened the position of the Turkish Cypriots vis-à-vis the Greek Cypriots. The Turkish Cypriot leadership feels that the Republic of Cyprus as established by the 1960 Constitution is legally in existence and that the constitutional rights of the Turkish Cypriot community must be upheld.[46]

---

sentatives," Law No. 2/1965: A Law to Make Interim Provisions for the Election of the Members of the Turkish Communal Chamber." For a description of the laws, see The Turkish Communal Chamber, "Text in English of the Laws and Decisions, Promulgated in the Official Gazette No. 2 Dated 30th July 1965, Published in Turkish Under the Authority of the Vice-President of the Republic," Nicosia, n.d. No elections have been held since the passage of the "Law No. 1/1965." However, following Makarios' proclamation for presidential elections, the Turkish Cypriot leadership proclaimed elections for the vice presidency to be held on February 25, 1968 (the same date as the Greek Cypriot elections). Since there was no opposition, Vice President Kuchuk was proclaimed the winner.

[44] *Ibid.*

[45] Interview of Dr. F. Kuchuk, Vice-President of the Republic of Cyprus with Mr. Alberto Ca Zorzi of the Italian Television, 29 August 1965. Quoted in *Special News Bulletin,* September 4, 1965.

[46] Dr. Kuchuk points out the following: "The Republic of Cyprus is still in existence legally and the Turkish Community continues to exercise its constitutional rights and powers as best it can under the circumstances. There has never been any doubt as to whether the Turks continue to consider themselves the citizens of the Republic of Cyprus. It is not the Turks but the Greeks who are trying to destroy the Republic of Cyprus. It is not the Turks but the Greeks who are trying to destroy the Republic of Cyprus with a view to annexing our island to Greece."
Interview of Dr. Fazil Kuchuk, Vice President of the Republic, with Mr. Ulrich Kienzle of West German Television, June 8, 1965; quoted in *Special News Bulletin,* July 7, 1965.

The Turkish Cypriot leadership contends that there are two distinct communities in Cyprus, and any attempt to define them as majority and minority is misleading and against the spirit of the 1960 Constitution. Rauf Denktash, the first President of the Turkish Communal Chamber, amplifies this position:

> There is no Cypriot nation and Cyprus is not a Greek Republic. It is a Republic of partnership between the Greeks and Turks, and, . . . it is the result of a compromise. This partnership was laid down in a constitution which was prepared by us and accepted by the communities of Cyprus at the 1960 elections . . .
> The Turks of Cyprus are a political entity with rights determined by the Constitution and guaranteed by international treaties. All Greek attempts to abrogate those rights and reduce us to the position of a mere minority are unjustified political manoeuvres aimed at opening the way to Enosis . . .[47]

Moreover, the Turkish Cypriot leadership accuses the Greek Cypriots of collaborating with Greece to bring about *Enosis,* the old Pan-Hellenic dream:

> The reason why the Greeks cannot show goodwill and are unable to see realities is that they are obsessed by a burning desire to dominate and enslave, if not to exterminate, the Turkish community of Cyprus and to annex the territory of our Republic to Greece to satisfy the latter country's Pan-Hellenic ambitions of territorial aggrandizement.[48]

In view of these existing realities, the Turkish Cypriot leadership points out that coexistence in a unitary state, as the Greek Cypriots propose, is unacceptable. The Turkish Cypriots emphasize that since the crisis of 1963, they have been deprived of their basic constitutional rights. This implies that even the 1960 constitutional framework failed to ensure the rights of the Turkish Cypriots. Consequently, the Turkish Cypriots feel that some form of physical and geographical separation is essential in order to safeguard their rights:

[47] United Nations, Security Council, *Provisional Verbatim Records of the Twelve Hundred and Thirty-Fifth Meeting, 5 August 1965,* (S/PV.1235, 5 August 1965), pp. 42 and 56.

[48] Interview of Dr. Kuchuk with Mr. Antonio Cifariello of the Italian television, December 1, 1965. Quoted in *Special News Bulletin,* December 25, 1965.

> The Turkish community [Vice President Kuchuk points out] has reached the definite conclusion that the physical separation of the two communities would be the only effective way of providing ironclad security of life and property for the Turks. This would be the only way to enable the two communities to live together in peace and cooperate for the good of the country as a whole within the framework of a federal system of government and without either community having the possibility of subjugating the other.[49]

The concept of physical and geographical separation is also encouraged by the Turkish Cypriot Press. In an editorial on August 23, 1965, the leading Turkish Cypriot newspaper *Halkin Sesi* pointed out that for centuries the two communities have retained their social, cultural, and religious institutions. Thus, any attempt to impose a unitary state is doomed to fail;[50] the Turkish Cypriot weekly, *Zafer,* editorialized that geographical separation is the only acceptable solution to the Turkish Cypriot community.[51] Moreover, the Turkish Cypriots refer to the "green line" in Nicosia and in the other cities, as the first step toward communal separation.[52]

Federation, a more subtle form of physical separation, envisaged by the Turkish Cypriot community,[53] is to be accomplished by compulsory exchange of population between the Greek and Turkish Cypriots so that each community will occupy distinctly Turkish and Greek parts in Cyprus. The dividing line, suggested by the Turkish Cypriots would give the Turkish Cypriot community the northern part of Cyprus, composed of 1,084 square miles or 38 percent of the total area of the Republic.[54] This would entail an exchange

[49] Interview of Dr. Fazil Kuchuk with Mr. Ulrich Kienzle of West German television, June 8, 1965. Quoted in *Special News Bulletin,* July 7, 1965.

[50] Reviewed in *Special News Bulletin,* August 24, 1965.

[51] *Ibid.,* June 19, 1965.

[52] The Turkish Cypriots claim the following: "After all the green lines are demarcations which ensure that the Greek Cypriots keep well away from the Turkish Cypriots. They are the first step for the separation of the two communities and might well constitute the foundation of their full and final separation in the future . . . In this country the Turkish Cypriots will not live together with the Greek Cypriots." *Special News Bulletin,* July 24, 1965.

[53] See editorial "Federation Will Come," in *Special News Bulletin, September 4, 1965.*

[54] United Nations, Security Council, *Report of the United Nations Mediator on Cyprus to the Secretary-General; Note by the Secretary-General,* (S/6253, 26 March 1965), p. 26.

of some 20,000 families, about 10,000 from each community.[55] The Turkish Cypriot position is supported by Turkey.[56]

GREEK CYPRIOT ATTITUDES: AN OPINION SURVEY

Essentially, the Greek Cypriot leadership feels that the agreements of Zurich and London, did not reflect the will of the Cypriots; rather they were imposed on Cyprus by "outside powers." [57] Therefore, the Constitution, which resulted from these agreements, proved to be unworkable, for it placed the Turkish Cypriot minority on the same political level with the Greek Cypriot majority. According to the Greek Cypriot leadership, the Turkish Cypriots should be treated as a minority with special guarantees for their cultural, religious, and educational rights. These guarantees should be based on the principles set forth by the European Convention for the Protection of Human Rights and Freedoms and in conformity with the Universal Declaration on Human Rights.[58]

In view of the fact that the 1960 Constitution proved to be "unrealistic," "undemocratic," and "unworkable," the Greek Cypriot leadership believes that any future settlement must be based on a completely new foundation. This new foundation must provide for a unitary state, completely independent and unfettered by any treaties encroaching upon Cyprus' constitutional development.

---

[55] *Ibid.* The necessity of exchange of population, if the Turkish Cypriot plan is applied, stems from the fact that the Greek and Turkish Cypriots live in an intermixed pattern all over the island. Thus, in Cyprus before the crisis, according to the United Nations Mediator's Report, out of 619 villages, 393 were wholly or predominantly Greek Cypriot; 120 were Turkish Cypriot and 106 were mixed. But the villages are not found in clusters where one community predominates. They are spread out all over the island. The towns, on the other hand, have mixed populations with the two ethnic communities concentrated in separate quarters. See *Ibid.,* p. 8.

[56] *Ibid.,* pp. 37-39. Since the November 1967 crisis, Turkey has pursued a Greco-Turkish dialogue for a Cyprus settlement. At the same time, the Turkish Cypriot leadership proclaims that it will propose its own constitutional solution. See, *Eleftheria* (Nicosia), February 21, 1968.

[57] Interview with Sypros Kyprianou, Foreign Minister, *op. cit.*

[58] Interviews with Glafcos Clerides, President of the House of Representatives; Tassos Papadopoulos, Minister of Labor; Constantinos Fanos, member of the House of Representatives; Antonios Anastassiades, member of the House of Representatives; Renos Solomides, Minister of Finance, *op. cit.* The Greek Cypriot leadership further state that they oppose the special right of self-determination for the Turkish Cypriot minority. If self-determination is granted to the Turkish Cypriot minority, the Greek Cypriots indicate, a precedent may be set up for minorities in all other countries which could cause a breakup of some existing political systems.

Thus, the Greek Cypriot leadership rejects any proposals for separation, federation, or partition.[59]

Moreover, the Greek Cypriot leadership argues that the internationally recognized right of self-determination cannot be denied to Cyprus. If the Cypriots, therefore, decide to unite with another country this should be decided by the majority of the Cypriots.[60] In essence, the Greek Cypriot leadership feels that if the majority decides to unite with Greece, this could not be denied to them, so long as the minority's fundamental rights are guaranteed. The Greek Cypriot leadership's position is supported by Greece.[61]

The Greek Cypriot leadership's attitudes regarding the causes of the 1963 crisis and its views toward settlement are also held by the Greek Cypriot community at large. According to a public opinion survey that I conducted among the Greek Cypriot community,[62] the Greek Cypriots, by and large, feel that the major cause of the 1963 crisis was the nature of the Zurich and London Agreements.

In replying to the question, "what do you consider to be the main causes of the present crisis?" as shown in Table 1, p. 124, three major classifications of answers appear: Zurich, NATO, and Turkish Cypriots. Of the 500 respondents, 85.8 percent stated that the present crisis can be attributed to the Zurich Agreement and NATO; 5 percent attributed the crisis to the Turkish Cypriots and 9.2 percent to "other" factors. Of the 85.8 percent blaming Zurich and NATO for the crisis, 55.8 percent blamed the Zurich Agreement

---

[59] Interview with Archbishop Makarios, President of the Republic of Cyprus, *op. cit.*

[60] *Ibid.*

[61] United Nations, Security Council, *Report of the United Nations Mediator on Cyprus to the Secretary-General; Note by the Secretary-General* (S/6253, 26 March 1965), pp. 36-37. With Greece having pulled her "illegal" troops out of Cyprus, Makarios has been following a more independent policy. It is expected that in the Spring of 1968 President Makarios will propose a new constitutional plan as a basis for negotiation with the Turkish Cypriots. *Eleftheria* (Nicosia), February 20, 1968.

[62] This public opinion survey was conducted in the summer and early fall of 1965 in Cyprus. It reflects only the attitudes of the Greek Cypriot community. The reasons for not conducting a similar opinion study among the Turkish Cypriots was that I was unable to enter the Turkish Cypriot enclaves. Thus, it was impossible to conduct a representative study. On advice by the United Nations Officials in Cyprus, I was discouraged from undertaking such a study in the Turkish Cypriot enclaves due to my Greek Cypriot ethnic background. For a sample of the questionnaire and the method of the survey, see Appendix "C." *Infra.* pp. 180-184.

TABLE 1

Distribution of Answers by Education, Age, and Place of Residence to the Question: "What Do You Consider to be the Main Causes of the Present Crisis?"

(by Percent)

EDUCATION	Zurich	NATO	Turkish Cypriots	Other
Grammar (Grades 0-6)	51.0	34.6	8.0	6.3
High School (Grades 7-12)	68.0	22.0	0.8	9.2
College (13 and above)	48.1	26.0	—	26.0
Total Per Cent	55.8	30.0	5.0	9.2

AGE	Zurich	NATO	Turkish Cypriots	Other
20 – 39	57.1	28.0	6.4	7.7
40 – 59	53.9	31.6	3.8	9.8
60 and above	57.0	27.0	3.2	12.7
Total Per Cent	55.8	30.0	5.0	9.2

PLACE OF RESIDENCE: URBAN/RURAL	Zurich	NATO	Turkish Cypriots	Other
Urban	47.0	30.5	10.5	11.5
Rural	61.6	29.7	1.3	7.6
Total Per Cent	55.8	30.0	5.0	9.2

n. Sample size—500 respondents

directly; and the other 30 percent widened their blame to include NATO. But in both sets of answers, the respondents indicated clearly that both factors, the Zurich Agreement and pressures from NATO resulted in imposing on the Cypriots an unworkable Constitution. All 85.8 percent of these respondents indicated that Greece and not Turkey was forced to make major concessions, thus making the 1960 Constitution an "unjust" one for the Greek Cypriot majority.

In analyzing the findings in Table 1 under the three variants of age, education, and place of residence, we find that there are practically no appreciable differences. About 85 percent within each age group stated that Zurich and NATO are responsible for the crisis. Under the variant of education, the ratio again shows a consistency. Thus, 85.6 percent of all of the grammar school and below respondents indicate that Zurich and NATO are to be blamed for the crisis; 84.1 percent of all college group respondents stated the same factors. Although 90 percent of all high school group respondents blamed Zurich and NATO, the proportional difference from the other educational groups is not significant to warrant explanation.

As far as the residence variant, Table 1 indicates that 91.3 percent of the rural population blames the Zurich Agreement and NATO, whereas only 77.5 percent of the urban dwellers blame Zurich and NATO. An explanation to the rural-urban opinion gap may be linked to the fact that a much higher proportion of urban dwellers blame the Turkish Cypriots for the crisis. Thus, 10.5 percent of all urban dwellers put the responsibility squarely on the Turkish Cypriot community, whereas only 1.3 percent of the rural population so indicates. Although one would expect to find more tolerance among urban dwellers, the Greek Cypriot rural population seems to be more tolerant toward a different ethnic community. This may be explained by the fact that most of the intercommunal fighting occurred in the cities, especially Nicosia. Thus, more urban dwellers were directly affected by the crisis.

That the rural dwellers show such an antipathy toward the Zurich Agreement and NATO, may be attributed to the Greek Cypriot leadership as an effective molder of rural opinion. It is no secret that from the very beginning, the Greek Cypriot leadership and the press initiated a propaganda campaign against the Zurich Agreement.

Only 5 percent of all 500 respondents stated that the Turkish Cypriots caused the crisis. It is significant to note that out of the total number of 25 respondents blaming the Turkish Cypriots, 24 have grammar school education or less. None from the college educated respondents blamed the Turkish Cypriots for the crisis.

Under the classification "other" of Table 1, the findings show 26 percent of all college-educated respondents attributing the cause of the crisis to "other" factors. Of these, 10 percent blame the Greek Cypriot officials for lacking responsible leadership in dealing with the Turkish minority. The same respondents blame the Greek Cypriot leadership for accepting the 1959 Zurich and London Agreements. The remaining 16 percent of college-educated respondents indicating "other" blame the "imperialistic" policies of the United States, Britain, and Turkey and the "incompetency" of the leadership in Greece.

To the question in Table 2, "under the present political circumstances, what do you consider to be the most realistic solution to the crisis," three important solutions are proposed: Independence, Self-Determination, and *Enosis*.

The findings show that 40.6 percent of all the respondents indicate a preference for Independence; 31.2 percent for Self-Determination; 18 percent for *Enosis;* and 10.2 percent indicate "other." All 40.6 percent, who prefer Independence indicate, without exception, that by independence they mean "without strings attached." They are alluding to the limitations of the 1960 Constitutional framework. It is interesting to note that practically all respondents indicating Independence stress their support for full guarantees for the Turkish minority. They do not, however, indicate what they mean by these guarantees other than expressing the opinion that these guarantees should be safeguarded by the United Nations.

In analyzing Table 2 under the age variant, there seems to be a greater proportion among the younger group, ages 20 to 39, preferring Independence than the higher age groups. Whereas 45 percent of the 20 to 39 age group respondents indicate preference for Inde-

TABLE 2

Distribution of Answers by Education, Age, and Place of Residence to the Question: "Under the Present Political Circumstances, What Do You Consider to be the Most Realistic Solution to the Crisis?"

(by Percent)

EDUCATION

	Independence	Self-Determination	Enosis	Other
Grammar (Grades 0-6)	44.0	33.0	19.0	4.0
High School (Grades 7-12)	42.0	28.7	18.6	10.6
College (13 and above)	16.0	28.0	10.0	46.0
Total Percent	40.6	31.2	18.0	10.2

AGE

	Independence	Self-Determination	Enosis	Other
20 – 39	45.0	27.2	18.1	9.4
40 – 59	36.7	34.9	17.4	10.6
60 and above	36.5	33.4	19.0	11.0
Total Percent	40.6	31.2	18.0	10.2

PLACE OF RESIDENCE: URBAN/RURAL

	Independence	Self-Determination	Enosis	Other
Urban	41.5	30.0	13.5	14.5
Rural	40.0	32.0	21.0	7.3
Total Percent	40.6	31.2	18.0	10.2

n Sample size—500 respondents

pendence, only 36 percent from each of the other two age groups indicate so. This gap may be explained by the fact that the younger group is beginning to entrench itself in the new governmental bureaucracy. Continued Independence may perpetuate their newly acquired status.

In analyzing Table 2 under the variant of education, there seems to be an appreciably smaller proportion among the college-educated respondents indicating preference for Independence than among the other two educational groups. Whereas 44 percent of the total grammar school and 42 percent of the total high school respondents indicate preference for Independence, only 16 percent of the total college respondents indicate so. The greatest proportion of the college-educated respondents (46 per cent) indicate "other" as a possible practical solution. This reveals a greater degree of awareness on the part of the upper educated strata, who express fears that Independence may not be possible under the "existing political circumstances." This they attribute to the power politics of NATO, Great Britain, Greece, and Turkey who may determine the political future of Cyprus. They tend to emphasize the military importance of Turkey to Britain and the United States and doubt the sincerity of the "Western powers" to bring about a "just and democratic solution" to Cyprus. By "just and democratic solution" these respondents indicate a government where the majority rules and the minority's political and social rights are guaranteed.

Characteristic of the respondents' attitudes, indicated in Table 2, is their low regard for *Enosis* as a practical solution. Only 18 percent of the total respondents indicate so. The low regard for *Enosis* as a practical solution may be explained by the fact that the old Hellenic ideal may not be so strong.

The E.O.K.A. underground struggle, the experience in running their internal and external political affairs, their ability to withstand crises, and their mistrust of the "foreign interested parties," have given the Greek Cypriots self-confidence and a desire to remain independent.

A further explanation may be the sense of realism among the Greek Cypriots in general that the United States and Great Britain are unwilling to allow *Enosis* because it would displease Turkey. Moreover, most Greek Cypriot respondents indicate that they have no faith in the Greek political leadership. They feel that Greece must be partly blamed for the Zurich Agreement. Moreover, the current political instability in Greece may have softened their desire for *Enosis*.

In analyzing Table 2, we find the answers given for self-determination difficult to assess; the concept of self-determination is an elusive term and has various implications. To some respondents "self-determination" may mean unfettered Independence; to others it may mean *Enosis;* to still others, it may have other meanings.

A clearer picture as to what the respondents mean by self-determination can be seen from our analysis of Table 3, p. 130. Thus, to the question, "ideally, what do you personally consider to be the most justifiable solution," there again appeared a three-way pattern of answers: Independence, self-determination and *Enosis*. Of the total respondents, 30 percent prefer Independence as an ideal solution; 15.8 percent self-determination; 53.4 percent *Enosis;* and 8 percent indicate "other."

Ideally, then, more than 53 percent of the total respondents indicate *Enosis* as their preference. This shows an increase of 35 percent over the Table 2 findings, which indicate only 18 percent preference for *Enosis* as a practical solution. It may be noted that more than half of those respondents indicating self-determination in Table 2 have now shifted their preference to *Enosis*. Whereas self-determination as a practical solution was the preference of 31.2 percent of all respondents, now under ideal conditions it drops to 15.8 percent. The shift from self-determination as practical to *Enosis* as an ideal solution, occurs in all variants without exception, that is, in education, age, and place of residence. We can assume, therefore, that *Enosis* may be cloaked in the concept of self-determination.

There is also a lowering of preference for Independence as an ideal solution from Independence as a practical solution. Thus, while Independence was the preference of 40.6 percent of all respondents as a practical solution (Table 2) now this drops to 30 percent as an ideal solution (Table 3).

There are, however, certain exceptions. The preference for Independence as an ideal solution increases in the education variant of the college group respondents and in the age variant of the 60 and

TABLE 3

Distribution of Answers by Education, Age, and Place of Residence to the Question: "Ideally, What Do You Personally Consider to be the Most Justifiable Solution?"

(by Percent)

EDUCATION

	Independence	Self-Determination	Enosis	Other
Grammar (Grades 0-6)	31.3	17.3	50.6	0.6
High School (Grades 7-12)	30.1	12.0	56.6	1.3
College (13 and above)	22.0	18.0	60.0	—
Total Percent	30.0	15.8	53.4	8.0

AGE

	Independence	Self-Determination	Enosis	Other
20 – 39	27.2	13.8	57.9	0.8
40 – 59	30.5	17.0	51.3	0.9
60 and above	38.0	19.0	42.8	—
Total Percent	30.0	15.8	53.4	8.0

PLACE OF RESIDENCE: URBAN/RURAL

	Independence	Self-Determination	Enosis	Other
Urban	38.5	17.0	42.5	1.5
Rural	24.0	15.0	61.0	0.3
Total Percent	30.0	15.8	53.4	8.0

n. Sample size—500 respondents

above group. This may indicate that some respondents from these groups, who as a practical solution indicated preference for self-determination or "other," now have shifted to Independence. Although the shifting to Independence from practical to ideal in these two groups is not more than 2 percent, it may be significant in the sense that the older age group and the college-educated group show more stability in their thinking. They may have more confidence in the Cypriots' ability toward governing themselves.

Viewed from the variant of residence, the preference of Independence, from practical to an ideal solution, shows no appreciable difference among the urban dwellers. However, there is a drastic difference among the rural dwellers. From 40 percent who expressed preference for Independence as a practical solution (Table 2), now 24 percent show the same preference as an ideal solution (Table 3). This may account for the substantial preference for *Enosis* among the rural dwellers as an ideal solution. Thus, 61 percent of all rural respondents showed preference for *Enosis* as an ideal solution, whereas only 21 percent indicated it as a practical solution.

The shifting to *Enosis* from practical to an ideal solution seems consistent in all variants. A marked difference, however, occurs among the college-educated respondents, who have shifted from 10 percent preference for *Enosis* as a practical solution to 60 percent as an ideal solution. This shifting among college educated respondents for *Enosis* may be explained in two ways. First, a high proportion of those shifting to *Enosis* as an ideal solution are school teachers. Traditionally, they have been the carriers of the Hellenic ideals and still express strong attachment to Greece. Second, the remaining college educated respondents shifting to *Enosis* as their ideal solution are, namely, doctors, lawyers, business executives, and engineers. This latter group's explanation for shifting, is that *Enosis* would be a lasting solution and would put an end to the present civil strife. To them, *Enosis* would prevent irresponsible elements of both communities from coming to power and thus leading an independent Cyprus to recurring crises; and *Enosis* would be more advantageous for the Turkish minority since Greece has proved to be capable of protecting its Turkish minority in the current Greco-Turkish rift over Cyprus.

TABLE 4
Distribution of Answers by Education, Age, and Place of Residence to the Question: "How Do You Feel Toward the Government's Policy [Greek Cypriot Leadership] During the Present Crisis?"
(by Percent)

EDUCATION	Proper Policy	Confused Policy	Other
Grammar (Grades 0-6)	88.3	3.7	8.0
High School (Grades 7-12)	82.7	8.7	8.6
College (13 and above)	64.0	22.0	14.0
Total Percent	84.2	7.0	8.8

AGE	Proper Policy	Confused Policy	Other
20 – 39	86.5	6.0	7.3
40 – 59	83.1	7.7	10.2
60 and above	82.5	7.9	9.6
Total Percent	84.2	7.0	8.8

PLACE OF RESIDENCE: URBAN/RURAL	Proper Policy	Confused Policy	Other
Urban	79.5	10.0	10.0
Rural	87.0	5.0	8.0
Total Percent	84.2	7.0	8.8

n. Sample size—500 respondents

To the question in Table 4, p. 132, "how do you feel toward the government's policy [Greek Cypriot leadership] during the present crisis," the overwhelming proportion of the respondents, 84 percent, indicated that their leadership is following the proper policy, whereas 7 percent indicated that the leadership was following a confused policy; and 8.8 percent indicated "other." There seems to be a great deal of unity among the Greek Cypriots. This factor is not difficult to explain, if we bear in mind that in times of crisis the people normally unite behind their leadership. Moreover, since the Greek Cypriot leadership has intermittently been using slogans such as *"Enosis,"* "Independence," "Self-Determination," most Greek Cypriots find it easy to identify themselves with their leadership's "policies."

Of the Greek Cypriots who are skeptical about their leadership, the most significant group are the college-educated respondents. Of all college-educated respondents, 22 percent consider the government's policy as "confused." Furthermore, an additional 14 percent who indicate "other," have reservations as to the leadership's policy. An important explanation given by those respondents who classify the government's policy as "confused" is that the present leadership contains incompetent and corrupt individuals. The respondents indicate that they have doubts about its ability to cope with the crisis.

The analysis of the bi-communal attitudes regarding the crisis discloses that both Greek and Turkish Cypriot communities have hardened their positions.

The Greek Cypriots attribute the cause of the crisis to the nature of the 1960 Constitution. They are unwilling to accept the pre-crisis arrangement. Moreover, they emphasize that "unfettered" Independence would be the only acceptable solution. Although the feeling for *Enosis* does not seem to run as strong among the Greek Cypriots, more than 50 percent of them still regard it as their ideal. The old idea of *Enosis* among Greek Cypriots has lost even more of its appeal since the April 1967 military coup in Greece. The way the Greek military leaders "mishandled" the Cyprus issue in November 1967 damaged even further the *Enosis* desire in Cyprus.

The fear of *Enosis* and the unwillingness of the Greek Cypriots to abide by the 1960 constitutional framework has made the Turkish Cypriot community's position adamant. The Turkish Cypriots feel that some form of physical separation would safeguard them from Greek Cypriot domination and would prevent *Enosis*.

The persistence of the crisis has made the positions of the two Cypriot communities more inflexible. The continuation of the crisis and the hardening of the bi-communal positions has had negative effects on the relations of Greece and Turkey and brought them, at times, to the brink of war. The role of Greece and Turkey in the affairs of Cyprus, as well as the interests of other external parties, are examined in the following chapter.

6

CYPRUS' DILEMMA: THE ENTRENCHMENT OF EXTERNAL INTERESTS

Cyprus' dilemma, the Greek and Turkish Cypriot inter-communal conflict, transcends the borders of the island Republic. Along with the constitutional deadlocks and enmity between the two Cypriot communities, the problem is heavily influenced by the involvement of a number of "interested parties." The nature and magnitude of the external involvements, therefore, explain, to a large extent, the inability and unwillingness of the Greek and Turkish Cypriots to function under constitutional government. In this chapter, through an analysis of the external involvement and interests in Cyprus, the complex roots of the inter-communal conflict are brought to the surface.

Cardinal among the issues involved are British strategic interests in the Middle East and Greco-Turkish relations. Through the 1960 Constitution, Greece, Turkey and Great Britain have permanently secured their interests in Cyprus. The constitutionalization of these interests, however, had negative effects. On the one hand, it placed Cypriot affairs within the context of international power politics. On the other hand, it placed the relations of the Greek and Turkish Cypriot communities into the realm of traditional animosity between Greece and Turkey. Thus, what in the pre-independence period may have essentially been a colonial problem between Britain and the Cypriots, eventually evolved into a fundamentally Greco-Turkish feud.

The Involvement of Greece, Turkey and Great Britain

Greece's interest in Cyprus stems from a number of factors based on a variety of arguments. Greek arguments have stressed that for over 3,000 years both Greece and Cyprus have kept alive the same historical and cultural traditions.[1]

The historical arguments of cultural, religious, racial, and traditional affinities have formed the basis for Greece's claim on Cyprus. In a sense, the Cyprus issue became interwoven with Greece's irredentist policy to reestablish the old Byzantine Empire. The catastrophic 1922 Asia Minor expedition put a temporary halt to Greece's irredentism, which eventually led to a rapprochement between Greece and Turkey and the signing of a Treaty of Friendship between Eleutherios Venizelos and Kemal Ataturk. However, the union of Cyprus with the "Hellenic World" remained one of the cornerstones of Greece's foreign policy. What strengthened Greece's claim on Cyprus was the persistent Greek Cypriot drive for *Enosis*. No Greek government could afford to disregard this age-old dream, and the Cyprus question has become the "national problem" for all Greek governments, especially in the post-World War II period.

The internal problems besetting Greece in the post-World War II period, especially civil war and reconstruction, prevented the Greek governments from pressing *Enosis* outside the Greco-British friendship. The end of the Greek Civil War and the improvement of Greece's international position, coupled with the changing British colonial policy, may have convinced the Greeks that Britain would take a more sympathetic view toward their claim on Cyprus.[2]

The unwillingness of Great Britain to accede to Greece's demands and to agree to Greco-British talks on Cyprus resulted in

---

[1] "Cyprus has always been regarded by historians and geographers as part of Greece, bound by ties of blood, culture, religion, tradition and sentiment. When for the first time the name of Cyprus appears in history, it is mentioned as being a Greek island. The successive conquests of the island that followed the fall of the Byzantine (Greek) Empire have been no more than passing, temporary and transitory influences. The Greek character alone has been the lasting element, the unalterable factor in the island of Cyprus. It is unique and awing. Three thousand five hundred years of history have not diminished one iota the Hellenic character of Cyprus—today, Cyprus is as Greek as Greece herself." Royal Greek Embassy Information Service, *Cyprus: Demands Self-Determination* (Washington, D. C., 1954) pp. 12-23.

[2] According to Stanley Mayes, another reason for Greece's increasing demand for Cyprus was her inability to receive any satisfaction of her claims to Northern Epirus, and "rectification of the Greek-Bulgarian frontier." Mayes, *op. cit.*, p. 106.

Greece's bringing the Cyprus issue to the United Nations under the form of self-determination. As was pointed out in Chapter Two, the Greek decision to bring the question of Cyprus to the United Nations in 1954 marked the beginning of the internationalization of the Cyprus problem, paving the way for Turkey's direct involvement.

For the first time, the United Nations debates revealed that the problem of Cyprus was closely interwoven with the interests of Britain, Greece, and Turkey. Greece's involvement is revealed by the statement of Alexis Kyrou during the December 1954 First Committee Meeting.[3]

Greece's claim was immediately counteracted by Turkey, which asserted its traditional interest in Cyprus. Turkey's involvement in Cyprus may be traced to the island's Ottoman occupation, which lasted for more than 300 years. Like Greece, Turkey advanced numerous arguments to justify her claim on Cyprus. These arguments ranged from geographical proximity, military security, and cultural affinity to the Turkish Cypriot community.

Turkey's interest in Cyprus, however, was not expressed openly so long as Britain retained sovereignty over the island. But, when Greece began to claim Cyprus under the principle of self-determination at the United Nations, Turkey asserted her own interest in the island. Thus, when it became clear to the Turks that Cyprus could become part of Greece, Turkey took a strong and active stand against Greece's "annexation aims." This stand falls in line with the age-old opposition by Turkey to any Greek claims to annex

---

[3] ". . . The history of the liberation movement in Cyprus was full of dramatic emotions shared by the Greek people . . . Under increasing pressure from public opinion in Cyprus and Greece, the Greek government had found itself obliged to apprise the United Nations of the continued refusal of the United Kingdom to grant the Cypriot people its right to self-determination. The Greek government had always been convinced that direct negotiations with the United Kingdom could lead to a solution. It had patiently continued its efforts for many years, in hope that it would eventually receive a favourable response . . . The British government had not allowed any occasion to pass without declaring that it would never discuss the status of Cyprus with Greece." United Nations. General Assembly. *Official Records,* Ninth Session. First Committee, 750th Meeting, 14 December 1954, pp. 547-548.

By 1958 Greece's position was hardened as revealed in the United Nations debates. See, United Nations. General Assembly. Thirteenth Session. First Committee *Verbatim Record of the One Thousand and Sixth Meeting,* (A/C.1/PV.1006, 3 December 1958) pp. 27-51.

Greek-speaking territories.[4] When Greece, in 1954, requested self-determination for Cyprus, Selim Sarper, the Turkish United Nations Representative, strongly rejected the Greek claims.[5] Subsequently, upon Turkey's increasing involvement, the Menderes regime used the issue of Cyprus as an important outlet to cover up domestic problems and unsatisfactory conditions at home.[6]

Turkey's direct involvement in the Cyprus dispute was welcomed and encouraged by Great Britain in attempting to counteract Greece's *Enosis* drive.[7] Although unwilling to submit to *Enosis* demands and surrender her sovereignty over Cyprus, Britain was willing to promote limited self-government[8] of the island. In essence, however, British policy toward limited self-government in Cyprus was directed toward perpetuating British economic and strategic interests in the Middle East. The British withdrawal from Palestine in 1948 and Suez in 1954 increased the value of Cyprus to

---

[4] For example, in the early 1920's, Turkey witnessed Greece's Asia Minor expedition which resulted in Greek troops marching outside Ankara. In spite of Greece's defeat in 1922, Turkey could not forget this. Furthermore, in 1947, Turkey tried to exert pressure to prevent the annexation of the Dodecanese Islands to Greece which lay close to Turkey's shores.

[5] ". . . Historically, after being administered by various states in ancient times, Cyprus had been a Turkish island for almost three and a half centuries. It had remained so from 1571 to 1923 prior to the acceptance of its annexation to the United Kingdom by virtue of the Treaty of Lausanne . . . On the other hand, it had never been administered by Greece . . . Turks of Anatolia had settled in Cyprus . . . They remained closely linked to the mother country, by race, custom and collective social sentiment . . . From the geographical, racial, historical and economic aspects . . . Turkey must be primarily affected by the status of the island . . . The activities of the Greek Government on behalf of the so-called application of the principle, but in reality [directed to] the annexation of the island . . . Its object was simply to take a territory away from the sovereignty of one State and place it under its own." United Nations. General Assembly. *Official Records.* Ninth Session. First Committee, 750th Meeting, 14 December 1954, pp. 551-553. The 1958 United Nations debates reflect a hardening of the Turkish position. See, United Nations. General Assembly. Thirteenth Session. *First Committee Verbatim Record of the One Thousand and Sixth Meeting,* (A/C.1/PV. 1006, 3 December 1958) pp. 2-25.

[6] Charles Foley points out that: "Foreign credit was already exhausted; no where in Turkey could you buy a cup of coffee and larger luxuries had long vanished from the market. Cyprus thus, provided the government with a welcome distraction for the Turkish public and might also prove a useful lever overseas." Foley, *Island in Revolt op. cit.,* p. 40.

[7] *The Economist* observes that "There is good reason for thinking that since 1953 the Foreign Office has been urging Ankara in the words of Othello's advisers, 'to consider the importance of Cyprus to the Turk,' a subject which had previously excited the Turks little . . ." *The Economist* (London), October 13, 1955.

[8] See *supra,* Chapter Two.

Britain. After pulling out of Suez, the British established their new Middle East headquarters in Cyprus; and the Conservative government in London gave every assurance to the "Suez rebels" that no withdrawal from Cyprus was contemplated.[9] The importance of Cyprus to British interest in the area is also evident in the 1954 United Nations debates.[10]

To the British, sovereignty over Cyprus was not only necessary but absolutely paramount. Any discussion concerning Cyprus would have to be considered within the broader context of Eastern Mediterranean politics, especially within British-Greek-Turkish relations.

The collusion of British and Turkish interests in Cyprus strengthened Turkey's role as an "interested party" in the dispute. Through membership in the Baghdad Pact, Turkey slowly emerged as one of the staunch allies of Britain, thus, on the one hand, preventing Russian penetration of the area; and, on the other, helping preserve British oil interests in the Middle East. The then British Prime Minister, Anthony Eden, emphasized the importance of the British-Turkish partnership: "I regard our alliance with Turkey as the first consideration in our policy in that part of the World." [11]

Additional British setbacks in the Middle East, namely, the 1956 Suez expedition, Jordan's dismissal of Glubb Pasha, the British military commander of its Arab League, the Lebanese Civil

---

[9] Foley, *Island in Revolt, op. cit.*, p. 11.

[10] Anthony Nutting, British delegate to the United Nations stated: "What must be clear for all to see was that Greece was now trying to use discussion at the United Nations to mobilize international pressure in order to acquire sovereignty over the territory for itself . . . The Committee should consider the repercussions which would be felt outside the territory itself were the long debate to continue in the Committee. The Eastern Mediterranean historically was not a peaceful area. Conflicts around its shores were still within the memories of many members of the Committee. But, as a result of painstaking diplomacy and political foresight and tolerance on the part of such statesmen as Venizelos and Kemal Ataturk, a happier state of affairs had been created in the area." United Nations. General Assembly. *Official Records.* Ninth Session. First Committee, 749th Meeting, 14 December 1954, pp. 545-552.

[11] Anthony Eden, *Full Circle* (London: Cassell, 1960) p. 414.

The significance of Turkey to Britain is closely tied with the creation of the Baghdad Pact. As Robert Stephens emphasizes: "With the evacuation of Egypt and the creation of the Baghdad Pact, British policy began to show signs of reverting, after seventy years, to the original idea which had inspired the Cyprus convention: protection of and support for Turkey as the shield for British interests in the Middle East, seen once more as lying chiefly in the Persian Gulf." Stephens, *op. cit.*, p. 138.

War of 1958, and the 1958 Iraqi Revolution weakening the Baghdad Pact, increased Britain's dependence on Turkey and increased Cyprus' importance as an advanced British base in the Mediterranean. Moreover, the membership of Britain, Greece and Turkey in NATO made the Cyprus dispute more complex. It brought other NATO allies into the dispute and eventually it became a Cold War issue as well. It was becoming evident that Cyprus could not be regarded as a simple colonial problem. The British Government indicated, therefore, that the Cyprus dispute not merely reflected the rival claims of the Greek and Turkish Cypriot communities, but it essentially reflected the national interests of Greece and Turkey and the strategic interests of Britain and NATO as well.[12]

The Cyprus problem as it unfolded in the late 1950's presented the following picture. It meant, on the one hand, that it was an absolute necessity to safeguard British interests in Cyprus; and, on the other, to reconcile Greek and Turkish interests for the sake of the Western alliance.

In view of these imperatives, the most important development at this time was a distinct change in British strategic requirements. By late 1957, it became evident that the British Government, on advice by its Chiefs of Staff, decided that it no longer needed Cyprus as a base but rather it needed "bases" in Cyprus. This change of British strategic considerations facilitated the eventual solution in 1959. The new outlook is reflected in the following analysis of Britain's position in the Middle East by the former Governor of Cyprus, Marshall Harding:

---

[12] Anthony Eden, speaking in the House of Commons, stated: ". . . I have never felt, and I do not believe now, that Cyprus is an Anglo-Greek question or can ever be treated as such. It is equally unrealistic to lecture Turkey as to the view she ought to take about an island no farther from her coast than is the Isle of Man from us. . . . Our duty if called on, . . . is to safeguard the strategic needs of our country and of our ally (Turkey). Neither the NATO obligations . . . nor the Baghdad Pact, nor any agreement in the Middle Eastern area or the Persian Gulf, or anything else, none of these can be speedily and effectively carried out today unless we have the assured and unfettered use of bases and the use of facilities in Cyprus . . . Her Majesty's Government must be concerned as every other government is concerned, to protect the vital interests of its own citizens. The welfare and indeed the lives of our people depends on Cyprus as a protective guard and staging post to take care of those interests, above all oil. This is not Imperialism. It should be plain duty of any government, and we intend to discharge it." *Parliamentary Debates* (1955-1956) Vol. 550, pp. 403-419.

> When I first went to Cyprus, there was a view which I shared at that time that we needed the use of the whole island for military purposes for an indefinite period. That time, I think, has now passed, and any support that we give to the Baghdad Pact and to the right flank of NATO in a military sense I think would have to be almost entirely by air power. To enable Cyprus to be used as our main operational air base in that part of the world—in the comparative role of that of the American Sixth Fleet, there are minimum conditions that would have to be fulfilled. We must have undisputed control of two air fields, and the communications system, rights to transportation systems, and access to the power system and the utility services of the island.[13]

Additional factors facilitated this change in British policy regarding Cyprus. The E.O.K.A. underground guerrilla warfare became an increasingly costly operation, and Britain was forced to keep more than 35,000 troops in Cyprus. Moreover, the intensifying Greco-Turkish conflict in Cyprus, which resulted in intercommunal violence, forced Britain to play the role of policeman. As a result, there was increasing pressure in Britain to abandon this thankless task of attempting to keep the peace between Greek and Turk.

With Britain willing to accede to an independent Cyprus, so long as her strategic interests were safeguarded, the burden for a "solution" on Cyprus fell upon the two parties "most directly concerned," Greece and Turkey. It became evident that Greece and Turkey had to search for a "solution" to safeguard their own interests in Cyprus, to secure British strategic interests, and to stabilize their respective roles within the Western alliance. Ironically, this meant that any "solution" which was acceptable to Greece and Turkey would be acceptable to Britain, so long as it secured British strategic interests in the Eastern Mediterranean. The Cyprus problem tended to evolve more and more into a Greco-Turkish problem.

Greece's abandonment of *Enosis* and self-determination for Cyprus may be attributed to several factors: persistent disappoint-

---

[13] Field Marshal The Lord Harding of Petherton, "The Cyprus Problem in Relation to the Middle East" *International Affairs* Vol. 34, No. 3 (London: July, 1958) p. 293.

ments in Greece resulting from Greece's failures at the United Nations; Greek fears that Britain, through the Macmillan Plan (which was analyzed in Chapter Two) would initiate partition of the island; and pressures by the United States for a solution in order to avoid weakening the Southeastern flank of the NATO Alliance. There is reason to believe that the increasing importance of Turkey as a strategic factor to the United States and Great Britain[14] resulted in the corresponding weakening of Greece's position within the alliance.

In view of the above, the Greek Government realized that it possessed neither the military nor the political means to gain a favorable solution. Finally, Greece accepted the invitation to negotiate her differences over Cyprus with Turkey. The acceptance of Turkish participation by Greece in the Cyprus problem was in line with the original Turkish position. Greece's willingness to negotiate proved, according to Turkey, a recognition of legitimate interests in Cyprus.

It was in this prevailing climate that "informal" discussions were held between Greek, Turkish and British foreign ministers in December 1958 during a NATO Council meeting. The three foreign ministers, after having reviewed the situation of Cyprus in the light of the 1958 United Nations debates, had agreed that bilateral negotiations would continue between the Greek and Turkish foreign ministers.[15] Britain, therefore, had given its blessings to the Greco-Turkish bilateral talks, on the condition that "British military requirements were met in a manner which could not be challenged."[16]

From the bilateral discussions, there resulted the Zurich Agreement between Greece and Turkey. The significant point regarding the agreements is that they essentially reflected the concerns of the "interested parties;" these interests were safeguarded through the Constitution of the Republic of Cyprus and international treaties. The settlement, however, was so complex that eventually it became

---

[14] Some analysts, for example, Thomas Anthem, point out that this reflects the "distorted and magnified view which the United States and Britain have of Turkey's military value as against that of Greece on the Eastern flank of NATO." Thomas Anthem "Greece and Cyprus" *Contemporary Review* Vol. 205, (London, April 1964) p. 170.

[15] *The New York Times,* January 4, 1959; see also *supra* pp. 50-52.

[16] Great Britain, *Cyprus* (Lonon: Her Majesty's Stationery Office, 1961) p. 1.

the basis for future friction, as analyzed in Chapters Three and Four.

The deep entrenchment and institutionalization of the interests of Greece and Turkey had negative effects on the constitutional and inter-communal life of Cyprus. The constitutionalized interference in the affairs of Cyprus resulted in continuous friction, thereby preventing the Cypriots, Greek and Turkish alike, from developing their own political consciousness. The two communities tended to look to their respective "mother" countries for support in solving Cypriot domestic problems. On the one hand, the Turkish Cypriots, who were numerically at a disadavantage in Cyprus, relied heavily on Turkey for directives. On the other hand, the Greek Cypriot leadership and press often provoked Turkish mistrust with their desire for *Enosis*.

The constitutional settlement in Cyprus can be understood by the respective roles of Greece and Turkey within the Western alliance. Turkey, playing an important role in British strategic plans in the Middle East, was able to obtain much more favorable terms. The disproportionate "guarantees" allotted to the Turkish Cypriot community [17] reveal dramatically the important role of Turkey in the Western alliance and the Eastern Mediterranean. The constitutional disequilibrium in Cyprus reflected the power configuration of Greece and Turkey within NATO and not the bi-communal structure of Cyprus. This constitutional disequilibrium had negative effects in Cyprus. It invited friction between the Greek and Turkish Cypriot communities as indicated in the constitutional tension areas discussed in Chapter Four. At the same time, it channeled the internal difficulties in Cyprus to Greece and Turkey. Thus, it became increasingly evident that as tension mounted in Cyprus, the Greco-Turkish rift became worse. In December 1963, when the inter-communal fighting broke out in Cyprus, Greece and Turkey once again were confronted with the choice of war or the responsibility of finding a solution. By this time, however, the political situation in Turkey and Greece was substantially affected by the Zurich and London Agreements.

[17] Namely, the Separate Majority Right; the Absolute Veto of the Vice President; the 70:30 in the Public Service; the 70:30 Representation in the House of Representatives and the Cabinet; the 60:40 Provision in the Army and the Separate Municipalities. See *supra* Chapters Three and Four.

The settlement of the Cyprus dispute was instrumental in the overthrow of the Menderes regime in Turkey. The end of the Cyprus problem brought to light Turkey's serious domestic problems, namely, administrative corruption, economic instability, severe inflation, curbing of the press, and attempts to silence the opposition. Unable to cope with these problems, the Menderes regime was overthrown in May 1960 by an Army coup. The following year, under a new constitution, General Gursel was elected President and General Ismet Inönu became the Prime Minister.[18]

The new regime focused its attention on internal politics, and Turkey attempted to play a moderate role toward the Cyprus Republic. In November 1962, President Makarios was invited to Turkey for a state visit. Turkey impressed upon the President of Cyprus that she would support his government so long as the provisions of the 1959 Agreements were strictly implemented. Ironically, it was in December 1962 that the Greek and Turkish Cypriots were deadlocked over the municipalities issue.[19] A serious constitutional breakdown was forthcoming, and Turkey demonstrated a readiness to interfere on behalf of the Turkish Cypriot community. In January, 1963, when a Turkish Cypriot delegation visited Ankara, the government of Turkey issued a communique pledging its staunch support to the Turkish Cypriot efforts for separate municipalities. Moreover, when in December, 1963, President Makarios proposed his thirteen points for amending the Cyprus Constitution, the Turkish Government took the initiative to reject Makarios' proposals first, even before the Turkish Cypriot leadership had an opportunity to respond to the Makarios request.[20] Turkey viewed Makarios' proposals as a threat to her own interest in Cyprus and her military commitments in the area.

In Greece, the government of Prime Minister Karamanlis, which was instrumental in the Zurich Agreement, ignored Greek Cypriot

[18] The Republican Party of Ismet Inönu gained 173 of 450 seats in the National Assembly. The Justice Party, which essentially appealed to former Menderes supporters gained 158 seats. Since neither party had a majority, a coalition government was formed with Inönu becoming the Prime Minister in 1961.

[19] See *supra* pp. 94-103.

[20] Foley, *Legacy of Strife op. cit.*, p. 165. Stephens writes "On December 16, 1963 in the bluntest language [Turkey] categorically rejected the entire memorandum." Stephens, *op. cit.*, p. 180; see also *supra* p. 107.

pressures to aid in revising their Constitution. At the same time, the political opposition in Greece also exerted strong pressures on Karamanlis, criticizing his government for selling out *Enosis*. With serious domestic problems and with increasing dependence on the United States for assistance, Karamanlis was anxious to maintain United States support. He was determined to follow a strong pro-Atlantic policy, and, in turn, a strong pro-Zurich policy. The Karamanlis regime was neither politically nor diplomatically in a position to initiate any changes regarding Cyprus. It was his Government which initiated and ratified the Zurich Agreement. Karamanlis' position, however, became increasingly precarious because of the opposition's continued accusations as to the unworkability of the Zurich and London Agreements.

When elections were held in November 1963, Karamanlis' party lost to the Center Union Party of George Papandreou and Sophocles Venizelos.[21] With the increasing political paralysis in Cyprus, the Cypriot issue tended to become more important in the Greek political spectrum. It is fair to argue that the Cyprus issue was one of the important factors in Karamanlis' defeat.[22]

With the outbreak of inter-communal violence in 1963, Cyprus once again became the apple of discord between Greece and Turkey, and brought the two countries to the brink of war. Turkey began military preparations for invasion of Cyprus, and Turkish Air Force jet airplanes flew over Nicosia. The Turkish Army con-

[21] The Center Union Party won 42 percent of the popular vote and 138 out of 300 seats in the Parliament. Papandreou, however, refused to collaborate with the leftist EDA to form a government, and he asked the King to call for new elections, eventually held in February 1964. In the latter elections, Papandreou's Center Union Party received 52.78 percent of the popular vote and an absolute majority in the Parliament of 173 seats. See Thomas Anthem "Greece and Cyprus" *Contemporary Review op. cit.*, p. 169.

[22] Thomas Anthem points out that: ". . . Cyprus loomed large in the minds of the overwhelming majority of the Greek people, (in the election campaign) . . . And though in November, at a press conference, Mr. Papandreou denied that his Government proposed to abrogate the Zurich and London Agreements, he has since made it clear that he intends to see the Greek Cypriot case go successfully through the formal stages at the United Nations, with revision of treaties at a minimum. The Greek Prime Minister is acutely aware that Cyprus is a burning question with the Greek nation, and that a large measure of voters' support that he has been accorded is due to his and their criticism of the handling of the issue by the Karamanlis Government from whose policy it is asserted stemmed the now discredited treaties which, in the words of Mr. Papandreou himself 'brought the Turkish nation back to Cyprus.' " *Ibid*.

tingent of 650 men stationed in Cyprus under the Treaty of Alliance moved out of its camp and took a position to support the Turkish Cypriot community.

At the same time, the Greek contingent of 950 men, stationed in Cyprus under the same treaty, moved to the aid of the Greek Cypriots. The more the tension in Cyprus heightened, the closer Greece and Turkey came to direct confrontation. The events of August 1964, as well as those of November 1967, testify to this effect.[23]

British Mediation Efforts and the Increase of External Involvements

The continued deadlock between Greece and Turkey, and the threat of war between two NATO allies, resulted in Great Britain's playing the role of the peace-keeper and mediator. British efforts were wholeheartedly encouraged and supported by the United States. While Britain undertook peace-keeping operations between the two Cypriot communities,[24] it initiated a conference in London between the interested parties in order to search for a political solution. The Conference which opened in London on January

---

[23] When in August 1964, inter-communal fighting in Cyprus was intensified and Turkish planes attacked Cyprus, Greece issued a warning of counter measure against Turkey. See, *The New York Times,* August 9, 10, 11, 1964. Again in November, 1967, when Turkey threatened to invade Cyprus, Greece mobilized her armies and the threat of a Greco-Turkish war over Cyprus seemed imminent. See, *The New York Times,* November 24, 1967; *The Sunday Telegraph* (London), November 26, 1967; *The Sunday Times* (London), November 26, 1967.

[24] From December 21 to 26, 1963, intense inter-communal fighting took place in Cyprus. Amidst rumors that Turkey would invade the island, the British made a move to initiate peace-keeping operations. With the consent of Makarios, the British agreed to form a tripartite peace force in which British soldiers along with the soldiers from the Greek and Turkish contingents on Cyprus would patrol the peace. The peace force was placed under British command. See, Foley, *Legacy of Strife op. cit.,* p. 170.

The British readiness to keep peace in Cyprus was interpreted as falling within their general interests in the area. Anthony Verrier indicates that: ". . . It is essential to correct the general impression that the British forces are in Cyprus solely to keep the peace. They are not. They are there first and foremost to preserve Britain's strategic interest in the Island, which through bases and other installations provide in thèory the facilities for operations in the Middle East. Since these interests cannot be preserved while the Island is in ferment, the garrison reinforced from the United Kingdom has perforce switched to internal security duties . . ." Anthony Verrier, "Cyprus: Britain's Security Role" *The World Today* (London, March, 1964) p. 131.

15, 1964, included Britain, Greece, Turkey, and delegations from the Greek and Turkish Cypriot communities. British mediation efforts at this Conference were unsuccessful. The Greek Cypriots supported by Greece insisted that the problem grew out of the unworkability of the Zurich and London Agreements, and they insisted on "unfettered" independence. The Turkish Cypriots, supported by Turkey, insisted that a physical separation of the Greek and Turkish communities was the only solution and that "Greeks and Turks cannot live together."

Since the task of arriving at a political solution was extremely difficult, Duncan Sandys, Secretary of State for Commonwealth Affairs and presiding officer of the Conference, directed the attention of the conferees to the immediate problem of peace-keeping operations in Cyprus. The British plan was to give NATO countries a greater role in peace-keeping operations already in existence.[25]

Although Turkey and Greece accepted the plan, President Makarios rejected it. Makarios asked that the contingents for the Cyprus peace-keeping force be selected by the United Nations Security Council.[26] President Makarios feared a NATO solution would be favorable to Turkey because of her importance in the alliance. Since Greece held a weak position in NATO, and since

---

[25] As was reported by *The New York Times:* "The force would be augmented by other countries that belong, like Britain, Greece and Turkey, to the North Atlantic Treaty Organization. The force would include up to 2,000 United States troops. The reinforcements, totaling at least 10,000 men, would serve on the Island for three months, during which time Turkey and Greece had agreed to suspend their right of intervention on the Island. The force would serve under a British Commander . . . On the political side, a mediator acceptable to the parties in the dispute would be chosen to look for a solution to the Cyprus question. He would be selected from a North Atlantic Treaty Organization nation other than the United States, Britain, Greece and Turkey." *The New York Times,* February 3, 1964.

The United States was originally reluctant to go along with the plan and join in a Cyprus peace force. The fact that Greece and Turkey were both members of NATO made the United States position extremely delicate. Thus, the three-month time limitation on the NATO peace plan was proposed by the United States, convinced that this would avoid "a protracted occupation." See, *The New York Times,* January 28, 31, 1964.

[26] The reason is reflected in a statement made by Greek Cypriot officials at the United Nations: "A Security Council commitment that the force would respect the independence and territorial integrity of Cyprus . . . A guarantee that Cyprus would not be partitioned between the Greek and Turkish communities as a result of any outside intervention in the fighting between Greek and Turkish Cypriots." *The New York Times,* February 6, 1964.

the Greek Cypriots believed that Britain and the United States were highly instrumental in bringing about the 1959 Cyprus settlement, President Makarios was trying to prevent another Zurich.

The failure of the British peace plan persuaded the United States to take a more active role in the problem of safeguarding United States interests within NATO. On February 9, 1964, George W. Ball, United States Under-Secretary of State, flew to London to assist in formulating a peace-keeping plan.[27] The United States revived the original British plan, by expanding it to include European troops from countries outside the NATO alliance. In addition, the United States formula was to have the peace-keeping force linked in principle, but not controlled, by the United Nations Security Council. Greece accepted the plan. Turkey insisted that Turkish forces be part of the peace force.

Under-Secretary Ball then flew to Nicosia "to convince President Makarios of the wisdom of accepting the United States-British proposals, which would establish an augmented international peace force loosely linked to, but not directly controlled by, the United Nations Security Council."[28] Makarios rejected the United States-British plan. The Soviet Union, which was basically hostile to NATO, supported Makarios' position. Already in a message to

---

[27] In connection with Secretary Ball's mission Mr. Robert J. McCloskey, State Department Deputy Director, Office of News, in a statement on February 8, 1964, indicated that: ". . . The United States welcomed the independence of Cyprus in 1960. It has always maintained close and cordial relations with the Republic. It has followed with sympathy and understanding the efforts to work out the problems that have arisen between the two communities in Cyprus.

The independence, territorial integrity, and security of Cyprus are the responsibility of the Government of Cyprus. They have been guaranteed by the Governments of Greece, Turkey and the United Kingdom. In January officials of the Government of Cyprus as well as of the three guarantor powers indicated their desire that the United States play a more active role in the increasingly difficult Cyprus situation . . . Against this background the United States has participated in discussions of the proposed creation of an international force that might help to bring about the maintenance of peace and order . . . The United States wants to make clear that it has no preconceptions or preferences as to the shape or form of final solutions that might be developed for the Cyprus problem . . . the United States must emphasize that it does have a major interest in the maintenance of peace in the eastern Mediterranean—an interest which it fortunately shares with many other nations. It will do whatever it can to assure that objective . . ." "Mr. Ball Leaves for London Talks on Cyprus," *United States Department of State Bulletin* Vol. 50 (Washington, D. C., February 24, 1964) p. 284.

[28] *The New York Times,* February 13, 1964.

NATO countries, Mr. Khrushchev had warned them about sending troops to Cyprus.[29] Thus, the Soviet Union became involved in the Cyprus dispute, a factor which the NATO plan tried to avert.

Since all efforts outside the United Nations failed,[30] on February 15, 1964, the British delegate, Sir Patrick Dean, requested a meeting of the Security Council:

> . . . My Government instructed me on 15 February to request that an early meeting of the Security Council be called to consider this urgent matter . . . With full regard to the rights and responsibilities of both the Cypriot communities, of the Government of Cyprus, and of the governments party to the Treaty of Guarantee.[31]

---

[29] Mr. Krushchev's message pointed out that: "Certain powers, tramping upon the United Nations Charter and the Generally accepted norms of the international law, are trying to impose on the people and government of Cyprus such a settlement of the problems, which are nobody's but the Cypriots' concern . . . The dispatch to Cyprus of NATO troops or the troops of separate NATO countries, although fundamentally all these variants have a single aim: actual occupation by the armed forces of NATO of the Republic of Cyprus which is conducting a policy of nonalignment with military blocs. In other words, the point at issue is crude encroachment on the sovereignty, independence and freedom of the Republic of Cyprus, an attempt to place this small neutral State under NATO's military control." Union of Soviet Socialist Republics, "N. S. Khrushchev's Message on Cyprus" Mission to the United Nations (New York: Press-Release No. 4, February 7, 1964) (mimeographed).

[30] Regarding efforts not to involve the United Nations in the peace-keeping operations, *The Economist* observes that: ". . . The determination of the British Government to try to keep the United Nations at arms' length is less easy to understand. One argument was that a force from NATO countries could be more quickly and efficiently organised. This seemed a good point when it was first made, but by now it has lost much of its validity. Another argument is that to try to organise a peace force through the Security Council may be to invite a Russian veto and open the door to Russian meddling. Keeping the Cyprus problem out of the United Nations will not prevent the Russians from meddling, as Mr. Khrushchev's letter last weekend demonstrated; but it could give them an excuse for doing so that many uncommitted countries would sympathise with.

The Russians may well object, as Mr. Khrushchev's letter implied, to sending an international force to Cyprus at all. But they might hesitate to veto it, just as they hesitated to veto the despatch of an international force to the Congo in 1960 although they disliked the idea. And if they did veto it, within 48 hours the matter could be referred to the General Assembly which would be very unlikely to refuse a two-thirds majority to any plan accepted by Archbishop Makarios . . ." See, *The Economist* (London) February 15, 1964.

[31] United Nations, Security Council, *Verbatim Record of the One Thousand and Ninety-Fifth Meeting.* (S/PV/1095, 18 February 1964) p. 41.

The Role of the United Nations

The debates in the Security Council centered around the establishment of a United Nations peace-keeping force in Cyprus. Although there were disagreements regarding the composition of the force and the role of a mediator for a political solution, all members essentially agreed on the need for an international peace-keeping operation. In the course of the debates, the Government of Cyprus sought from the Security Council a guarantee of the Republic's independence and territorial integrity and protection from an invasion by Turkey.[32] The Greek Cypriot position was wholeheartedly supported by the Greek government.[33] Turkey, however, insisted on the adherence to international treaties, alluding to the Treaty of Guarantee, which Turkey believed gave her the right to intervene.[34] Britain and the United States, while agreeing with the need for an international peace force, emphasized the importance and sanctity of international treaties.[35] The Soviet Union took this opportunity to verbally attack the military forces of the "NATO bloc" and to give its general support to the position of Cyprus.[36] However, although the Soviet Union was against peace-keeping operations in principle, it did not oppose the Cyprus peace force plan.

---

[32] *Ibid.,* p. 46-71.

[33] *Ibid.,* pp. 103-105. Greece was careful in stating her position not to offend her allies; but also not to offend Archbishop Makarios.

[34] United Nations. Security Council. *Verbatim Record of the One Thousand and Ninety-Fifth Meeting.* (S/PV/1095, 18 February 1964) pp. 87-96. Although Turkey would have preferred a NATO peace-force plan, she went along with the British and United States efforts at the Security Council. As it is indicated in *The Economist:* "Turkey was bound to support Britain and the United States in the Security Council because it was agreed during Mr. Ball's visit to Ankara on February 11, that it would do so . . . At bottom, the Turks are deeply worried about their lack of friends in the world. That is their basic doubt about the United Nations. Even their fellow Moslems . . . have looked askance. Most of the Arabs are clearly on the other side. Even Turkey's Central Treaty Organization ally, Persia, has not spoken . . ." *The Economist* (London), February 22, 1964.

[35] United Nations. Security Council. *Verbatim Record of the One Thousand and Ninety-Fifth Meeting.* (S/PV/1095, 18 February 1964) pp. 44-45; United Nations. Security Council. *Verbatim Record of the One Thousand and Ninety-Sixth Meeting.* (S/PV/1096, 19 February 1964) pp. 38-40.

[36] *Ibid.,* pp. 6-17.

On March 4, 1964, the Security Council adopted the resolution which became the foundation of the United Nations peace-keeping operations in Cyprus and the establishment of mediation for a political solution. Essentially the Security Council resolution provided the following:

> . . .
>
> 1. *Calls upon* all Member States, in conformity with their obligations under the Charter of the United Nations, to refrain from any action or threat of action likely to worsen the situation in the sovereign Republic of Cyprus, or to endanger international peace;
>
> . . .
>
> 4. *Recommends* the creation, with the consent of the Government of Cyprus of a United Nations peace-keeping force in Cyprus. The composition and size of the force shall be established by the Secretary-General, in consultation with the Governments of Cyprus, Greece, Turkey and the United Kingdom . . .
>
> 5. *Recommends* that the function of the force should be, in the interest of preserving international peace and security, to use its best efforts to prevent a recurrence of fighting and, as necessary, to contribute to the maintenance and restoration of law and order and a return to normal conditions;
>
> . . .
>
> 7. *Recommends further* that the Secretary General designate, in agreement with the Government of Cyprus and Governments of Greece, Turkey and the United Kingdom, a mediator, who shall use his best endeavours with the representatives of the communities and also with the aforesaid four Governments, for the purpose of promoting a peaceful solution and an agreed settlement of the problem confronting Cyprus . . .[37]

On March 27, 1964, the United Nations Peace Force in Cyprus (UNFICYP) became operational, and it was placed under the

[37] United Nations. Security Council. *The Cyprus Question,* Resolution 186 (1964) [s/5575], 4 March 1964, in Security Council, *Official Records,* Nineteenth Year, Resolutions and Decisions (S.INF/19/Rev. 1), pp. 2-4.

command of Lieutenant General P. S. Gyani.[38] With the establishment of the peace-keeping force, and in accordance with the resolution of March 4, 1964, the Secretary-General, with the consent of the governments of Cyprus, Greece, Turkey and the United Kingdom, appointed the Finnish diplomat, Sakari S. Tuomioja as mediator.[39]

The United Nations peace-keeping forces in Cyprus were faced with armed "irregulars" on both sides, the problem of Turkish refugees, and the physical and psychological "greenlines" separating the Greek and Turkish Cypriot communities. UNFICYP's task was made even more complicated by the divergent views regarding its function.

To the Greek Cypriots and Greece, the United Nations' presence in Cyprus was regarded as a means of ending the Turkish Cypriot

[38] United Nations, Security Council, *Report By The Secretary-General On The Organization and Operation Of The United Nations Peace-Keeping Force in Cyprus,* S/5579, 6 March 1964, p. 1.

By June 8, 1964, the strength of UNFICYP was 6,411. The composition of the Force at that time was as follows:

(1) *Military*		(2) *Police*	
Austria	55	Australia	40
Canada	1,122	Austria	33
Denmark	676	Denmark	40
Finland	1,000	New Zealand	20
Ireland	639	Sweden	40
Sweden	954	Total	173
United Kingdom	1,792		
Total	6,238		

United Nations, Security Council, *Report By The Secretary-General To The Security Council On The United Nations Operation in Cyprus, For The Period 26 April to 8 June 1964,* S/5764, 15 June 1964, p. 2.

As of June 7, 1967 the strength of UNFICYP was 4,622, composed as follows:

(1) *Military*		(2) *Police*	
Austria	51	Australia	39
Canada	880	Austria	35
Denmark	645	Denmark	39
Finland	607	New Zealand	20
Ireland	523	Sweden	40
Sweden	616	Total	173
United Kingdom	1,127		
Total	4,449		

United Nations, Security Council, *Report By The Secretary-General On The United Nations Operations In Cyprus (For the period 6 December to 12 June 1967),* S/7969, 13 June 1967, pp. 4-5.

[39] United Nations, Security Council, *Report By The Secretary-General On The Organization And Operation Of The United Nations Peace-Keeping Force In Cyprus,* S/5625, 26 March 1964, pp. 1-2.

"rebellion" and of helping the government of Cyprus defend itself against Turkish invasion. To the Turkish Cypriots and Turkey, the United Nations Peace Force was a means of protecting the Turkish Cypriot community from threats and domination by the Greek Cypriots and Greece. The United Nations Peace Force, however, was directed to make efforts to reconcile the two sides rather than help one dominate the other. Moreover, it had no authority to use force, except in self-defense, and no authority to remove fortifications and to disarm armed "irregulars." Consequently, it relied on methods of persuasion and negotiation for effectiveness.[40]

In spite of the complexities of the situation and the intransigence of the respective parties, the United Nations Peace Force has, by and large, been instrumental in improving the situation in Cyprus. During its first three and a half years, in spite of recurring violence, it was able to ease tension. UNFICYP was instrumental in improving freedom of movement of the population in many areas, in removing fortifications, in preventing armed clashes, and in assisting the Turkish refugees.[41] Thus, amidst explosive conditions, the United Nations played an important role in preventing dangerous confrontations between the two Cypriot communities from exploding into an all-out war between Greece and Turkey.[42]

---

[40] The guiding principles governing the operation of the United Nations Peace Force were essentially as follows: "(a) The Force is under the exclusive control and command of the United Nations at all times. The Commander of the Force is appointed by and responsible exclusively to the Secretary-General . . . The troops of the Force carry arms which, however, are to be employed only for self-defense, should this become necessary in the discharge of its function, in the interest of preserving international peace and security, of seeking to prevent a recurrence of fighting, . . . The personnel of the Force must act with restraint and with complete impartiality towards the members of the Greek and Turkish Cypriot communities . . . "self-defense" includes the defense of United Nations posts, premises and vehicles under armed attack, . . . When acting in self-defense, the principle of minimum force shall always be applied and armed force will be used only when all peaceful means of persuasion have failed . . ." United Nations, Security Council, *Report By The Secretary-General On The United Nations Operation In Cyprus,* S/5950, 10 September 1964, p. 4.

[41] For a recent analysis of the United Nations performance in Cyprus, see United Nations, Security Council, *Report By The Secretary-General On The United Nations Operation in Cyprus,* S/7969, 13 June 1967, *passim.*

[42] The neutralizing effect of the United Nations is indicated in its role during the August 1964 Turkish air attacks on Cyprus and the resulting threat of Greco-Turkish confrontation. See, United Nations, Security Council, *Verbatim Record Of The Eleven Hundred And Forty-Second Meeting,* S/PV.1142, 8 August 1964, *passim;* United Nations, Security Council,

The United Nations mediation efforts toward a political solution of the problem met with little success. Mr. Tuomioja, the first mediator, died on September 9, 1964, and he was replaced by Galo Plaza of Ecuador on September 16, 1964. Mr. Plaza undertook a comprehensive study of the situation in Cyprus. In March 1965, he submitted his report to the Security Council.[43] After a careful examination of the internal aspects of the Cyprus problem and the positions of the parties concerned, namely, Greece, Turkey, and Great Britain, Mr. Plaza made specific observations on the prospects for solution. Under the heading of "Independence-Self-determination and International Peace," Mr. Plaza first examined the Greek and Greek Cypriot position and made the following observation:

> . . . the Greek Cypriot leadership and the basis of their political claims—in which they have the support of the Government of Greece—is that the independence and sovereignty of the Republic . . . were impaired by the Treaties of 16 August 1960 which formed an integral part and governed the nature of the Constitution of the same date. The effect of these Treaties was indiputably to forbid the people of Cyprus from amending their own Constitution, or at any rate the basic articles which determined the structure of the State; to prohibit the union of Cyprus with any other State; and to forbid the partitioning of the country. The Greek Cypriot leadership claims to have accepted these restrictions under duress, in that the only alternative at the time would have been to suffer an attempt to partition the country. The political objective of the Greek Cypriots has therefore been to secure for Cyprus an "unfettered independence" . . .[44]

Verbatim Record Of The Eleven Hundred And Forty-Third Meeting, S/PV.1143, 9 August 1964, *passim;* United Nations, Security Council, *Verbatim Record Of The Resumed Eleven Hundred And Forty-Third Meeting,* S/PV.1143, 11 August 1964, *passim.* Along with other diplomatic efforts, the United Nations played an instrumental role in helping to avert a Greco-Turkish war over Cyprus in November, 1967. Secretary-General U Thant made a dramatic "appeal on Cyprus," *The New York Times,* November 23, 1967; and he dispatched his special representative, Jose Rolz-Bennett, to Athens, Ankara and Nicosia to calm tensions. *The New York Times,* November 26, 1967.

[43] The Plaza Report was submitted to the Security Council on March 26, 1965. United Nations, Security Council, *Report Of The United Nations Mediator on Cyprus To The Secretary-General, Note By The Secretary-General,* S/6253, 26 March 1965.

[44] *Ibid.,* p. 50.

Mr. Plaza then proceeded to make the following observations regarding the position of Turkey and the Turkish Cypriots:

> The Turkish Cypriot leaders and the Government of Turkey do not dispute the restrictive nature of the conditions under which Cyprus acceded to independence. From their standpoint, however, these limitations were deliberate and essential: to secure for the Turkish Cypriots their treatment not as a minority but as a community with distinct political rights, and to secure for Turkey the maintenance of an equilibrium in the eastern Mediterranean which, in the Turkish Government's view, would be especially seriously disturbed should Cyprus become Greek territory.[45]

From the observations regarding the positions of the above two sides in the dispute, Mr. Plaza concluded that:

> . . . It is still possible to read into the positions of the two sides an objective which, so long as it is stated in very broad terms, would seem acceptable to them both: namely, an independent Cyprus with adequate safeguards for the safety and the rights of all its people.[46]

In his analysis, Mr. Plaza noted that *Enosis* is the most explosive issue separating the Greek and Turkish Cypriot communities and endangering the relations between Greece and Turkey:

> I am certain in my own mind that the question of *Enosis* is the most decisive and potentially the most explosive aspect of the Cyprus problem.[47]

However, although Mr. Plaza felt that *Enosis* was a very explosive concept, at the same time, he indicated that a federal system in Cyprus would be unworkable and extremely dangerous.

> . . . The establishment of a federal regime requires a territorial basis, and this basis does not exist . . . It would seem to require a compulsory movement of the people concerned—many thousands on both sides—contrary to all the enlightened

[45] *Ibid.*
[46] *Ibid.*, p. 51.
[47] *Ibid.*, p. 52.

> principles of the present time, including those set forth in the Universal Declaration of Human Rights . . . Geographical separation of the two communities under a federal system of government have not convinced me that it would not inevitably lead to partition and thus risk creating a new national frontier between Greece and Turkey, a frontier of a highly provocative nature, through highly volatile peoples who would not hesitate to allow their local differences to risk involving the two home countries in conflict and consequently endangering international peace and security.[48]

Thus, Mr. Plaza concluded that in the interest of all parties concerned, Cyprus should become a demilitarized and "fully independent" state. However, under such a solution, a major problem would be the "protection of individual and minority rights," and the Turkish minority's participation in government. In this sense Mr. Plaza noted that the most "rigorous" safeguards for the Turkish Cypriot community should be implemented. The mediator felt, however, that the Zurich and London Agreements failed in this objective:

> It will need not to be forgotten that the Turkish Cypriot community obtained from the Zurich and London Agreements a series of rights greatly superior to those which can realistically be contemplated for it in the future . . . Some special measures should be applied in order to ensure to the members of the minority community a proper voice in their traditionally communal affairs and also, without weakening the unity of the State, an equitable part in the public life of the country as a whole . . . This might be done by a system of proportional representation or reservation of seats in the parliament, and also, perhaps by the appointment of a Turkish Cypriot Minister responsible for the affairs of his community—without prejudice, of course, to other Turkish Cypriots being elected or appointed on merit . . .[49]

Mr. Plaza's proposals were intended to provide a basis for a possible solution to the Cyprus problem. The United Nations was

---

[48] *Ibid.*, pp. 58-59.
[49] *Ibid.*, pp. 61-63.

to play an active role in this endeavor. The Turkish Cypriots and Turkey, however, rejected the Plaza Report as unacceptable,[50] while the Greek Cypriots and Greece received it, by and large, favorably.[51] Moreover, Turkey stressed that: "Mr. Galo Plaza's report contains sections which exceed his terms of reference [therefore] there can be no further usefulness in the continuation of Mr. Plaza in his function." [52] Thus, United Nations mediation efforts came to a halt and no progress has been made since.[53]

The Intensification of External Involvements

While the United Nations Peace Force was in Cyprus and mediation efforts were being undertaken for a peaceful solution, Cyprus was becoming increasingly more explosive. Armed "irregulars" from both Cypriot communities and infiltration of military personnel from Greece and Turkey constantly increased. By July 1964, at least 5,000 men arrived in Cyprus from Greece and more than 600 from Turkey.[54] The infiltration of troops by Greece and Turkey was intended to assist their respective communities and to strengthen their positions on the island. Turkey's claim was that her troops were needed to protect Turkish Cypriots, who were outnumbered on the island by four to one. Greece's claim was that her troops were intended to strengthen the defenses of Cyprus against Turkish invasion. This continued military buildup increased the possibility of direct confrontation between Greece and Turkey in Cyprus.

---

[50] United Nations, Security Council, *Exchange Of Letters Between The Permanent Representative Of Turkey And The Secretary-General Regarding The Effort Of The United Nations Mediator On Cyprus, 1. Letter dated 31 March 1965 from the Permanent Representative of Turkey addressed to the Secretary-General,* S/6267, 2 April 1965.

[51] United Nations, Security Council, *Letter Dated 8 April 1965 From The Minister For Foreign Affairs Of Greece Addressed To The Secretary-General,* S/6280, 9 April 1965.

[52] United Nations, Security Council, *Exchange Of Letters Between The Permanent Representative Of Turkey And The Secretary-General Regarding The Report Of The United Nations Mediator On Cyprus, Addendum, Letter Dated 6 April 1965 From The Permanent Representative Of Turkey Addressed To The Secretary-General,* S/6267/Add. 1, 7 April 1965.

[53] United Nations, Security Council, *Report By The Secretary-General On The United Nations Operations On Cyprus (For the period 6 December 1966 to 12 June 1967),* S/7969, 13 June 1967, p. 68.

[54] Before Greece began to pull her troops out of Cyprus in November 1967, it was estimated that there were 10,000 "illegal" Greek Troops and 1,200 "illegal" Turkish troops on the island.

There were also ulterior motives regarding Greco-Turkish military moves on the island. In the first place, Greece, through her military presence in Cyprus, hoped to curb possible Russian penetration in the area. In the second place, through General George Grivas, who arrived in Cyprus in June 1964, Greece hoped to control Makarios and to ensure a continuation of the *Enosis* struggle. In this sense, Archbishop Makarios was to be discouraged from pursuing an independent and neutralist policy. Thus, the presence of General Grivas in Cyprus, adversely affected Makarios' independence policy.[55] At the same time, Grivas' stand on *Enosis* invited stronger reaction by Turkey and the Turkish Cypriots and had negative effects on mediation efforts.

General Grivas' arrival in Cyprus coincided with renewed American concern in initiating efforts for solving the Cyprus conflict. In June 1964, President Johnson met in Washington first with the Prime Minister of Turkey, Ismet Inönu, and later with the Prime Minister of Greece, George Papandreou, in an effort to mediate the dispute between the two NATO allies. At the same time, in July 1964, the President sent Dean Acheson to Geneva as his special envoy to undertake "informal" meetings with representatives of Turkey and Greece. The results of the United States mediation efforts were expressed in the "Acheson Plan" calling for union of Cyprus with Greece and the establishment of two Turkish cantons in Cyprus. Moreover, the Acheson Plan called for the establishment of a Turkish military base on Cyprus and the ceding to Turkey of one small Greek island in the Aegean.[56]

---

[55] *The Economist* observes that: ". . . by supporting Archbishop Makarios wiih arms and troops, Mr. Papandreou is forestalling Mr. Khrushchev. In other words that if Archbishop Makarios did not get military backing from Greece at this stage he would get it from the Russians." *The Economist* (London), July 18, 1964. Regarding Grivas' role, *The Economist* adds that: ". . . The question of Generai Grivas's hard core supporters will also certainly cause increasing difficulty. Now that their leader is back they naturally expect a greater say in Greek-Cypriot counsels, but they may be disappointed . . . If Archbishop Makarios should show any hint at all of compromising with the Turks, they will work for a coup d'etat . . . General Grivas's presence has given a tremendous impetus to the cause of *Enosis*. At the same time, with the General breathing down his neck, it seems out of the question that Archbishop Makarios (or for that matter Mr. Papandreou) can make any concessions to the Turks." *The Economist* (London) July 4, 1964.

[56] *The New York Times,* July 31, 1964.

Both Greece and the Greek Cypriots rejected the plan as unacceptable, indicating that this was another form of "double *Enosis*" or partition. Turkey, on the other hand, although accepting the Acheson Plan as a basis for negotiations, insisted that the Turkish base in Cyprus should be large enough to eventually engulf most of the Turkish Cypriot population.[57]

The United States' active role in the Cyprus dispute was intended to safeguard the Southeastern flank of the NATO Alliance and to curb Soviet infiltration of the area.[58] However, the Soviet Union, which had all along supported the Cyprus government, objected to NATO and "foreign intervention" in the internal affairs of Cyprus.[59] The Soviets used the Cyprus issue to undermine Western interests in the Eastern Mediterranean. Russia's role was facilitated by Makarios' mistrust of NATO plans and his willingness to accept Soviet diplomatic and military help against Turkish invasion. However, when Turkish Air Force jets strafed Cypriot villages in Northwestern Cyprus, in August 1964, the Soviet Union not only did not come to the aid of Cyprus but appealed to Makarios to use his "influence to prevent further bloodshed." [60]

---

[57] Stephens, *op. cit.,* p. 201.

[58] As Charles Foley points out: "Once Turkey had been induced to accept union of Cyprus with Greece trouble would end between the two NATO members . . . An Athenian government could be trusted to take a firm line with the Communists and the influence which America had exercised in Greece since the [Greek] Civil War would be extended to her newest province." Foley, *Island in Revolt op. cit.,* pp. 184-185.

[59] As it was stated in *Pravda:* ". . . The Soviet Union supports the legitimate endeavors of the people of Cyprus to insure its independence, sovereignty and territorial integrity and condemns any attempts of foreign intervention in the internal affairs of the Cypriot Republic . . . Tass has been authorized to state that the leading circles of the Soviet Union hope that international complications which could jeopardize the cause of peace in the area will not materialize over Cyprus . . ." "Aggressive Schemes Against Cyprus: Threat to International Security—Tass Statement" *Current Soviet Documents* Vol. II, No. 6 (New York, February 10, 1964) p. 12. Furthermore, Mr. Khrushchev speaking to a correspondent of *Izvestia* on May 5, 1964 stressed that: "The Soviet government has been and is now firmly and consistently opposed to each and every foreign interference in the affairs of Cyprus, all attempts from the outside to impose a solution of the Republic's internal problems on the Cypriots . . . In the interests of the NATO military bloc, they want to turn the Island into a bridge-head, or as they say, into an 'unsinkable air craft carrier' of NATO anchored in the Eastern Mediterranean." "N. S. Khrushchev Replies to *Izvestia* Correspondents on Cyprus," *Current Soviet Documents,* Vol. II, No. 21 (New York, May 25, 1964) pp. 27-28.

[60] *The Economist* (London), August 15, 1964.

Significant developments in Soviet involvement in the Cyprus problem occurred following the August 1964 Turkish air attacks. Makarios, unable to obtain military aid from Western sources, negotiated an agreement with the Soviet Union for anti-aircraft weapons to strengthen Cyprus' defenses against future Turkish air attacks.[61] However, Soviet double diplomacy was beginning to take effect. The Soviet Union began to use the Cyprus dispute to lure Turkey away from the NATO Alliance.

At this time Turkey was amenable to Soviet influences. The United States' attempts to promote *Enosis* as a safeguard against Communism in the area had negative effects in Turkey. Turkey was beginning to believe that the West was more sympathetic to the cause of Hellenısm than to the suffering of the Turkish Cypriot community and to Turkey's interests in the area. Moreover, Turkey interpreted the presence of General Grivas in Cyprus as an encouragement by the United States for *Enosis*. Turkey's disillusionment led to a Soviet-Turkish rapprochement. Thus, Turkey, which at the time was the most anti-Communist of the NATO allies, and traditionally hostile to Soviet intrigues, began to pursue a more independent foreign policy. In essence, the Soviet Union's antipathy toward *Enosis* coupled with Prime Minister Inönu's belief that Turkey's dependence on the West cost her bargaining power over Cyprus, paved the way for this Soviet-Turkish rapprochement.[62] Turkey was eventually able to get Soviet support for an "independent Federated Cyprus."[63]

---

[61] *The Economist* views Moscow's relations with Makarios' regime as follows: "The Greek Cypriots want submarines and aircraft in case of another Turkish attack; Moscow undoubtedly want Cyprus to commit itself to a policy of non-aligned independence with all bases removed . . . Certain basic factors are perceptible: the Russians want the maximum credit with minimum military involvement; the Cypriots want the maximum military aid, but are not at all sure about the question of involvement." *The Economist* (London) August 22, 1964.

[62] For an additional analysis, see Alain Guiney, "Turkey Plays it Cool" *New Outlook* Vol. 8, No. 1 (Tel Aviv: January/February, 1965) pp. 33-37.

[63] Foreign Minister Andrei Gromyko, in an interview with *Izvestia* on January 21, 1965, indicated that: "The Soviet government believes that the question of Cyprus should be settled on the basis of respect for the independence and territorial integrity of the Republic of Cyprus with due account to be taken of the legitimate rights of the Cypriots of both Greek and Turkish communities, the rights insuring their peaceful life . . . The people of Cyprus wll be able to choose independently and as a sovereign state any form of government that will make it possible to take into account the spe-

The continued stalemate on Cyprus, in conjunction with Soviet-Turkish rapprochement and the inability of the United Nations to solve the problem, led to increasing Turkish pressures for bilateral talks with Greece. Turkey began to expel the Greek citizens from Turkey and threaten the existence of the Ecumenical Patriarchate in Istanbul.[64] These pressures, however, had negative effects on Greco-Turkish relations and made Greece's position more intransigent. When Prime Minister Suleyman Demirel came to power in October 1965, he, too, demanded Greco-Turkish talks for the settlement of the Cyprus dispute. However, the political instability in Greece, which occurred in July 1965, when the Government of Prime Minister George Papandreou was forced to resign because of a conflict with King Constantine over the control of the army, made a meaningful dialogue impossible.

The prospects for a dialogue on Cyprus between Greece and Turkey took a new turn after the April 21, 1967, Greek military coup. The Greek military regime was instrumental in initiating a conference on Cyprus between the Greek and Turkish prime ministers on September 9, 1967.[65] At this conference, which was held at Evros (Eastern Thrace), Greece offered Turkey a large military base on Cyprus in return for union of the island with Greece.[66] Since this was the first major concession by any Greek government,

---

cific position of the national communities—the Greek and the Turkish—within the bounds of a single sovereign and united Cypriot state and that would meet their interests. They may also choose the *federal form.*" (My emphasis). *"Izvestia* Interview with USSR Foreign Minister, A. A. Gromyko" *Current Soviet Documents* Vol. III, No. 7 (New York, February 15, 1965) pp. 25-26. Furthermore, during a Soviet Parliamentary Delegation's visit to Turkey the same views were expressed: "It was no more than natural that the members of parliament (Turkish Parliament) should be particularly interested in the problem of Cyprus. We explained the Soviet attitude. The Soviet Union, we said, has consistently urged a peaceful settlement in the interest of all Cypriots based on absolute respect of the Republic's independent sovereignty and territorial integrity, and upon absolute observance of the lawful rights of the two communities the Greeks and the Turks. "The Soviet and Turkish Peoples Want to Live in Peace and Friendship" *New Times,* No. 7 (Moscow: February 17, 1965) p. 5.

[64] *The Economist* comments as follows: "The decision to expel . . . Greeks from Turkey (most of whom live in Istanbul) is an irritation rather than a serious worry to the Greek government. Greeks have been repatriated from there, and the addition of more will cause only mounting annoyance. It is the question of the ecumenical patriarchate that is causing anxiety." *The Economist* (London), April 24, 1965.

[65] *The New York Times,* September 9, 10, 11, 1967.

[66] *The New York Times,* September 11, 1967.

it seems that the military regime in Greece took this opportunity to exploit the Cyprus issue to cover up their internal difficulties and to improve their position in the Western alliance. Turkey rejected Greece's plan.

The precarious position of the Greek military regime was exposed during the 1967 Greco-Turkish confrontation when Turkey was able to extract major concessions. At this writing, the full details of the Turkish demands agreed upon by the military regime are not fully known. It should be pointed out, however, that the manner in which the military leaders in Greece submitted to Turkish demands may prove detrimental to their position at home. Cyprus is an emotional issue, and no Greek government accused of losing face to Turkey could survive such an accusation.

The agreement to remove General Grivas from the Cyprus scene, to withdraw all "illegal" Greek and Turkish troops on Cyprus and the tacit consent to demilitarize the island, may have the following effects: first, the pan-Hellenic policy of *Enosis* may become a decreasing possibility; second, the influence of Greece on President Makarios and his policies will increasingly diminish, and the Cyprus Government will be forced to pursue a more independent policy, including a meaningful rapprochement with the Turkish Cypriot community. Thus, a settlement may be possible if the United Nations plays an active role in successfully disengaging the entrenched external interests in Cyprus; and, at the same time, promoting pacification and a successful political settlement.

7

CONCLUSION: WHAT PROSPECTS FOR CYPRUS?

The 1963 crisis in Cyprus resulted from the inability of two unequal and distinct ethnic communities to function under the 1960 constitutional framework. The inability of the Greek and Turkish Cypriots to function under constitutional government can be explained by the following: first, the absence of a Cypriot political consciousness, resulting from the nature of bi-communal Cyprus, and the persistence of the *Enosis* movement; second, the absence of any serious attempts on the part of the British colonial administration to promote genuine self-government and bi-communal cooperation; third, the deep entrenchment of external interests, especially those of Britain, Greece, and Turkey; fourth, the inability and unwillingness of the Greek and Turkish Cypriots to function within the 1960 constitutional framework.

Cyprus throughout its history has retained a multi-communal character. Its present bi-communal society, Greek and Turkish Cypriot, is characterized by linguistic, religious, and cultural differences and divergent political aspirations. There were never any genuine attempts to promote political integration between the Greeks and Turks of Cyprus. The Greek national character of the Greek Cypriots has been retained and strengthened by the Orthodox Church of Cyprus. The Turkish national character has also been retained and strengthened by the Turkish Cypriots. The strengthening of the Greek and Turkish national characters in Cyprus tended to entrench the direct interests of Greece and Turkey in Cypriot developments.

Bi-communal differences were strengthened during the British rule in Cyprus from 1878 to 1960. The British colonial administration did not encourage communal cooperation. Indeed, the British, from the very beginning, accentuated bi-communalism when they placed the administration of education under bi-communal authorities. The Greek Orthodox Church directed the schools of the Greek

Cypriot community and thus enhanced the Greco-Byzantine tradition. The Turkish Cypriots controlled their own school system and thereby strengthened their Turkish national tradition. Thus, education served as a non-integrating factor. Moreover, it tended to fortify the historical and cultural bonds of the two Cypriot communities with their respective "mother countries" Greece and Turkey.

The development of a Cypriot political consciousness was greatly hindered by the *Enosis* movement. The Church persistently demanded union of Cyprus with Greece. The persistence of the *Enosis* demand, however, tended to antagonize the British colonial administration and to invite reaction from the Turkish Cypriot community. At the same time, the *Enosis* movement was morally and actively supported by Greece and eventually invited strong reaction from Turkey. Turkey interpreted the Greek demands as an example of Greece's irredentism. Thus, *Enosis* eventually became the basis for deterioration of the relations between Greece and Turkey.

Britain's primary concern, that of utilizing Cyprus as a base, failed to realize the magnitude of the Greek Cypriot *Enosis* drive. The British viewed the demand for union with Greece as a nuisance and had no intention of acceding to it. To offset the drive for *Enosis,* the British attempted to promote limited self-government. However, the British attempts to promote limited self-government were unsuccessful because they were either half-hearted or divisive in character.

The political framework of the 1882 Constitution resulted in further polarizing the Greek and Turkish Cypriots. The Legislative Council, established under the 1882 Constitution, served as a means to accentuate the differences between the two communities and to hinder cooperation.

The alliance between the officially appointed members and the Turkish Cypriot elected members in the Legislative Council counteracted and antagonized the Greek Cypriot elected members. The Greek Cypriot members in the Council acted as the permanent opposition. In view of the fact that the Greek Cypriots constituted the majority of the population and continually found themselves in permanent opposition, they did not cooperate with the colonial government; and the 1882 constitutional framework failed to achieve any form of legitimacy. On the contrary, the Greek Cypriot members used the Council to agitate for *Enosis* and demand genuine constitutional reforms. The increasing bi-polarity between the British colonial administration and the Greek Cypriots led to the 1931 uprising, the collapse of the 1882 constitutional framework, and the institution of direct rule.

In the post-World War II period, the British again attempted to promote limited self-government. These attempts were intended to thwart the Church's *Enosis* drive and to secure British strategic interests in the Middle East. Because the British plans were either half-hearted or untimely, along with the intensification of the *Enosis movement,* they were unsuccessful. Thus the 1948 Constitutional Plan, the Harding-Makarios constitutional negotiations, the Radcliffe Proposals and the Macmillan Plan never materialized; and self-government was never implanted.

The Church leadership exhibited a complete lack of foresight by persisting on *Enosis* as its only political goal. It has never occurred to the Cypriot Church leadership that full self-government, independence, and probably union of Cyprus with Greece could result from limited self-government. Consequently, the Greek Cypriots rejected all plans short of *Enosis*. Moreover, the Church leadership disregarded the Turkish Cypriot community, as well as the role of Turkey. The Church leadership was unable to realize that the Turkish Cypriot community, with its cultural, religious, and linguistic differences, coupled with its support by Turkey, was an important factor and had to be accounted for in any Cypriot political development. The Church, by its persistent demands for *Enosis,* invited distrust and increasing tension between the two communities. It also invited the more active involvement of Greece and Turkey in Cyprus, which resulted in revitalizing the traditional Graeco-Turkish feud. This antagonism in Cyprus, which was channeled to Greece and Turkey, was accentuated by the E.O.K.A. underground struggle.

Although the E.O.K.A. struggle hastened the departure of the British, it did so at a price. On the one hand, the British, in order to retain their sovereignty in Cyprus and safeguard their strategic interests, actively encouraged the traditional Graeco-Turkish animosity. On the other hand, Turkey, in support of the Turkish Cypriot community, reacted strongly. As a result, extremist elements in Cyprus, as well as nationalistic fervor in Greece, and Turkey, exerted increasing influence in any future settlement.

Thus, the E.O.K.A. struggle brought Greek and Turkish nationalistic antagonism to the surface, which resulted in increasing direct involvement of Greece and Turkey in the political and constitutional future of Cyprus. In fact, it was Greece and Turkey, together with Britain, which drafted the basic principles of the 1960 Cypriot constitutional framework.

The Zurich and London Agreements, establishing the foundation of the Republic of Cyprus, reflect *par excellence* the intricate involvement of the "interested parties." On the one hand, the British strategic interests were enabled to take hold by two sovereign British bases in Cyprus; on the other, the direct interests of Greece and Turkey were secured by the stationing of Greek and Turkish troops in Cyprus under the Treaty of Alliance. Furthermore, Britain, Greece, and Turkey secured a direct voice in the constitutional developments of the Republic under the Treaty of Guarantee, thus acting as constitutional "philosopher kings."

The entrenching of diverse interests within the framework of the Cypriot Constitution hindered the development of constitutional government. The constitutional life of the Republic, prescribed under rigid rules, proved to be unworkable. The 1963 intercommunal conflict testifies to this effect.

Contributing to the failure of the Constitution to serve as a basis for promoting constitutional government were two defects. First, it did not reflect the actual composition of the Cypriot society; rather it reflected the bargaining power of the interested parties. In this sense, Turkey, which exercised a stronger position in the Western alliance, was able to secure for the Turkish-Cypriot community guarantees disproportionate to their numerical strength within the Cypriot society. This alienated the Greek Cypriot majority. Second, the Constitution went to extremes to institutionalize the differences of the two Cypriot communities. In this manner, the very nature of the Constitution discouraged communal cooperation.

In all spheres of government, the Greek and Turkish Cypriots were recognized not as citizens of Cyprus, but primarily as members of their respective communities with political and constitutional rights. These features of the Constitution prevented it from becoming a unifying symbol.

In an attempt to safeguard the minority community's participation in government, the framers of the 1960 Constitution institutionalized a communal balance of interests through the following: fixed numerical ratios in all spheres of government, final veto power in the Executive branch, and separate majority vote in the Legislative branch. The provisions of the Constitution devised to ensure Turkish Cypriot participation in government, invited strong reaction by the Greek Cypriot majority.

The theoretical basis of the Constitution was intended to prevent a tyranny by the majority; but the framers of the 1960 Cypriot Constitution, in their attempt to safeguard the minority community's interests, alienated the majority community. The constitutional guarantees intended to assure Turkish Cypriot participation in government failed. The Greek Cypriots refused to cooperate in the implementation of those constitutional provisions which they considered as "disproportionate" and favoring the Turkish Cypriot minority. The Turkish Cypriots, on the other hand, faced with the opposition of the Greek Cypriot majority, used their constitutional rights to extract concessions from the Greek Cypriot majority. The net result was increasing antagonism between the Greek and Turkish Cypriots. This growing antagonism in Cyprus left its mark on relations between Greece and Turkey, both of which naturally supported the positions of their respective communities.

From the very beginning of the constitutional life of the Republic, there developed constitutional deadlocks in establishing a Cypriot Army and in implementing the constitutional provisions of the seventy-thirty in the Public Service. The refusal of the Greek Cypriot community to fully implement the seventy-thirty ratio in the Public Service led to the refusal of the Turkish Cypriots to vote for tax legislation. This left the government without the power to tax. In turn, the Greek Cypriots refused to extend the Municipalities law—fearful that municipal separation would lead to partition.

The persistent constitutional deadlocks led to the Greek Cypriots' proposing sweeping amendments, which in effect would have established a unified state and majority rule. Makarios' proposals were strongly rejected by Turkey. Turkey perceived these proposals as being a threat to her interests in Cyprus and in the area. There followed a confrontation between the two Cypriot communities, which brought Greece and Turkey to the brink of war.

Since the December 1963 crisis, the two communities, by and large physically separated, are functioning under crisis government; and the United Nations is policing an uneasy peace. It has so far been unable to mediate a political solution.

Crisis government is carried out under two authorities, strictly bi-communal, with the leadership of each community leading the affairs of its respective community. Greece and Turkey, in an attempt to support their respective communities during the crisis, have since infiltrated the island with armed personnel and equipment. This has increased the danger of direct confrontation between Greece and Turkey as clearly indicated by the November 1967 threat of a Graeco-Turkish war over Cyprus.

With the crisis in Cyprus having entered its fifth year, we may ask: Are there any prospects of a constitutional settlement under which both Cypriot communities could function, or will the external interests of Greece and Turkey prevent permanent settlement and promote continuing political instability?

Regarding the prospects of political and constitutional settlement in Cyprus, Greek Cypriots supported by Greece and Turkish Cypriots supported by Turkey have proposed their respective plans for solution. These proposals, however, are by their very nature uncompromising and thus unable to bring the two communities under a workable constitutional framework.

Any constitutional settlement in Cyprus must be based on bi-communal compromise, which in essence must reflect the needs of the Cypriot political spectrum. Such a compromise presupposes the disengagement of Greece and Turkey's involvement in the affairs of Cyprus. Parallel with this Graeco-Turkish disengagement, an increase in the United Nations' role is necessary. Settlement must, by necessity, exclude *Enosis* and federation. The desire for *Enosis* is adhered to by the Greek Cypriots and is identified with Greece's irredentist plans; the desire for federation is adhered to by Turkish Cypriots, and it is identified with Turkish plans for partition.

Enosis is completely unacceptable to the Turkish Cypriots and Turkey. Therefore, it is unrealistic as a solution. The Turkish Cypriot community refuses to be absorbed by Greece, believing that it would thereby become an insignificant minority, and Turkey objects to Greek expansionism. Thus, the Greek Cypriot majority, if it desires to cooperate with the Turkish Cypriot minority in establishing constitutional government in Cyprus, must abandon *Enosis;* in turn, Greece must also abandon *Enosis.*

Federation, proposed by the Turkish Cypriot community, and supported by Turkey, must also be excluded as a solution. Federation is totally unacceptable to the Greek Cypriot majority, and thereby it too is unrealistic as a basis for communal cooperation. The Greek Cypriots have displayed the same degree of hostility toward a federal solution as the Turkish Cypriots have toward *Enosis.* Federation, furthermore, is inapplicable in Cyprus, except by force, for there is no territorial basis on which a federal system of government could be established.

Turkish Cypriot proposals encouraged by Turkey stipulating the movement of more than 10,000 families from each community, in order to create a territorial division, would result in forced human displacement and would also create a permanent border of friction. In an island of less than 600,000 people, proposals to move more than 100,000 of its people in order to secure territorial separation would have negative effects; it would create more tension and unrest than it professes to solve.

If *Enosis* and federation are excluded as prospective solutions, our investigation must conclude that some form of independence could be a possible compromise. The major question is, however, what form of independence? Independence, as envisaged in the Zurich and London Agreements, is unrealistic. This experiment has failed, and any attempt to re-institute it will probably be unsuccessful. Moreover, if by independence we mean "unfettered independence," where the majority rules and the minority's rights are guaranteed, this solution must be excluded for the following reasons: First, neither the bi-communal character of the Cypriot society, nor the political climate in Cyprus, is conducive to this form of independence; "unfettered independence" would entail the right of self-determination, which may lead to *Enosis;* second, the

Greek Cypriot majority has not exhibited the magnanimity required of a majority to obtain the trust and cooperation of the minority community; third, the Turkish Cypriot community, supported by Turkey, fears Greek Cypriot domination and thereby resents such an arrangement.

What is needed in Cyprus is a constitutional framework providing for a working system of government and promoting communal cooperation, thus reducing Greek and Turkish Cypriot differences. Perhaps the alarming Greco-Turkish confrontation of November 1967 may have dramatized the futility of the persistent deadlock. The expressed intent of both Greece and Turkey to eventually accept a demilitarized Cyprus as a political fact may pave the way to permanent compromise. Undue optimism, however, can be misleading. Unless the United Nations is given a stronger voice in formulating a permanent settlement in Cyprus outside the sphere of external interests, no constitutional settlement can be envisioned.

Constitutional formulas to fit the complex political situation in Cyprus cannot be easily devised. What is more, constitutional formulas are even more meaningless when devised on a theoretical level. The question is not how to provide for complicated constitutional machinery to satisfy the framer's imagination, but how to promote the growth of Cypriot communal cooperation, thereby encouraging a conscious attempt to promote allegiance to a Cypriot constitution.

In essence, what constitutional framers are faced with in Cyprus is, first, how to pave the way for intercommunal cooperation, which will facilitate the implanting of a constitutional government. To succeed, the framers of a constitution must avoid imposing solutions; rather they must encourage the growth of trust and cooperation within the Cypriot society between the Greek and Turkish communities.

Any settlement must reflect magnanimity on the part of the Greek Cypriot community and restraint on the part of the Turkish Cypriot community. The constitutional framework should be devised in such a manner as to give no cause to the majority to believe that it has an absolute moral right to rule, and at the same time to give no cause to the minority community to believe that it has a right to perpetual veto.

APPENDIXES

APPENDIX A

THE ZURICH AGREEMENT*

English Translation of the Documents Agreed in the French Texts and Initialled by the Greek and Turkish Prime Ministers at Zurich on February 11, 1959

Basic Structure of the Republic of Cyprus

1. The State of Cyprus shall be a Republic with a presidential regime, the President being Greek and the Vice-President Turkish elected by universal suffrage by the Greek and Turkish communities of the Island respectively.

2. The official languages of the Republic of Cyprus shall be Greek and Turkish. Legislative and administrative instruments and documents shall be drawn up and promulgated in the two official languages.

3. The Republic of Cyprus shall have its own flag of neutral design and colour chosen jointly by the President and the Vice-President of the Republic.

Authorities and communities shall have the right to fly the Greek and Turkish flags on holidays at the same time as the flag of Cyprus.

The Greek and Turkish communities shall have the right to celebrate Greek and Turkish national holidays.

4. The President and the Vice-President shall be elected for a period of five years.

In the event of absence, impediment or vacancy of their posts, the President and the Vice-President shall be replaced by the President and the Vice-President of the House of Representatives respectively.

In the event of a vacancy in either post, the election of new incumbents shall take place within a period of not more than 45 days.

The President and the Vice-President shall be invested by the House of Representatives, before which they shall take an oath of loyalty and respect for the Constitution. For this purpose, the House of Representatives shall meet within 24 hours after its constitution.

---

* Quoted from: Great Britain, *Conference on Cyprus: Documents Signed and Initialled at Lancaster House on February 19, 1959,* (London: Her Majesty's Stationery Office, 1964), Cmnd 679, pp. 5-9

5. Executive authority shall be vested in the President and the Vice-President. For this purpose they shall have a Council of Ministers composed of seven Greek Ministers and three Turkish Ministers. The Ministers shall be designated respectively by the President and the Vice-President who shall appoint them by an instrument signed by them both.

The Ministers may be chosen from outside the House of Representatives.

Decisions of the Council of Ministers shall be taken by an absolute majority.

Decisions so taken shall be promulgated immediately by the President and the Vice-President by publication in the official gazette.

However, the President and the Vice-President shall have the right of final veto and the right to return the decisions of the Council of Ministers under the same conditions as those laid down for laws and decisions of the House of Representatives.

6. Legislative authority shall be vested in a House of Representatives elected for a period of five years by universal suffrage of each community separately in the proportion of 70 per cent for the Greek community and 30 per cent for the Turkish community, this proportion being fixed independently of statistical data. (N.B.—The number of Representatives shall be fixed by mutual agreement between the communities.)

The House of Representatives shall exercise authority in all matters other than those expressly reserved to the Communal Chambers. In the event of a conflict of authority, such conflict shall be decided by the Supreme Constitutional Court which shall be composed of one Greek, one Turk and one neutral, appointed jointly by the President and the Vice-President. The neutral judge shall be president of the Court.

7. Laws and decisions of the House of Representatives shall be adopted by a simple majority of the members present. They shall be promulgated within 15 days if neither the President nor the Vice-President returns them for reconsideration as provided in Point 9 below.

The Constitutional Law, with the exception of its basic articles, may be modified by a majority comprising two-thirds of the Greek members and two-thirds of the Turkish members of the House of Representatives.

Any modification of the electoral law and the adoption of any law relating to the municipalities and of any law imposing duties or taxes shall require a simple majority of the Greek and Turkish members of the House of Representatives taking part in the vote and considered separately.

On the adoption of the budget, the President and the Vice-President may exercise their right to return it to the House of Representatives, if in their judgment any question of discrimination arises. If the House maintains its decisions, the President and the Vice-President shall have the right of appeal to the Supreme Constitutional Court.

8. The President and the Vice-President, separately and conjointly, shall have the right of final veto on any law or decision concerning foreign affairs, except the participation of the Republic of Cyprus in international organisations and pacts of alliance in which Greece and Turkey both participate, or concerning defence and security as defined in Annex I.

9. The President and the Vice-President of the Republic shall have, separately and conjointly, the right to return all laws and decisions, which may be returned to the House of Representatives within a period of not more than 15 days for reconsideration.

The House of Representatives shall pronounce within 15 days on any matter so returned. If the House of Representatives maintains its decisions, the President and the Vice-President shall promulgate the law or decision in question within the time-limits fixed for the promulgation of laws and decisions.

Laws and decisions, which are considered by the President or the Vice-President to discriminate against either of the two communities, shall be submitted to the Supreme Constitutional Court which may annul or confirm the law or decision, or return it to the House of Representatives for reconsideration, in whole or in part. The law or decision shall not become effective until the Supreme Constitutional Court or, where it has been returned, the House of Representatives has taken a decision on it.

10. Each community shall have its Communal Chamber composed of a number of representatives which it shall itself determine.

The Communal Chambers shall have the right to impose taxes and levies on members of their community to provide for their needs and for the needs of bodies and institutions under their supervision.

The Communal Chambers shall exercise authority in all religious, educational, cultural and teaching questions and questions of personal status. They shall exercise authority in questions where the interests and institutions are of a purely communal nature, such as sporting and charitable foundations, bodies and associations, producers' and consumers' co-operatives and credit establishments, created for the purpose of promoting the welfare of one of the communities. (N.B.—It is understood that the provisions of the present paragraph cannot be interpreted in such a way as to prevent the creation of mixed and communal institutions where the inhabitants desire them.)

These producers' and consumers' co-operatives and credit establishments, which shall be administered under the laws of the Republic, shall be subject to the supervision of the Communal Chambers. The Communal Chambers shall also exercise authority in matters initiated by municipalities which are composed of one community only. These municipalities, to which the laws of the Republic shall apply, shall be supervised in their functions by the Communal Chambers.

Where the central administration is obliged to take over the supervision of the institutions, establishments, or municipalities mentioned in the two preceding paragraphs by virtue of legislation in force, this supervision shall be exercised by officials belonging to the same community as the institution, establishment or municipality in question.

11. The Civil Service shall be composed as to 70 per cent of Greeks and as to 30 per cent of Turks.

It is understood that this quantitative division will be applied as far as practicable in all grades of the Civil Service.

In regions or localities where one of the two communities is in a majority approaching 100 per cent, the organs of the local administration responsible to the central administration shall be composed solely of officials belonging to that community.

12. The deputies of the Attorney-General of the Republic, the Inspector-General, the Treasurer and the Governor of the Issuing Bank may not belong to the same community as their principals. The holders of these posts shall be appointed by the President and the Vice-President of the Republic acting in agreement.

13. The heads and deputy heads of the Armed Forces, the Gendarmerie and the Police shall be appointed by the President and the Vice-President of the Republic acting in agreement. One of these heads shall be Turkish and where the head belongs to one of the communities, the deputy head shall belong to the other.

14. Compulsory military service may only be instituted with the agreement of the President and the Vice-President of the Republic of Cyprus.

Cyprus shall have an army of 2,000 men, of whom 60 per cent shall be Greek and 40 per cent Turkish.

The security forces (gendarmerie and police) shall have a complement of 2,000 men, which may be reduced or increased with the agreement of both the President and the Vice-President. The security forces shall be composed as to 70 per cent of Greeks and as to 30 per cent of Turks. However, for an initial period this percentage may be raised to a maximum of 40 per cent of Turks (and consequently reduced to 60 per cent of Greeks) in order not to discharge those Turks now serving in the police, apart from the auxiliary police.

15. Forces, which are stationed in parts of the territory of the Republic inhabitated, in a proportion approaching 100 per cent, by members of a single community, shall belong to that community.

16. A High Court of Justice shall be established, which shall consist of two Greeks, one Turk and one neutral, nominated jointly by the President and the Vice-President of the Republic.

The President of the Court shall be the neutral judge, who shall have two votes.

This Court shall constitute the highest organ of the judicature (appointments, promotions of judges, etc.).

17. Civil disputes, where the plaintiff and the defendant belong to the same community, shall be tried by a tribunal composed of judges belonging to that community. If the plaintiff and defendant belong to different communities, the composition of the tribunal shall be mixed and shall be determined by the High Court of Justice.

Tribunals dealing with civil disputes relating to questions of personal status and to religious matters, which are reserved to the competence of the Communal Chambers under Point 10, shall be composed solely of judges belonging to the community concerned. The composition and status of these tribunals shall be determined according to the law drawn up by the Communal Chamber and they shall apply the law drawn up by the Communal Chamber.

In criminal cases, the tribunal shall consist of judges belonging to the same community as the accused. If the injured party belongs to another community, the composition of the tribunal shall be mixed and shall be determined by the High Court of Justice.

18. The President and the Vice-President of the Republic shall each have the right to exercise the prerogative of mercy to persons from their respective communities who are condemned to death. In cases where the plaintiffs and the convicted persons are members of different communities the prerogative of mercy shall be exercised by agreement between the President and the Vice-President. In the event of disagreement the vote for clemency shall prevail. When mercy is accorded the death penalty shall be commuted to life imprisonment.

19. In the event of agricultural reform, lands shall be redistributed only to persons who are members of the same community as the expropriated owners.

Expropriations by the State or the Municipalities shall only be carried out on payment of a just and equitable indemnity fixed, in disputed cases, by the tribunals. An appeal to the tribunals shall have the effect of suspending action.

Expropriated property shall only be used for the purpose for which the expropriation was made. Otherwise the property shall be restored to the owners.

20. Separate municipalities shall be created in the five largest towns of Cyprus by the Turkish inhabitants of these towns. However:—

a — In each of the towns a co-ordinating body shall be set up which shall supervise work which needs to be carried out jointly and shall concern itself with matters which require a degree of cooperation. These bodies shall each be composed of two members chosen by the Greek municipalities, two members chosen by the Turkish municipalities and a President chosen by agreement between the two municipalities.

b — The President and the Vice-President shall examine within four years the question whether or not this separation of municipalities in the five largest towns shall continue.

With regard to other localities, special arrangements shall be made for the constitution of municipal bodies, following, as far as possible, the rule of proportional representation for the two communities.

21. A Treaty guaranteeing the independence, territorial integrity and constitution of the new State of Cyprus shall be concluded between the Republic of Cyprus, Greece, the United Kingdom and Turkey. A Treaty of military alliance shall also be concluded between the Republic of Cyprus, Greece and Turkey.

These two instruments shall have constitutional force. (This last paragraph shall be inserted in the Constitution as a basic article.)

22. It shall be recognised that the total or partial union of Cyprus with any other State, or a separatist indepedence for Cyprus (i.e., the partition of Cyprus into two independent States), shall be excluded.

23. The Republic of Cyprus shall accord most-favoured-nation treatment to Great Britain, Greece and Turkey for all agreements whatever their nature.

This provision shall not apply to the Treaties between the Republic of Cyprus and the United Kingdom concerning the bases and military facilities accorded to the United Kingdom.

24. The Greek and Turkish Governments shall have the right to subsidise institutions for education, culture, athletics and charity belonging to their respective communities.

Equally, where either community considers that it has not the necessary number of schoolmasters, professor or priests for the working of its institutions, the Greek and Turkish Governments may provide them to the extent strictly necessary to meet their needs.

25. One of the following Ministries—the Ministry of Foreign Affairs, the Ministry of Defence or the Ministry of Finance—shall be entrusted to a Turk. If the President and the Vice-President agree they may replace this system by a system of rotation.

26. The new State which is to come into being with the signature of the Treaties shall be established as quickly as possible and within a period of not more than three months from the signature of the Treaties.

27. All the above Points shall be considered to be basic articles of the Constitution of Cyprus.

APPENDIX B

This Appendix consists of letters by Dr. Fazil Kuchuk, Vice President of the Republic of Cyprus to the Secretary-General of the United Nations. They express the Turkish Cypriot community's feelings regarding the crisis in Cyprus.

*Letter by Vice President Kuchuk to the Secretary-General, Nicosia, March 6, 1965.**

> The Turkish Cypriot leadership has been trying to show all along that the real aim of Greece and of the Cypriot Greek leaders is to annex the island of Cyprus to Greece in order to satisfy Greece's age-old ambitions of territorial aggrandizement and that the real reason why the Greeks in Cyprus, in collusion with the Greek Government, have resorted to a campaign of violence and extermination against the Turks since 21 December 1963, is because the Turkish Community is and has always been against Enosis as Turks know for certain that Enosis would mean their total ruin. This has not been an easy task because, in order to achieve their aim of recolonization of Cyprus . . . both Greece and the Greek Cypriots have been trying to hide behind internationally-accepted principles such as self-determination and sovereignty . . .
>
> Can the denial of fundamental human rights and liberties to the Turks as individuals and to the Turkish Cypriot Community as such, who are a subject of international law, be shrouded behind the ostensibly impenetrable cloak of sovereignty despite those numerous provisions in the United Nations Charter which recognize that the treatment of even the individual citizen is no longer a matter solely of domestic concern? Sovereignty in the sense the

* United Nations, Security Council, *Letter Dated 8 March 1965 from the Permanent Representative of Turkey Addressed to the Secretary-General,* (S/6223, 9 March 1965). This submits the above letter of Dr. Kuchuk.

Greeks claim to exercise, and for which they demand the help of the United Nations in Cyprus, until such time as they are ready, both politically and militarily, to impose Enosis, means absolute and unlimited freedom of national will, unrestricted by law for only one of the two national communities in a bi-communal country, while the other community and its members as individuals are condemned to complete and permanent deprivation of all such rights and freedoms. Is this not a denial of the very object and *raison d'etre* of the world Organization itself, particularly in the case of Cyprus where its sovereignty and independence are regulated by international treaties and are shared by two national communities?

It is my earnest hope that the honourable members of the Security Council will examine the situation in Cyprus in their forthcoming meeting under the light of these facts.

*Letter by Vice President Kuchuk to the Secretary-General, Nicosia, July 25, 1965.**

As I am sure it is already reported to you by your special representative in Cyprus, the Greek members of the House of Representatives, having prevented Turkish members from attending the meeting of the House, proceeded to enact electoral legislation of a nature and in a manner repugnant to and inconsistent with the basic articles of the Republic's Constitution. By this legislation an attempt has been made to destroy completely the constitutional structure of the country and to put up in its place a structure which will disregard completely the existence of the Turkish Community in Cyprus and do away with the Turkish share in the sovereignty and administration of the Republic of Cyprus, thus eliminating one of the two pillars on which this structure can validly stand.

Though these enactments are devoid of any legal or constitutional basis, yet the fact that they are to be given the force of law by the use of arms leaves no room for doubt that they tend to worsen the situation and to impose the will of one community over the other by the use of brute force. Such action is no doubt contrary to the Security Council's resolution of 4 March 1964, which lays down specifically that the parties should refrain from any action which would worsen the situation and that any final political settlement should be brought about by agreement of all parties concerned.

I shall be grateful if Your Excellency will give urgent consideration to the matter and will invite the attention of the Security

---

* United Nations, Security Council, *Letter Dated 26 July 1965 from the Permanent Representative of Turkey Addressed to the Secretary-General,* (S/6562, 26 July 1965). This submits the above letter of Dr. Kuchuk.

Council to this delicate and highly grave and explosive situation which the Greeks have deliberately brought about in order to suppress the Turkish Community in the island and rob them of their constitutional rights with a view to making it impossible for the Turkish Community to continue in existence as an equal party in finding an agreed solution to the Cyprus problem.

*Letter by Vice President Kuchuk to the Secretary-General, Nicosia, September 21, 1965.**

In a new letter addressed to Your Excellency, a representative of the Greek Cypriot leadership claims that the Turkish proposal for a federal solution in Cyprus is a confession that the Zurich Constitution of 1960 has proved unworkable. The Turkish federation proposal carries no such meaning whatsoever. The fact is that, like every other constitution, the Constitution of Cyprus depended for successful implementation primarily on the goodwill of people who swore allegiance to it and undertook to apply it faithfully. It is not a reflection on the Constitution itself if these people, acting with ulterior motives and with racial fanaticism and religious bigotry, have failed to abide by their solemn pledge to fulfill their obligations under the Constitution and the relevant international agreements. What the Turkish federation proposal envisages is that in view of the methods of barbarism employed by the Greeks in their armed onslaught on the Turkish Community since December 1963, more concrete and physical guarantees are required for the Turks' security of life and property in Cyprus. The only practical and fair and just way to achieve this would be to find a geographical basis for our Constitution which already provides for a federal system of government based on the existence of two national communities in Cyprus. Was it because the Constitution was unworkable that over 100 Turkish villages were razed to the ground by the Greeks in a frenzy of sheer hatred after their inhabitants had evacuated them in order to save their lives by taking shelter in Turkish-controlled areas and after many hundreds of Turks who remained in their places were killed in attacks on Turkish villages and towns?

The representative in question also claims that the federation proposal means partition and that it does not serve the interests of the people of Cyprus as a whole . . .

The overall and real interests of the people of Cyprus as a whole (i.e., of both the Turkish and the Greek Communities) require the creation of permanent conditions conducive to peaceful inter-com-

* United Nations, Security Council, *Letter Dated 21 September 1965 from the Permanent Representative of Turkey Addressed to the Secretary-General,* (S/6708, 24 September 1965). This submits the above letter of Dr. Kuchuk.

munal coexistence and co-operation without either of the two communities being able to destroy and/or dominate and enslave the other (this is the Turkish case) and not a solution that would enable the Greek Community to condemn the Turks, surreptitiously, to extinction or serfdom in their own homeland (this is the Greek case). The crux of the matter is that people who can actually attempt to use methods of genocide in the second half of the twentieth century (and they openly declare that they will repeat this if Turkey attempts to use her treaty rights) and who were prevented from consummating their plans by the United Nations and by Turkey's deep interest in Cyprus, are not entitled to exploit respected principles when it suits them in order to keep the Turks permanently at the mercy of the Greeks.

I wish also to point out that contrary to what the Greek representative in question tries to imply, the Government of Cyprus, as mentioned in the Security Council resolution of 4 March 1964, is not and cannot be the insurgent and arbitrary administration of Archbishop Makarios who placed himself above the law, for the simple reason that the Security Council cannot be a party to the Greek plot to destroy the independence of a United Nation's Member country and to satisfy Greece's well-known "Megali Idea" expansionism by depriving the Turkish Community of its own country—a requirement that must take precedence over every other consideration. It is not up to me to reply to wild accusations against Turkey, but I must point out that Turkey is morally and legally obliged to protect the Turkish Community of Cyprus. The Greek Cypriot leadership, wishing that the Turkish Community were left unprotected so that they could carry out their plans of extermination without any hindrance, wilfully misconstrue the protective shield provided by Turkey for us and thus impute certain ambitions to Turkey. Unfortunately for the Greeks, the world knows what is going on in Cyprus.

APPENDIX C

Public Opinion Survey of the Greek Cypriot Community Conducted in the Summer and Early Fall of 1965

The purpose of the Opinion Survey was to ascertain the attitudes of the Greek Cypriot community toward the 1963 political and constitutional crisis. The major weakness of this Survey, is that it does not include the Turkish Cypriot attitudes. The intercommunal tension, coupled with my Greek Cypriot ethnic background, prevented me from entering the Turkish Cypriot enclaves for the purpose of conducting a similar Opinion Survey. However, irrespective of its limitation, this survey is important because it represents the attitudes of the Greek Cypriot community, comprising over 78 per cent of the population of Cyprus.

The Opinion Survey* which was based on a proportionate sample plan was conducted as follows:

1. Demographically, Cyprus was divided into three segments: villages of under 2,000 population; small rural towns over 2,000 population; and the six major cities. A stratified random sample was used to select a number of villages and small rural towns to be included in the sample. From these villages and small towns a random sample was drawn representing the rural population. All six major cities** were included in the Survey and were used to draw a sample representing the urban population. The distribution for the sample was chosen to reflect the urban/rural distribution of the Cypriot population. Thus, 60 per cent of the sample was drawn from the rural population, and 40 per cent from the urban.†

2. The sample as a whole (urban and rural) was placed under the following restrictions:

a — All persons under 20 years of age were excluded from the sample due to the political nature of the study.

b — Education was chosen as an important variant, because of its significance in forming political opinions. All those interviewed were classified proportionately according to the following educational levels: 60 per cent within the 0 to 6 grades; 30 per cent within the 7 to 12 grades; and 10 per cent within the 13 and above grades. A higher proportion of college and high school educated persons were included in the sample because of their importance in molding political attitudes and influencing political decision-making.‡

3. A sample survey of 600 individuals was drawn based on the restrictions regarding residence, age and education. After the second recall, the non-respondents were dropped, thereby reducing the sample

---

* For an analysis of survey procedures, see Frederick F. Stephen and Philip J. McCarthy *Sampling Opinions,* (New York: John Wiley and Sons, 1963).

** Nicosia, Famagusta, Limassol, Larnaca, Paphos and Kyrenia.

† According to the official census of 1960, the population of Cyprus was 64 per cent rural and 34 per cent urban. Cyprus, *Annual Report 1961, op. cit.,* p. 20.

‡ The 1960 census indicates that of all individuals over 20 years of age, 80 per cent have an elementary school education or less, 17 per cent are high school graduates and 3 per cent have a college education. Cyprus, Statistics and Research Department, *Statistical Abstract* (Nicosia: Printing Office of the Republic, 1963), p. 80.

from 600 to 500. By statistical standards, this is a high ratio of respondents—83.3 per cent of the total sample.

In devising the questionnaire, I used the open-end type of question, thereby giving an opportunity to those interviewed to comment freely. This was devised in order to avoid interview bias. The limitations of an open-end questionnaire, which often discourage respondents, did not materialize. This is indicated by the high ratio of respondents and their willingness to comment freely on at least four out of a total of six questions.

The results of the Survey are classified in Tables "C-I," "C-II," "C-III," and "C-IV" in this Appendix and in Tables 1, 2, 3, and 4 in Chapter 5 above.

Occupation was not used as a variant in the Tables, because occupational status is difficult to ascertain in Cyprus. Furthermore, occupational status is closely reflected in the educational variant. Question 4 of the questionnaire was not analyzed because respondents either avoided answering the question or expressed similar comments as on question 5.

The Questionnaire

The following questions form part of a special study on Cyprus conducted in a University overseas.

Please answer the following about yourself:

Occupation ______________________________.

Education—Graduate or years of attendance in:

a. Elementary __________________________.

b. High School __________________________.

c. College ______________________________.

Sex __________________.

Age __________________.

Place of Residence—Name of city, suburb or village:

____.

Name foreign countries you have visited

____.

1. What do you consider to be the main causes of the present crisis?
2. Under the present political circumstances, what do you consider to be the most realistic solution to the crisis?
3. Ideally, what do you personally consider to be the most justifiable solution?

4. Name ten persons who you feel have potential political leadership in Cyprus. Do not limit yourself to individuals presently holding government positions. Name individuals who you feel can provide political leadership in Cyprus irrespective of their occupational status. (i.e., lawyers, farmers, doctors, teachers, businessmen, etc.)

1.	6.
2.	7.
3.	8.
4.	9.
5.	10.

5. How do you feel toward the government's policy during the present crisis?
6. Additional comments.

TABLE C-I

Distribution of Respondents by Age Group

Age	Number of Persons Interviewed	Percentage of Persons Interviewed
20 - 39	231	46.2
40 - 59	206	41.2
60 and above	63	12.6
Total	500	100.0

n. Sample size—500 respondents.

TABLE C-II

Distribution of Respondents by Number of Years of Formal Education

Age	Number of Persons Interviewed	Percentage of Persons Interviewed
Grammar (Grades 0-6)	300	60.0
High School (Grades 7-12)	150	30.0
College (Grades 13 and above)	50	10.0
Total	500	100.0

n. Sample size—500 respondents.

TABLE C-III

Distribution of Respondents by Place of Residence

Place of Residence	Number of Persons Interviewed	Percentage of Persons Interviewed
Urban	199	39.8
Rural	301	60.2
Total	500	100.0

n. Sample size—500 respondents

TABLE C-IV

Distribution of Respondents by Education, Age and Place of Residence

Age	Grammar (Grades 0-6)		High School (Grades 7-12)		College (Grades 13 and above)		Total	
	Rural	Urban	Rural	Urban	Rural	Urban	Abs. No.	Per Cent
20 – 39	83	55	43	27	14	9	231	46.2
40 – 59	74	50	37	25	12	8	206	41.2
60 and above	23	15	11	7	4	3	63	12.6
Total Number	180	120	91	59	30	20	500	–
Total Percent	36.0	24.0	18.2	11.8	6.0	4.0	–	100.0

n. Sample size—500 respondents

BIBLIOGRAPHY

Public Documents

*A. Cyprus**

1. Published

CYPRUS. *Annual Report 1961.* Nicosia: Printing Office of the Republic of Cyprus, 1962.

——. *Annual Report 1962.* Nicosia: Printing Office of the Republic of Cyprus, 1963.

——. *Annual Report of the Department of Public Works* (1961 through 1966). Nicosia: Printing Office of the Republic of Cyprus, 1962-1967.

——. *Annual Report of the Ministry of Commerce and Industry* (1961 through 1966). Nicosia: Printing Office of the Republic of Cyprus, 1962-1967.

——. *Annual Report of the Ministry of Health* (1961 through 1966). Nicosia: Printing Office of the Republic of Cyprus, 1962-1967.

——. *Annual Report of the Ministry of Labour and Social Insurance* (1961 through 1966). Nicosia: Printing Office of the Republic of Cyprus, 1962-1967.

——. *Budget for 1965. Nicosia:* Printing Office of the Republic of Cyprus, 1966.

——. *Demographic Report 1965.* Nicosia: Printing Office of the Republic of Cyprus, 1966.

——. *Financial Report* (1961 through 1966). Nicosia: Printing Office of the Republic of Cyprus, 1962-1967.

——. *Five-Year Programme of Economic Development: Address of the President of the Republic, Archbishop Makarios, to the House of Representatives on the 21st August, 1961.* Nicosia: Printing Office of the Republic of Cyprus, 1961.

——. *Monthly Publications of Judgments of the Supreme Court of Cyprus, December 1964.* Part 5. Nicosia, 1964. (Mimeographed.)

——. *Monthly Publications of Judgments of the Supreme Court of Cyprus, June 1965.* Part 6. Nicosia, 1965. (Mimeographed.)

——. *Official Documents and Statements on U.N. Mediation and the Report of the U.N. Mediator Senor Galo Plaza on Cyprus.*

* Published documents and Parliamentary Minutes issued after December 1963 are not recognized by the Turkish Cypriots as documents of the Government of Cyprus.

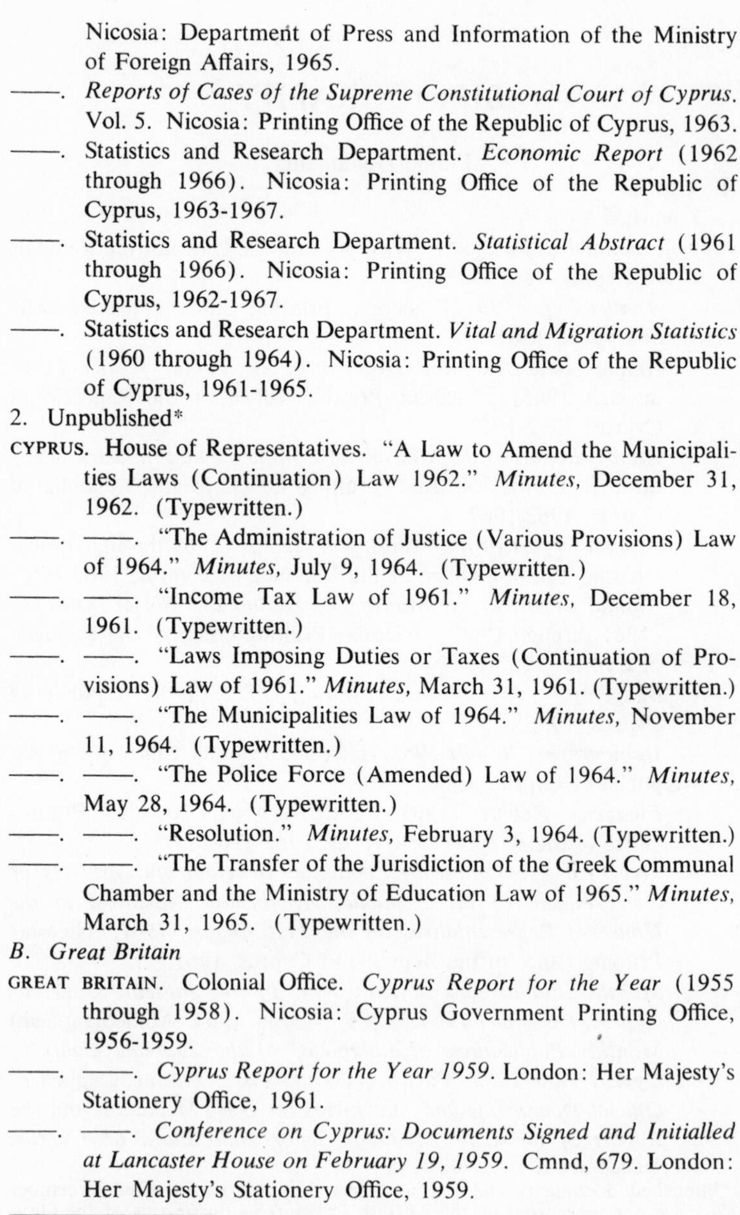

Nicosia: Department of Press and Information of the Ministry of Foreign Affairs, 1965.

——. *Reports of Cases of the Supreme Constitutional Court of Cyprus.* Vol. 5. Nicosia: Printing Office of the Republic of Cyprus, 1963.

——. Statistics and Research Department. *Economic Report* (1962 through 1966). Nicosia: Printing Office of the Republic of Cyprus, 1963-1967.

——. Statistics and Research Department. *Statistical Abstract* (1961 through 1966). Nicosia: Printing Office of the Republic of Cyprus, 1962-1967.

——. Statistics and Research Department. *Vital and Migration Statistics* (1960 through 1964). Nicosia: Printing Office of the Republic of Cyprus, 1961-1965.

2. Unpublished*

CYPRUS. House of Representatives. "A Law to Amend the Municipalities Laws (Continuation) Law 1962." *Minutes,* December 31, 1962. (Typewritten.)

——. ——. "The Administration of Justice (Various Provisions) Law of 1964." *Minutes,* July 9, 1964. (Typewritten.)

——. ——. "Income Tax Law of 1961." *Minutes,* December 18, 1961. (Typewritten.)

——. ——. "Laws Imposing Duties or Taxes (Continuation of Provisions) Law of 1961." *Minutes,* March 31, 1961. (Typewritten.)

——. ——. "The Municipalities Law of 1964." *Minutes,* November 11, 1964. (Typewritten.)

——. ——. "The Police Force (Amended) Law of 1964." *Minutes,* May 28, 1964. (Typewritten.)

——. ——. "Resolution." *Minutes,* February 3, 1964. (Typewritten.)

——. ——. "The Transfer of the Jurisdiction of the Greek Communal Chamber and the Ministry of Education Law of 1965." *Minutes,* March 31, 1965. (Typewritten.)

B. Great Britain

GREAT BRITAIN. Colonial Office. *Cyprus Report for the Year* (1955 through 1958). Nicosia: Cyprus Government Printing Office, 1956-1959.

——. ——. *Cyprus Report for the Year 1959.* London: Her Majesty's Stationery Office, 1961.

——. ——. *Conference on Cyprus: Documents Signed and Initialled at Lancaster House on February 19, 1959.* Cmnd, 679. London: Her Majesty's Stationery Office, 1959.

* All unpublished documents are in Greek.

——. ——. *Constitutional Proposals for Cyprus: Report Submitted to the Secretary of State for the Colonies by the Right Hon. Lord Radcliffe, C.B.E.* Cmnd, 42. London: Her Majesty's Stationery Office, 1956.

——. *Cyprus.* Cmnd, 1093. London: Her Majesty's Stationery Office, 1960.

——. *Cyprus: Correspondence Exchanged Between the Governor and Archbishop Makarios.* Cmnd. 9708. London: Her Majesty's Stationery Office, 1956.

——. *Cyprus: Statement of Policy.* Cmnd, 455. London: Her Majesty's Stationery Office, 1958.

——. *Parliamentary Debates.* (Commons.) Vol. 427 (1946).

——. *Parliamentary Debates.* (Commons.) Vol. 531 (1954).

——. *Parliamentary Debates.* (Commons.) Vol. 543 (1955).

——. *Parliamentary Debates.* (Commons.) Vol. 547 (1956).

——. *Parliamentary Debates.* (Commons.) Vol. 550 (1956).

——. *Parliamentary Debates.* (Commons.) Vol. 562 (1957).

——. *Parliamentary Debates.* (Commons.) Vol. 589 (1958).

——. *Parliamentary Debates.* (Commons.) Vol. 626 (1960).

——. *Parliamentary Debates.* (Commons.) Vol. 627 (1960).

——. *The Tripartite Conference on the Eastern Mediterranean.* Cmd. 9594. London: Her Majesty's Stationery Office, 1955.

C. United Nations

UNITED NATIONS. General Assembly. *Application Under the Auspices of the United Nations, of the Principle of Equal Rights and Self-determination of People in the Case of the Population of the Island of Cyprus.* Resolution 814(IX), 17 December 1954. (General Assembly. *Officials Records,* Ninth Session, Supplement No. 21[A/2890]).

——. ——. *Greece: Request for the Inclusion of a Supplementary Item in the Provisional Agenda of the Ninth Session.* A/2703, 20 August 1954, (General Assembly, *Official Records,* Ninth Session, Annexes. Agenda Item 62).

——. ——. *Official Records,* Ninth Session. General Committee, 93rd Meeting, 23 September 1954.

——. ——. *Official Records,* Ninth Session. First Committee, 749th Meeting, 14 December 1954.

——. ——. *Official Records,* Ninth Session. First Committee, 750th Meeting, 14 December 1954.

——. ——. *Official Records,* Tenth Session. General Committee, 102nd Meeting, 23 September 1955.

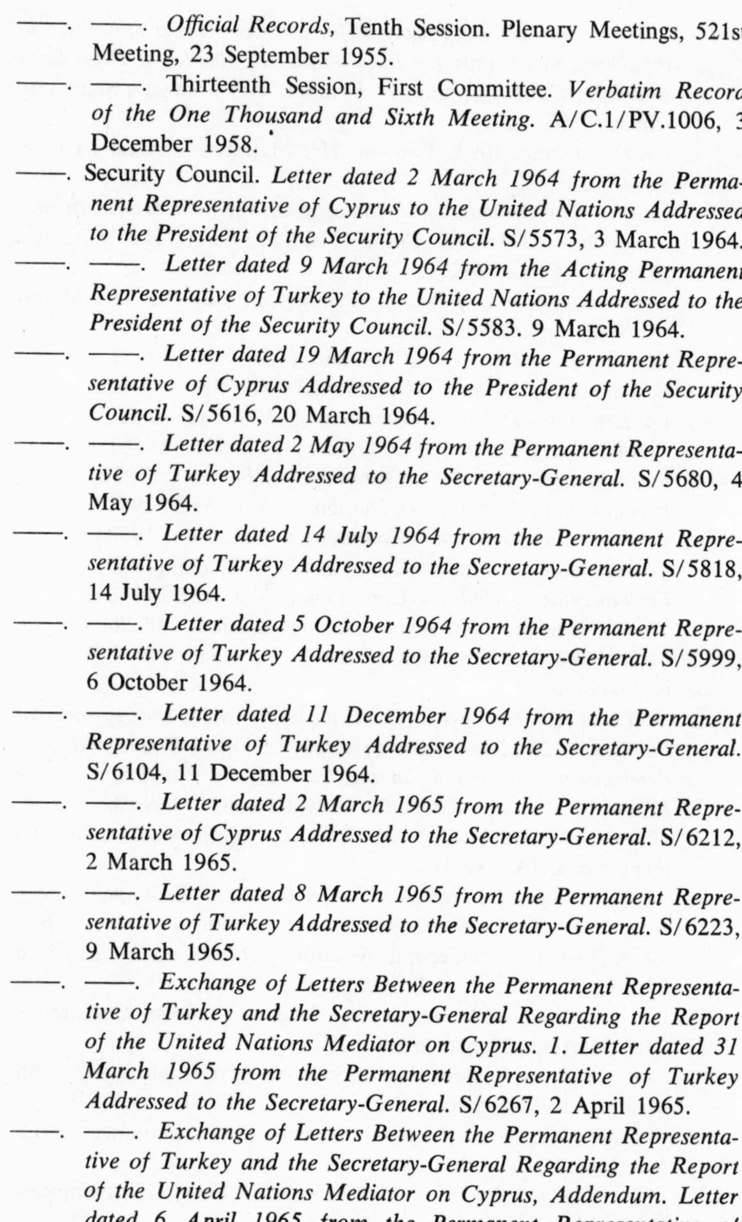

——. ——. *Official Records,* Tenth Session. Plenary Meetings, 521st Meeting, 23 September 1955.

——. ——. Thirteenth Session, First Committee. *Verbatim Record of the One Thousand and Sixth Meeting.* A/C.1/PV.1006, 3 December 1958.

——. Security Council. *Letter dated 2 March 1964 from the Permanent Representative of Cyprus to the United Nations Addressed to the President of the Security Council.* S/5573, 3 March 1964.

——. ——. *Letter dated 9 March 1964 from the Acting Permanent Representative of Turkey to the United Nations Addressed to the President of the Security Council.* S/5583. 9 March 1964.

——. ——. *Letter dated 19 March 1964 from the Permanent Representative of Cyprus Addressed to the President of the Security Council.* S/5616, 20 March 1964.

——. ——. *Letter dated 2 May 1964 from the Permanent Representative of Turkey Addressed to the Secretary-General.* S/5680, 4 May 1964.

——. ——. *Letter dated 14 July 1964 from the Permanent Representative of Turkey Addressed to the Secretary-General.* S/5818, 14 July 1964.

——. ——. *Letter dated 5 October 1964 from the Permanent Representative of Turkey Addressed to the Secretary-General.* S/5999, 6 October 1964.

——. ——. *Letter dated 11 December 1964 from the Permanent Representative of Turkey Addressed to the Secretary-General.* S/6104, 11 December 1964.

——. ——. *Letter dated 2 March 1965 from the Permanent Representative of Cyprus Addressed to the Secretary-General.* S/6212, 2 March 1965.

——. ——. *Letter dated 8 March 1965 from the Permanent Representative of Turkey Addressed to the Secretary-General.* S/6223, 9 March 1965.

——. ——. *Exchange of Letters Between the Permanent Representative of Turkey and the Secretary-General Regarding the Report of the United Nations Mediator on Cyprus. 1. Letter dated 31 March 1965 from the Permanent Representative of Turkey Addressed to the Secretary-General.* S/6267, 2 April 1965.

——. ——. *Exchange of Letters Between the Permanent Representative of Turkey and the Secretary-General Regarding the Report of the United Nations Mediator on Cyprus, Addendum. Letter dated 6 April 1965 from the Permanent Representative of*

Turkey Addressed to the Secretary-General. S/6267/Add. 1, 7 April 1965.

——. ——. *Letter dated 8 April 1965 from the Minister for Foreign Affairs of Greece Addressed to the Secretary-General.* S/6280, 9 April 1965.

——. ——. *Letter dated 23 June 1965 from the Permanent Representative of Cyprus Addressed to the Secretary-General.* S/6473, 24 June 1965.

——. ——. *Letter dated 26 July 1965 from the Permanent Representative of Turkey Addressed to the Secretary-General.* S/6562, 26 July 1965.

——. ——. *Letter dated 30 July 1965 from the Permanent Representative of Turkey Addressed to the Security Council.* S/6571, 30 July 1965.

——. ——. *Letter dated 30 July 1965 from the Permanent Representative of Cyprus Addressed to the President of the Security Council.* S/6573, 30 July 1965.

——. ——. *Letter dated 9 August 1965 from the Permanent Representative of Turkey Addressed to the Secretary-General.* S/6602, 10 August 1965.

——. ——. *Letter dated 25 August 1965 from the Permanent Representative of Cyprus Addressed to the Secretary-General.* S/6631, 26 August 1965.

——. ——. *Letter dated 21 September 1965 from the Permanent Representative of Turkey Addressed to the Secretary-General.* S/6708, 24 September 1965.

——. ——. *Letter dated 21 February 1966 from the Permanent Representative of Cyprus Addressed to the Secretary-General.* S/7155, 21 February 1966.

——. ——. *Letter dated 2 May 1966 from the Permanent Representative of Cyprus Addressed to the Secretary-General.* S/7276, 2 May 1966.

——. ——. *Letter dated 24 June 1966 from the Permanent Representative of Turkey Addressed to the Secretary-General.* S/7377, 24 June 1966.

——. ——. *Official Records,* Nineteenth Year, 1099 Meeting, 28 February 1964.

——. ——. *Official Records,* Nineteenth Year, Supplement for January, February and March 1964.

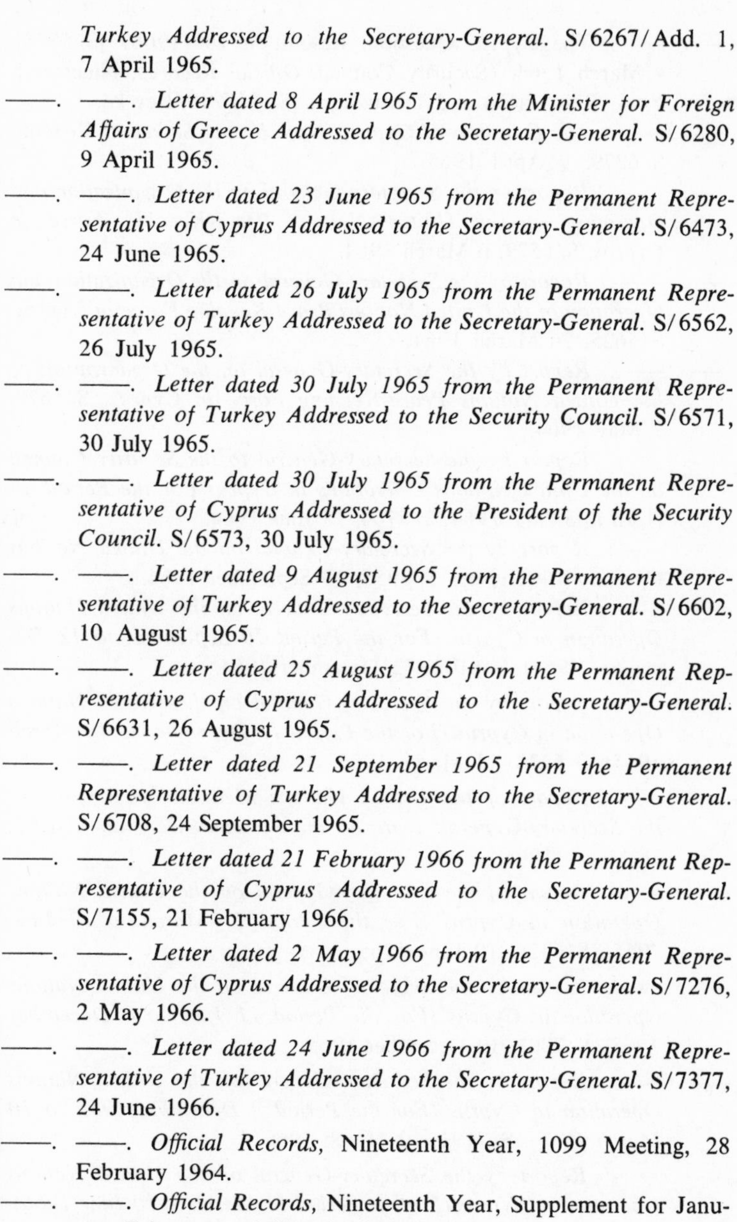

——. ——. The Cyprus Question. Resolution 186(1964) [S/5575], 4 March 1964, (Security Council, *Official Records,* Nineteenth Year, Resolutions and Discussions [S/INF/19/Rev.1.].

——. ——. *The Question of Cyprus: Note by the Secretary-General.* S/6279, 9 April 1965.

——. ——. *Report by the Secretary-General on the Organization and Operation of the United Nations Peace-Keeping Force in Cyprus.* S/5579, 6 March 1964.

——. ——. *Report by the Secretary-General on the Organization and Operation of the United Nations Peace-Keeping Force in Cyprus.* S/5625, 26 March 1964.

——. ——. *Report by the Secretary-General on the Organization of the United Nations Peace-Keeping Force in Cyprus.* S/5679, 2 May 1964.

——. ——. *Report by the Secretary-General to the Security Council on the United Nations Operations in Cyprus For the Period 26 April to 8 June 1964.* S/5764, 15 June 1964.

——. ——. *Report by the Secretary-General on the United Nations Operation in Cyprus.* S/5950, 10 September 1964.

——. ——. *Report by the Secretary-General on the United Nations Operation in Cyprus (For the Period 10 September to 12 December 1964).* S/6102, 12 December 1964.

——. ——. *Report by the Secretary-General on the United Nations Operation in Cyprus (For the Period 13 December to 10 March 1965).* S/6228, 11 March 1965.

——. ——. *Report of the United Nations Mediator on Cyprus to the Secretary-General; Note by the Secretary-General.* S/6253, 26 March 1965.

——. ——. *Report of the Secretary-General on the United Nations Operation in Cyprus (For the Period 11 March to 10 June 1965).* S/6426, 10 June 1965.

——. ——. *Report by the Secretary-General on the United Nations Operation in Cyprus (For the Period 11 June to 8 December 1965).* S/7001, 10 December 1965.

——. ——. *Report by the Secretary-General on the United Nations Operation in Cyprus (For the Period 9 December 1965 to 10 March 1966).* S/7191, 10 March 1966.

——. ——. *Report by the Secretary-General on the United Nations Operation in Cyprus (For the Period 11 March to 10 June 1966).* S/7350, 10 June 1966.

——. ——. *Report by the Secretary-General on the United Nations Operation in Cyprus (For the Period 11 June to 5 December 1966).* S/7611, 8 December 1966.

——. ——. *Report by the Secretary-General on the United Nations Operation in Cyprus (For the Period 6 December 1966 to 12 June 1967).* S/7969, 13 June 1967.

——. ——. *Report by the Secretary-General on the United Nations Operation in Cyprus (For the Period 13 June to 8 December 1967).* S/8286, 8 December 1967.

——. ——. *Verbatim Record of the One Thousand and Ninety-Fifth Meeting.* S/PV/1095, 18 February 1964.

——. ——. *Verbatim Record of the One Thousand and Ninety-Sixth Meeting.* S/PV/1096, 19 February 1964.

——. ——. *Verbatim Record of the Eleven Hundred and Forty-Second Meeting.* S/PV/1142, 8 August 1964.

——. ——. *Verbatim Record of the Eleven Hundred and Forty-Third Meeting.* S/PV/1143, 9 August 1964 and 11 August 1964.

——. ——. *Provisional Verbatim Record of the Twelve Hundred and Thirty-Fifth Meeting.* S/PV/1235, 5 August 1965.

——. ——. *Provisional Verbatim Record of the Thirteen Hundred and Eighty-Third Meeting.* S/PV/1383, 24 November 1967.

Books

ALASTOS, DOROS. *Cyprus Guerilla: Grivas, Makarios and the British.* London: Heinemann, 1960.

——. *Cyprus in History: A Survey of 5,000 Years.* London: Zeno Publishers, 1955.

ALMOND, GABRIEL A. and COLEMAN, JAMES S. (eds.). *The Politics of the Developing Areas.* Princeton: Princeton University Press, 1960.

ALMOND, GABRIEL A. and POWELL, BINGHAM G. *Comparative Politics: A Developmental Approach.* Boston: Little, Brown and Co., 1966.

ANDERSON, ANTHONY DOLPHIN. *The Structure of the Ottoman Dynasty.* Oxford: Clarendon Press, 1956.

ANDREWS, WILLIAM G. (ed.). *Constitutions and Constitutionalism.* Princeton: D. Van Nostrand Company, Inc., 1961.

ANGELIDES, G. "The Constitution of Cyprus." Unpublished Master of Laws Thesis, University of Birmingham, 1960 (Typewritten).

APPLEBY, JOHN. *The Bad Summer.* London: Hodder and Stoughton, 1958.

ARISTOTLE. *The Politics.* Translated and edited by Ernest Barker. New York: Oxford University Press, 1962.

ARNOLD, PERCY, *Cyprus Challenge*. London: The Hogarth Press, 1956.

BALFOUR, PATRICK. *The Orphaned Realm*. London: P. Marshall, 1951.

BARKER, DUDLEY. *Grivas: Portrait of a Terrorist*. New York: Harcourt, Brace and Company, 1960.

BEER, SAMUEL H. *et. al. Patterns of Government*. 2nd. ed., revised. New York: Random House, 1964.

BYFORD-JONES, W. *Grivas and the Story of E.O.K.A.* London: Robert Hale Ltd., 1959.

CAMPBELL, JOHN C. *Defense of the Middle East*. New York: Harper & Brothers, 1958.

CASSON, STANLEY. *Ancient Cyprus*. London: Methuen, 1937.

CHRISTIDES, CHR. *Cyprus and Greco-Turkish Relations 1953-1967*. Athens: 1967. (In Greek).

COBHAM, CLAUDE DELAVAL. *An Attempt at the Bibliography of Cyprus*. Ed. G. Jeffery. Nicosia: Government Printing Office, 1929.

——. *Excerpta Cypria: Materials for a History of Cyprus*. Cambridge: Cambridge University Press, 1908.

DE SMITH, S. A. *The New Commonwealth and Its Constitutions*. London: Stevens, 1964.

DI CESNOLA, LOUIS PALMA. *Cyprus: Its Ancient Cities, Tombs and Temples*. New York: Harper and Brothers, 1878.

DURRELL, LAWRENCE. *Bitter Lemons*. New York: Dutton, 1957.

EDEN, ANTHONY. *Full Circle*. London: Cassell, 1960.

EMILIANIDES, ACHILLEUS K. *The Greekness of Cyprus*. Nicosia: Mouson Press, 1944. (in Greek).

FLINN, WILLIAM HENRY. *Cyprus: A Brief Survey of its History and Development*. Nicosia: W. J. Archer, 1924.

FOLEY, CHARLES. *Island in Revolt*. London: Longmans, 1962.

——. *Legacy of Strife: Cyprus From Rebellion to Civil War*. Baltimore: Penguin, 1964.

FOOT, HUGH (Sir). *A Start in Freedom*. New York: Harper and Row, 1964.

FOOT, MICHAEL and JONES, MERVYN. *Guilty Men 1957: Suez and Cyprus*. New York: Rinehart & Company, Inc., 1957.

FOOT, SYLVIA. *Emergency Exit*. London: Chatto and Windus, 1960.

FRIEDRICH, CARL J. *Constitutional Government and Democracy*. rev. ed. New York: Ginn and Company, 1950.

——. *Man and His Government*. New York: McGraw-Hill Book Company, Inc., 1963.

GRIVAS, GEORGE (General). *General Grivas on Guerrilla Warfare*. Translated by A. A. Pallis. New York: Frederick A. Praeger, 1965.

——. *The Memoirs of General Grivas.* Edited by Charles Foley. New York: Frederick A. Praeger, 1964.

GYALISTRAS, SERGE. *Hellas and Cyprus.* Translated by G. A. Trypanis. Athens, 1955.

HACKETT, JOHN. *History of the Orthodox Church in Cyprus.* Translated by Ch. I. Papaioannou. 3 vols. Athens: Sakellariou and Eleftheriou, 1923-1932. (in Greek.)

HADJICOSTA, ISMENE. *Cyprus and its Life.* Nicosia: Zavalliss Press, 1943.

HILL, GEORGE (Sir). *A History of Cyprus.* 4 vols. Cambridge: Cambridge University Press, 1940-1952.

HOME, GORDON C. *Cyprus Then and Now.* London: J. M. Dent, 1960.

INSTITUTE FOR MEDITERRANEAN AFFAIRS. *The Cyprus Dilemma: Options for Peace.* New York: Marstin Press, 1967.

JENNESS, DIAMOND. *The Economics of Cyprus.* Montreal: McGill University Press, 1962.

KEPIADES, GEORGIOS. *Memoirs of the 1821 Tragic Events in Cyprus.* Alexandria, 1888. (in Greek).

KIRK, GEORGE E. *A Short History of the Middle East.* 6th rev. ed. New York: Frederick A. Praeger, 1959.

KOSLIN, ADAMATIA POLLIS. "The Megali Idea: A Study in Greek Nationalism," Unpublished Ph.D. dissertation, Johns Hopkins University, 1958. (Typewritten).

KOURITOS, I. F. *The Orthodox Church of Cyprus.* Nicosia, 1907 (in Greek).

KRANIDIOTIS, NIKOS. *Cyprus in the Struggle for Freedom.* Athens, 1957. (in Greek.)

KYRRIS, COSTAS P. *Cyprus Between East and West Today.* Nicosia, 1964. (in Greek.)

LANITIS, N. C. *Our Destiny.* Nicosia, 1963.

LE GEYT, P. S. *Makarios in Exile.* Nicosia: Anagennisis Press, 1961.

LEE, DWIGHT E. *Great Britain and the Cyprus Convention Policy.* (Harvard Historical Studies, Vol. XXXVIII.) Cambridge: Harvard University Press, 1934.

LEKKAS, G. P. *Cyprus: The Occupied Greece.* Athens, 1952. (in Greek).

LERNER, DANIEL. *The Passing of Traditional Society.* New York: The Free Press, 1965.

LIPSET, SEYMOUR MARTIN. *Political Man.* Garden City: Doubleday and Co., 1963.

LUKE, HARRY C. (Sir). *Cyprus: A Portrait and an Appreciation.* 2nd. rev. ed. London: G. G. Harrap, 1964.

——. *Cyprus Under the Turks, 1571-1878.* London: Oxford University Press, 1921.

MACRIDIS, ROY C. and BROWN, BERNARD E. (eds). *Comparative Politics: Notes and Readings.* Homewood, Illinois: The Dorsey Press, Inc., 1961.

MAYES, STANLEY. *Cyprus and Makarios.* London: Putnam Press, 1960.

MC ILWAIN, CHARLES HOWARD. *Constitutionalism: Ancient and Modern.* Ithaca: Cornell University Press, 1947.

MEYER, ALBERT J. and VASSILIOU, SIMOS. *The Economy of Cyprus,* Cambridge: Harvard University Press, 1962.

MILBRATH, LESTER W. *Political Participation.* Chicago: Rand McNally and Co., 1965.

MONROE, ELIZABETH. *Britain's Moment in the Middle East—1914-1956.* London: Chatto and Windus, 1963.

MYRIANTHOPOULOS, CLEOVOULOS I. *Education in Cyprus from the British Occupation 1878-1946.* Limassol: Papatsiakou Press, 1946. (in Greek).

NEWMAN, PHILIP. *A Short History of Cyprus.* London: Longmans, Green and Co., 1953.

ORR, C. W. J. *Cyprus Under British Rule.* London: Robert Scott, 1918.

PALLIS, A. A. *Greece's Anatolian Venture and After.* London: Methuen, 1937.

PANA, K. *Cyprus is Greek: 3,000 Years of Greek Life.* Athens, n.d. (in Greek.)

PAPADOPOULLOS, THEODORE. *Texts and Studies of the History of Cyprus: Social and Historical Data on Population 1570-1881.* Nicosia: Cyprus Research Centre, 1965.

PAPADOPOULLOS, CHRYSOSTOMOS. *The Church of Cyprus Under the Turks.* Athens, 1929. (in Greek.)

PARIS, PETER. *The Impartial Knife: A Doctor in Cyprus.* London: Hutchinson, 1962.

PERISTIANES, K. I. *General History of Cyprus.* Nicosia, 1910. (in Greek).

PUSEY, G. B. *Cyprus: Past, Present, Future.* Nicosia: Pusey Press, 1943.

——. *Cyprus: Yours? Mine? Ours?* Nicosia: Pusey Press, 1944.

PYE, LUCIEN W. *Aspects of Political Development.* Boston: Little, Brown and Co., 1965.

——. and Verba, Sidney (eds). *Political Culture and Political Development.* Princeton: Princeton University Press, 1965.

RHALLYS, I. G. *Cyprus: That Hellenic Island.* Athens, 1954.

ROSSITER, CLINTON L. *Constitutional Dictatorship: Crisis Government in the Modern Democracies.* Princeton: Princeton University Press, 1948.

ROYAL INSTITUTE OF INTERNATIONAL AFFAIRS. *Cyprus, Background to Enosis.* London: Chatham House, 1958.

——. *Cyprus: The Dispute and the Settlement.* London: Chatham House, 1959.

SABINE, GEORGE. *A History of Political Theory.* 3rd. ed. New York: Holt, Rinehart and Winston, Inc., 1961.

SILVERT, K. H. (ed.). *Expectant Peoples: Nationalism and Development.* New York: Random House, 1963.

SPYRIDAKIS, COSTAS. *A Brief History of Cyprus.* Nicosia: Greek Communal Chamber, 1964.

STEPHEN, FREDERICK P. and MC CARTHY, PHILIP J. *Sampling Opinions: An Analysis of Survey Procedure.* New York: John Wiley and Sons, 1965.

STEPHENS, ROBERT. *Cyprus: A Place of Arms.* London: Pall Mall Press, 1966.

STORRS, RONALD (Sir). *A Chronology of Cyprus.* Nicosia: Government Printing Office, 1930.

——. *The Memoirs of Sir Ronald Storrs.* New York: G. P. Putnam's Sons, 1937.

——. *Orientations.* London: Nicholson and Watson, Ltd., 1937.

STYLIANOU, DEMETRIOS. *The Inner Life of Cyprus.* Nicosia, 1931.

THEODORIDES, G. M. *Cyprus: Its Civilization, Struggles and Tribulations.* Athens, 1958. (in Greek).

TREMAYNE, PENELOPE. *Below the Tide: War and Peace in Cyprus.* Boston: Houghton Mifflin, 1959.

VEZANIS, DEMETRIOS S. *The Cyprus Problem.* Athens, 1959. (in Greek).

VUCINICH, WAYNE S. *The Ottoman Empire, Its Record and Legacy.* Princeton: Van Nostrand, 1965.

UNITED STATES DEPARTMENT OF THE ARMY. *U.S. Army Area Handbook for Cyprus.* Washington, D. C.: U. S. Government Printing Office, 1964.

WEIR, W. W. *Education in Cyprus.* Nicosia: Cosmos Press, 1952.

ZANNETOS, PHILIOS. *Cyprus During the Struggle for Revival 1921-1930.* Athens: D. Delis and Tsipis, 1930. (in Greek).

——. *History of the Island of Cyprus.* 3 vols. Larnaca: Philokalias Press, 1910-1912. (in Greek).

ZOTIADES, GEORGE. *The Ethnic Composition and the Geographic Distribution of the Population of Cyprus.* Athens, 1959. (in Greek).

——. *The Idea of Partitioning Cyprus.* Athens, 1959. (in Greek).

ZURCHER, ARNOLD J. (ed.). *Constitutions and Constitutional Trends Since World War II.* 2nd. rev. ed. New York: New York University Press, 1955.

Greek and Greek Cypriot Pamphlets and Publications

Appeal by the Greek Cypriot Trade Union Federations and Organizations to their Turkish Colleagues. Nicosia, 20 February 1964.

ARCHBISHOP MAKARIOS. *Crusade for Freedom.* New York: Cyprus Federation of America, 1958.

CENTRAL COMMITTEE OF THE PROGRESSIVE PARTY OF THE WORKING PEOPLE (A.K.E.L.). *A.K.E.L. Newsletter.* Nicosia, 1964-1965.

——. NEOS DEMOCRATES (New Democrat). Monthly. Nicosia, 1964-1965. (in Greek).

COMMITTEE OF THE STRUGGLE OF CYPRUS. *Position on the National Problem: Objective—Enosis; Mean—Self-Determination.* Nicosia: Geka Press, 1964. (in Greek.)

CYPRUS DEPUTATION TO LONDON. *Memorandum on the Island of Cyprus.* London: Hesperia Press, 1919.

THE CYPRUS ETHNARCHY OFFICE. *Memorandum of the Educational Council of the Cyprus Ethnarchy on the Educational Situation in Cyprus.* Nicosia: Cyprus Ethnarchy Office, 1957.

The Cyprus Plebiscite and the Greek Parliament. London: Cypriot National Delegation, 1950.

CYPRUS WORKERS' CONFEDERATION (S.E.K.). *Cyprus: Historical Notes and Analysis of the Present Tragedy.* Nicosia, 1964.

EVANGELIDES, SOCRATES. *Cyprus Has Never Belonged to Turkey—Not Even for a Day.* Nicosia, n.d. (Mimeographed.)

EVDOKAS, T. *The Demand for Enosis: Psychological Obstacles.* Nicosia: Geka Press, 1965. (in Greek).

GREEK COMMUNAL CHAMBER (Cyprus). *Cyprus Today.* Nicosia, 1963-1965.

——. *Facts About Cyprus.* Nicosia, 1965.

——. *Political Documents.* Nicosia, 1964-1966.

——. *Cyprus: A Handbook on the Island's Past and Present.* Nicosia, 1964.

KOULLIS, L. K. *Greek Education in Cyprus.* Nicosia: The Education Office, Greek Communal Chamber, 1964.

KYPRIANOU, SPYROS. *The Cyprus Question.* Athens, 1956.

LOIZIDES, SAVVAS. *Cyprus Demands Self-Determination.* Athens: National Committee for Self-Determination of Cyprus, 1956.

——. *The Cyprus Question: Its Evolution—Present Aspects After the Plebiscite of January 1950.* Nicosia: The Ethnarchy of Cyprus, 1950.

——. *The Right of Peoples to Self-Determination and the Cyprus Question*. New York, 1957.

NATIONAL COUNCIL FOR PUBLIC ENLIGHTENMENT. *Truth About Greece: Cyprus*. Athens, 1954.

THE OFFICE OF THE DIRECTOR OF THE HOUSE OF REPRESENTATIVES. *Outline of the Negotiations Regarding the Question of the Municipalities in the Five Towns*. Nicosia, n.d. (Mimeographed).

——. *The Problem of the 70 to 30 Ratio in the Participation of the Two Communities in the Civil Service of the Republic*. Nicosia, n.d. (Mimeographed.)

PANCYPRIAN FEDERATION OF LABOR (PEO). *Report on the Activities of PEO*. Nicosia: December 1956. (in Greek.)

——. *Report on the Activities of PEO*. Nicosia: April 1959. (in Greek).

——. *Report on the Activities of PEO*. Nicosia: March 1961. (in Greek.)

——. *13th Convention of PEO*. Nicosia: December 1963. (in Greek).

ROSSIDES, ZENON G. *The Island of Cyprus and Union With Greece*. Nicosia: The Ethnarchy Council, 1954.

ROYAL CONSULATE GENERAL OF GREECE. Press and Information Service. "Background to the Cyprus Problem," New York: July, 1964. (Mimeographed).

——. ——. "The Cyprus Question: Policy of the Greek Government," New York: July 11, 1964. (Mimeographed).

ROYAL GREEK EMBASSY INFORMATION SERVICE. *British Views on Cyprus*. Washington, D. C., 1955.

——. *Cyprus Demands Self-Determination*. Washington, D. C., 1954.

——. *Statement of His Eminence Archbishop Makarios*. Washington, D. C., n.d.

SOLOMIDES, R. MINISTER OF FINANCE. "Comments of the Minister of Finance on the paper entitled 'Federation and Cyprus Economy,' Prepared by the Turkish Communal Chamber and dated the 6 June 1964." Nicosia, 1964. (Mimeographed.)

SPYRIDAKIS, COSTAS. *The Educational Policy of the English Government in Cyprus, 1878-1954*. Nicosia: Cyprus Ethnarchy Office, 1954.

——. *The Greek Secondary Education of Cyprus*. Nicosia: The Cyprus Ethnarchy Office, 1959.

——. President of the Greek Communal Chamber. "Review of the Activities of the Greek Communal Chamber from August 21, 1960 to the present." Nicosia, March 16, 1965. (Mimeographed). (in Greek).

——. *Summary of the Report on the Work of the Office of Greek Education.* Nicosia, 1962.

UNION OF JOURNALISTS OF THE ATHENS DAILY NEWSPAPERS. *Cyprus: Touchstone for Democracy.* Athens, 1958.

Turkish and Turkish Cypriot Pamphlets and Publications

BAYULKEN, UMIT HALUK. *Turkish Minority in Greece.* The text of a talk given at the London School of Economics and Political Science, on March 13, 1958. Ankara, 1964.

BEDEVI, VERGI H. *Cyprus Has Never Been A Greek Island.* Nicosia: Cyprus Turkish Historical Association, 1964.

Cyprus is Turkish Party. *Greek Atrocities Against the Turks.* Nicosia, 1956.

——. *Intercommunal Strife in Cyprus.* Nicosia, 1958.

CYPRUS TURKISH ASSOCIATION. *Cyprus.* London, n.d. (Mimeographed).

CYPRUS TURKISH CULTURAL ASSOCIATION. *Cyprus: Why? Why?* Ankara, 1964.

CYPRUS TURKISH HUMAN RIGHTS COMMITTEE. *Events of Cyprus.* Nicosia, n.d.

CYPRUS TURKISH INFORMATION CENTRE. *Turks and Cyprus.* Nicosia, n.d.

——. *Turks Say No To Enosis.* Nicosia, n.d.

KUCHUK, FAZIL. *Cyprus: Turkish Reply to Archbishop Makarios' Proposals.* Nicosia, n.d.

RIZA, HALIT ALI. *The House of Representatives: The Separate Majority Right.* Nicosia: Halkin Sesi Press, 1963.

TURKISH COMMUNAL CHAMBER (Cyprus). *A Report on Cyprus.* Nicosia, 1965.

——. *Federation and the Cyprus Economy.* Nicosia, 1964.

——. *History Speaks: A Documentary Survey.* Nicosia, 1964.

——. *Looking Back: An Official Briefing.* Nicosia: Halkin Sesi Press, 1963.

——. *Special News Bulletin.* Nicosia, 1964-1967.

——. "Text in English of the Laws and Decisions, Promulgated in the Official Gazette No. 2 Dated 30 July 1965, Published in Turkish Under the Authority of the Vice-President of the Republic." Nicosia, n.d.

——. *Turks and Cyprus: Introduction to the Problem of Cyprus.* Nicosia, n.d.

——. *Turkish Answers to Greek Charges on Cyprus.* Nicosia, n.d.

——. *The Turkish Case: 70:30 and the Greek Tactics.* Nicosia: Halkin Sesi Press, 1963.

——. *Turkish Cypriot Community: Struggling for Existence.* Nicosia, 1964.

TURKISH EMBASSY. *The Diary of A Cypriot Turk 1963-1965.* Washington, D. C., 1965.

——. *Dictionary of Greek Cypriot Politics.* Washington, D. C., 1965.

TURKISH NATIONAL PARTY, CYPRUS. *Who Is At Fault?* Nicosia: Halkin Sesi Press, 1964.

TURKISH TOURISM AND INFORMATION BUREAU. *Turkish Minority in Greece—Greek Minority in Turkey.* New York, n.d.

——. *Cyprus: Past, Present, Future.* New York, n.d.

——. *Turkish Views on Cyprus.* New York, 1956.

——. *Turkish Views on Cyprus.* New York, 1965.

TURKISH TOURISM AND INFORMATION OFFICE. *Cyprus: Greek Expansionism or Independence.* New York, n.d.

VICE PRESIDENT, *et al. The Cypriot Turkish Case and Greek Atrocities in Cyprus.* Nicosia: Halkin Sesi Press, 1964.

Articles and Periodicals

ADAMS, T. W., COTTRELL, ALVIN J. "The Cyprus Conflict," *Orbis,* VIII, No. 1 (Philadelphia, Spring 1964), pp. 66-83.

"Aggressive Schemes Against Cyprus: Threat to International Security —Tass Statement," *Current Soviet Documents,* Vol. II, No. 6 (New York, February 10, 1964) pp. 9-12.

ANTHEM, THOMAS. "Crisis in Cyprus: President Makarios Talks to the Contemporary Review," *Contemporary Review,* Vol. 204 (London, August 1963), pp. 57-67.

——. "Cyprus Imbroglio," *Contemporary Review,* Vol. 205 (London, October 1964) pp. 518-522.

——. "Greece and Cyprus," *Contemporary Review,* Vol. 205 (London, April 1964), pp. 169-174.

BAKER, ERIC. "The Settlement in Cyprus," *The Political Quarterly,* Vol. 30, No. 3 (London, July-September 1959), pp. 244-253.

——. "Spotlight on Cyprus," *The Progressive,* Vol. 23, No. 2 (Madison, Wisconsin: February 1959), pp. 35-37.

BECKINGHAM, C. F. "The Cypriot Turks," *Royal Central Asian Journal,* XLIII, Part II, (London, April 1956), pp. 126-130.

——. "The Turks of Cyprus," *The Journal of the Royal Anthropological Institute of Great Britain and Ireland,* Vol. 87, Part II (London, July-December 1957), pp. 165-174.

"Clouds Over Cyprus," *New Times,* No. 7 (Moscow: February 19, 1964), pp. 3-5.

"The Constitutional System of the Republic of Cyprus," *Bulletin of the International Commission of Jurists,* No. 11 (Geneva, December 1960), pp. 20-23 .

"Current Crisis in Cyprus," *United States Department of State Bulletin,* Vol. 50 (Washington, D. C., March 2, 1964), pp. 332-333.

"Cyprus: A New Republic," *International Affairs,* (Moscow: September 1960), pp. 89-91.

"Cyprus: Part I," *Current Notes on International Affairs,* Vol. 31, No. 11 (Canberra, Australia: November 1960), pp. 617-624.

"Cyprus: Part II," *Current Notes on International Affairs,* Vol. 31, No. 12 (Canberra, Australia: December 1960), pp. 694-702.

"Cyprus—The Turkish Case," *Asian Review,* LIII, No. 193 (London, January 1957), pp. 47-59.

DEMING, W. EDWARDS. "On Errors in Surveys," in *Marketing Research.* ed. Hiram C. Barksdale. (New York: The Ronald Press, 1966), pp. 407-423.

ENNIS, CLARE. "Cyprus: A Critical Survey," *Contemporary Issues,* Vol. 8, No. 29 (London, February-March, 1957), pp. 353-379.

"Enosis and Its Background: Race and Religion in Cyprus," *The Round Table,* Vol. 47, No. 186 (London, March 1957), pp. 121-140.

ERGIN, FERIDUN. "Island of Strife: The History of Cyprus and the Turks on the Island," *Turkish Economic Review,* IV, No. 10 (Ankara, January 1964), pp. 14-16.

EVATT, CLIVE Q. C. "Cyprus: Tory Colonialism Exposed," *Labour Monthly,* Vol. 40, No. 8 (London: August 1958), pp. 347-351.

FAIRFIELD, ROY P. "Cyprus: Revolution and Resolution," *The Middle East Journal,* Vol. 13, No. 3 (Washington, D. C., Summer 1959), pp. 235-248.

FLANZ, GISBERT H. "Comparative Study of Constitutions and Constitutionalism," *Seoul Law Journal,* Vol. 4, No. 1-2 (Seoul: Seoul National University, 1962), pp. 48-54.

GUINEY, ALAIN. "Turkey Plays It Cool," *New Outlook,* Vol. VIII, No. 1 (Tel Aviv: January-February 1965), pp. 33-37.

"Hands Off Cyprus," *New Times,* No. 8 (Moscow: February 26, 1964), p. 3.

HARDING, J. (LORD). "The Cyprus Problem in Relation to the Middle East," *International Affairs,* Vol. 34, No. 3 (London, April 1958), pp. 291-296.

HUGHS, JAMES. "The Cypriot Labyrinth," *New Left Review,* No. 29 (London: January-February 1965) pp. 41-52.

"International Law and Some Recent Developments in the Commonwealth," *The American Journal of International Law,* Vol. 55, No. 2 (Washington, D. C., April 1961), pp. 440-444.

"*Izvestia* Interview with U.S.S.R. Foreign Minister A. A. Gromyko," *Current Soviet Documents,* Vol. III, No. 7 (New York: February 15, 1965), pp. 24-26.

JACKSON, COLIN. "Cyprus and Malta: What Answers Will Makarios Find?" *New Commonwealth,* Vol. 39 (London, January 1961), pp. 17-20.

KANAAN, HAVIV. "Cyprus on the Verge," *New Outlook,* Vol. III, No. 4 (Tel Aviv: February 1960), pp. 15-19.

KONDRATYEV, V. "The Plot Against Cyprus," *New Times,* No. 4 (Moscow: January 29, 1964), pp. 16-18.

MACKAY, MERCEDES. "Cyprus: The First Year," *New Commonwealth,* Vol. 39 (London, October 1961), pp. 641-644.

MEIER, VICTOR. "Cyprus—Constitutional Problems," *Swiss Review of World Affairs,* XIII, No. 6 (Zurich, September 1963), pp. 3-8.

MELAMID, ALEXANDER. "The Geographical Distribution of Communities in Cyprus," *The Geographical Review,* XLVI, No. 3 (New York, July 1956), pp. 355-374.

——. "Partitioning Cyprus: A Class Exercise in Applied Political Geography," *The Journal of Geography,* LIX, No. 3 (Chicago, March 1960), pp. 118-122.

"Mr. Ball Leaves for London Talks on Cyprus," *United States Department of State Bulletin,* Vol. 50 (Washington, D. C., February 24, 1964), pp. 284-285.

NAHUMI, MORDECHAI. "Cyprus: The Solution and Its Dangers," *New Outlook,* Vol. II, No. 10 (Tel Aviv, July-August 1959), pp. 3-10.

"N. S. Khrushchev's Comments Concerning Cyprus," *Current Soviet Documents,* Vol. II, No. 36 (New York, September 7, 1964), pp. 9-11.

"N. S. Khrushchev Replies to Izvestia Correspondents on Cyprus," *Current Soviet Documents,* Vol. II, No. 21 (New York, May 25, 1964), pp. 27-28.

PEFKOS, GEORGE. "Cyprus: Self-Determination," *Labour Monthly,* Vol. 46, No. 2 (London, February 1964), pp. 80-83.

PIPINELIS, PANAYOTIS. "The Greco-Turkish Feud Revived," *Foreign Affairs,* Vol. 37, No. 2 (New York, January 1959), pp. 306-316.

"President Johnson Expresses Hope for End of Strife in Cyprus," *United States Department of State Bulletin,* Vol. 50 (Washington, D. C., January 20, 1964), p. 90.

"President Johnson Replies to Soviet Letter on Cyprus," *United States Department of State Bulletin,* Vol. 50 (Washington, D. C., March 23, 1964), pp. 446-447.

RADCLIFFE, D. J. R. (LORD). "The Problem of Cyprus," *United Empire,* XLIV, No. 1 (London, January-February 1958), pp. 15-19.

"The Republic of Cyprus," *Contemporary Review,* Vol. 197 (London, February 1960), pp. 78-81.

"The Republic of Cyprus: From the Zurich Agreement to Independence," *The World Today,* Vol. 16, No. 12 (London, December 1960), pp. 526-540.

ROSSI, MARIO. "Cyprus: Defense vs. Nationalism," *Foreign Policy Bulletin,* Vol. 35, No. 14 (New York, April 1, 1956), pp. 105-107.

——. "NATO Gains by Cyprus Settlement," *Foreign Policy Bulletin,* Vol. 38, No. 16 (New York, May 1, 1959), pp. 121-122.

"The Settlement in Cyprus: A Complex and Rigid Constitution," *The Round Table,* Vol. 49, No. 195 (London, June 1959), pp. 256-265.

"The Situation in Cyprus," *United States Department of State Bulletin,* Vol. 50 (Washington, D. C., February 24, 1964), p. 283.

"The Soviet and Turkish Peoples Want to Live in Peace and Friendship," *New Times,* No. 7 (Moscow, February 17, 1965), pp. 3-6.

"Statement on Cyprus," *United States Department of State Bulletin,* Vol. 43 (Washington, D. C., September 19, 1960), pp. 457-458.

Tachau, Frank. "The Cyprus Controversy," (New Brunswick, New Jersey, 1964). (mimeographed).

——. "The Face of Turkish Nationalism: As Reflected in the Cyprus Dispute," *The Middle East Journal,* Vol. 13, No. 3 (Washington, D. C., Summer, 1959), pp. 262-272.

"Trouble on the Southern Flank," *New Times,* No. 12 (Moscow, March 25, 1964), pp. 1-2.

"United Nations Force to Cyprus," *The Commonweal,* Vol. LXXX, No. 1 (New York, March 27, 1964), pp. 4-6.

"United States and Cyprus Reaffirm Common Objective," *United States Department of State Bulletin,* Vol. 47 (Washington, D. C., July 16, 1962), p. 103.

"United States Favors Peacekeeping Force for Cyprus," *United States Department of State Bulletin,* Vol. 50 (Washington, D. C., March 9, 1964), pp. 374-376.

"United States Welcomes Agreement on Solution of Cyprus Problem," *United States Department of State Bulletin,* Vol. 40 (Washington, D. C., March 16, 1959), pp. 367-368.

UNION OF SOVIET SOCIALIST REPUBLICS. Mission to the United Nations. "N. S. Khrushchev's Message on Cyprus," Press-Release No. 4 (New York, February 7, 1964). (Mimeographed.)

VERRIER, ANTHONY. "Cyprus: Britain's Security Role." *The World Today,* Vol. 20, No. 3 (London, March 1964), pp. 131-137.

WALSH, FRANK R. and WALSH, MARIA T. "Church and State in Cyprus," *The Texas Quarterly,* III (Austin, Autumn 1960), pp. 268-273.

Newspapers

The Cyprus Mail (Nicosia), 1947, 1955, 1958, 1960-1967.

The Economist (London), 1955, 1956, 1959, 1964-1967.

Eleftheria (Freedom, Athens), 1948, 1955, 1959, 1965, 1967.

Eleftheria (Freedom, Nicosia), 1942-1967.

Eleftheros Cosmos (Free World, Athens), 1967.

Ergatiki Foni (Worker's Voice, Nicosia), 1965.

Ethniki (National, Nicosia), 1959-1966.

Ethnos (Nation, Nicosia), 1946-1960.

Foni Ton Agroton (Voice of the Farmers, Nicosia), 1962, 1965.

Halkin Sesi (Voice of the People, Nicosia), 1960, 1961, 1963, 1965, 1967.

Haravghi (Dawn, Nicosia), 1959-1967.

I Mahi (Struggle, Nicosia), 1961-1967.

I Niki (Victory, Nicosia), 1964.

I Patris (Fatherland, Nicosia), 1965-1967.

The Manchester Guardian (London), 1951, 1955, 1956, 1959-1961, 1963-1967.

The New York Times, 1955-1967.

Nei Kaeri (New Times, Nicosia), 1960, 1963-1965.

Neos Democrates (New Democrat, Nicosia), 1949, 1955.

New Statesman (London), 1960, 1964-1967.

O Agon (Contest, Nicosia), 1965, 1967.

The Observer (London), 1956, 1964, 1967.

Phileftheros (Liberal, Nicosia), 1959-1967.

Spectator (London), 1956, 1964-1967.

The Times (London), 1948, 1954-1960, 1963, 1964, 1967.
The Times of Cyprus (Nicosia), 1955-1960.
To Fos (Light, Nicosia), 1960-1964.
To Tharros (Courage, Nicosia), 1962-1967.
Tribune (London), 1955, 1967.

Personal Interviews

AKYAMAC, AHMET. Special Adviser to the United Nations Turkish Delegation; formerly a Member of the United Nations Cyprus Delegation, New York, July 14, 1966.

ANASTASSIADES, ANTONIOS P. Member of the House of Representatives, Nicosia, August 12, 1965.

ARAOUZOS, ANDREAS. Minister of Commerce and Industry, Nicosia, July 15, 1965.

ARCHBISHOP MAKARIOS. President of the Republic of Cyprus, Nicosia, September 4, 1965.

CLERIDES, GLAFCOS. President of the House of Representatives, Nicosia, August 13, 1965.

DEMETRIADES, CHRYSIS. Leading Member of the *Progressive Party of the Working People* (A.K.E.L.); Member of the House of Representatives, Nicosia, August 12, 1965.

DEMETRIOU, NIKOS. Leading businessman and formerly President of Cyprus Chamber of Commerce and Industry, Larnaca, September 3, 1965.

DERVIS, THEMISTOCLES. Leader of the pro-Enosis *Democratic Union*, Nicosia, July 31, 1965.

FANOS, CONSTANTINOS. Parliamentarian of the *Patriotic Front*, Nicosia, August 24, 1965.

EVDOKAS, TAKIS. Psychiatrist, Nicosia, June 21, 1965.

GEORGADJIS, POLYCARPOS. Minister of the Interior, Nicosia, September 8, 1965.

GRIVAS, GEORGE (General). Ex-leader of E.O.K.A., Nicosia, August 11, 1965.

KOSHIS, NICOS. Member of the House of Representatives, Nicosia, August 5, 1965.

KYPRIANIDES, GEORGE. Director of the Office of the House of Representatives, July 21, 1965; August 12, 13, 1965.

KYPRIANOU, SPYROS. Foreign Minister, Nicosia, July 16, 1965.

KYRIAKIDES, RENOS. Brother of the Bishop of Kyrenia; Leading anti-Makarios figure. Nicosia, August 26, 1965.

LANITIS, N. C. Leading businessman, Nicosia, September 3, 1965.

MOUSHOUTAS, DINOS. Consul General of Cyprus in New York, New York, June 28, 1966.

ORPHANOS, PANAYIOTIS. Secretary-General of *Cyprus Farmers Union* (P.E.K.), Nicosia, August 19, 1965.

PAPADOPOULOS, ANDREAS. Minister of Public Works, Nicosia, July 13, 1965.

PAPADOPOULOS, TASSOS. Minister of Labor, Nicosia, September 2, 1965.

PAPAFOTIS, FOTIS. Editor of the staunch pro-Enosis and anti-Makarios newspaper *I Patris,* Nicosia, September 4, 1965.

PAPAIOANNOU, EZEKIAS. Secretary-General of the *Progressive Party of the Working People* (A.K.E.L.); Member of the House of Representatives, Nicosia, August 19, 1965.

PETRIDES, FRIXOS. Leading Educator; Headmaster of Pancyprian Gymnasium, Nicosia, July 16, 1965.

SAVVA, ANDREAS. Secretary to the Public Service Commission, Nicosia, August 28, 1965.

SAVVIDES, MICHALAKIS. President of the Cyprus Chamber of Commerce and Industry; Member of the House of Representatives, Nicosia, August 28, 1965.

SIVITANIDES, PANIKOS. Member of the House of Representatives, Nicosia, August 12, 1965.

SOLOMIDES, RENOS. Minister of Finance, Nicosia, August 12, 1965.

SOULIOTI, STELLA. Minister of Justice, July 17, 1965.

SPYRIDAKIS, COSTAS. First President of the Greek Communal Chamber; presently, Minister of Education, Nicosia, August 31, 1965.

THEOCHAROUS, RIGINOS. President of the Bank of Cyprus; formerly, Minister of Finance, Nicosia, August 27, 1965.

TOUMAZIS, PANAYIOTIS. Member of the House of Representatives, Nicosia, July 21, 1965.

UNITED NATIONS OFFICIALS WITH UNFICYP, Nicosia, July 6, August 10, August 26, 1965.

VASSILIADES, G. Supreme Court Justice. Nicosia, August 24, 1965.

YIANGOU, ANDREAS. Member of the House of Representatives; formerly, Secretary-General of the *Cyprus Farmers Union* (P.E.K.), August 13, 1965.

ZIARTIDES, ANDREAS. Leader of the *Pancyprian Federation of Labor* (P.E.O.); Member of the House of Representatives, Nicosia, August 21, 1965.

ZIVANAS, NIKOS. Secretary-General of the *Cyprus Workers' Confederation* (S.E.K.), (a right-wing labor union), Nicosia, August 31, 1965.

INDEX